"*Counseling Under the Cross* ex my appreciation for Luther and given me a new perspective on Luther as a pastoral counselor. I pray that the Lord will be pleased to use this book to call us back to the cross of Christ, that we might more fully follow the example of Paul in 1 Corinthians 2:2 and Galatians 6:14 by glorying in the cross above all else. I am personally grateful for Bob and for the clear and practical teaching he has provided in this book about the centrality of the cross in counseling and by extension the entire Christian life and ministry."

Wayne Mack, ACBC Member of the Academy; Director and Professor at Strengthening Ministries Training Institute; Counseling Pastor at Lynnwood Baptist Church; author of *Preparing for Marriage God's Way*

"And I thought I knew something about Luther! *Counseling Under the Cross* is such a well-researched and beautifully written book. Because Martin Luther desperately needed gospel counseling himself, he developed a perspective of soul care that reaches deeply into the heart of broken sinners who long for (and yet fear) intimacy with God. And although he wrote 500 years ago, we still need his perspective—a perspective that proclaims God's self-giving love for anxious sinners demonstrated by the perfect life and substitutionary death of the Son he loved. Perhaps if the church had paid more attention to Luther's paradigm for soul-care, she wouldn't have given herself over to the futile philosophies of the world as she has. Bob Kellemen has given us a gift that has been sorely needed by the church: a revival of Luther's deep, gentle, and loving counsel. What a gift!"

Elyse M. Fitzpatrick, Author of *Counsel from the Cross*

"In *Counseling Under the Cross*, Bob Kellemen has written an insightful work concerning the implications of Luther's theological observation that will greatly help the Christian pastor and biblical counselor address serious issues of the heart. Living under the cross changes people for the better! If you want to learn the theological impact of this truth, you must read this book! The transformation that occurred in the heart of Martin Luther happened because he was a fervent student of the Word. His observations concerning Romans 1:17 and Galatians 3:11 were completely life-transforming because he learned salvation was wholly a work of God, solely secured by the work of Christ on the cross."

John D. Street, Chair, Biblical Counseling Graduate Programs, The Master's University & Seminary; President, Association of Certified Biblical Counselors (ACBC)

"We all know Martin Luther, the Reformer who recovered the bedrock scriptural principles summarized in the great solas. Five hundred years later, as the church stands in need of a recovery of biblical soul care, Bob Kellemen introduces us to Luther the biblical counselor. In *Counseling Under the Cross*, Bob shows how Luther faithfully ministered God's Word to those in his day who were simultaneously sinners and sufferers. Bob also shows how Luther addresses the challenges faced by biblical counselors today, including the proper balance of the gospel indicatives and the corresponding imperatives. One of the greatest benefits of this book is that it offers the reader the cream of Kellemen's years of extensive research in a very concise and readable format. I highly recommend it."

Jim Newheiser, Director of the Christian Counseling Program, Associate Professor of Counseling and Practical Theology, Reformed Theological Seminary, Charlotte, NC

"I LOVE this book! I'm with Bob. Martin Luther has instructed and encouraged and reformed my life and ministry, too. Beyond the helpful unpacking of the key elements of Luther's theology and methodology, *Counseling Under the Cross* reminds us that the issues that we wrestle with in our current soul care ministries are not new. What must be renewed in each generation is the courage to challenge the status quo—even within the church—with practical, biblical answers. This book will help you with that reforming process."

Wayne A. Vanderwier, Executive Director, Overseas Instruction in Counseling

"Think you know Martin Luther? Think again! Bob Kellemen has done a masterful job at highlighting the Augustinian monk's heart and pastoral care. Meticulously researched and thoughtfully presented, in *Counseling Under the Cross*, Kellemen brings his trademark organizational skill, creative writing, and warmth along with a compelling insight into an oft-overlooked aspect of Luther's ministry. Join Kellemen on this journey to the past and be encouraged that gospel-centered counseling is not so new after all."

Jonathan Holmes, Pastor of Counseling, Parkside Church; Council Member, Biblical Counseling Coalition

"Bob Kellemen's decades of experience as a counselor, teacher, leader, and author make *Counsel Under the Cross* a rare gift for pastors and counselors. This book provides an inspiring account of Luther's journey from fear to faith, a comprehensive explanation of the classic forms of pastoral counseling, a practical theology for helping sufferers and sinners, and a Christ-centered focus throughout—all leading to 'faith working through love.' Read *Counseling Under the Cross* and be encouraged, instructed, and equipped."

Pat Quinn, Director of Counseling Ministries, University Reformed Church

"When I first heard Dr. Kellemen talk about Luther as a soul physician, I was somehow surprised. After all, Luther is the bold Reformer, not a caring shepherd of suffering people. However, *Counseling Under the Cross* proved me wrong. Bob masterfully describes the transformation of a fearful monk into a faithful, bold, and loving pastor. And he does so not in a merely historical fashion, but by applying eternal truths for today. Praise God for the work of the Cross then, now, and forever."

    Alexandre "Sacha" Mendes, Associate Pastor (Brazil); Director for Vision and Expansion of the Brazilian Association of Biblical Counselors (ABCB); Member of Board of Directors, Biblical Counseling Coalition

"Most know of Luther's preaching, but Bob Kellemen powerfully and practically shows the commitment Luther had for using God's Word in biblical counseling. Bob creatively shows how that commitment was rooted in the same great gospel that initially rocked Luther's world at salvation. Luther, more than any other from the Reformation, has been the one I return to again and again. I love his passion, his raucous laughter, and the way he not only preached great sermons but poured his life into others at close range. *Counseling Under the Cross* demonstrates that in living color."

    Brad Bigney, ACBC Certified Counselor; Lead Pastor, Grace Fellowship Church; author of *Gospel Treason*

"Would it surprise you to know that Luther, the Reformer, was also very much Luther, the tender shepherd? Passion for soul care grows best in the soul that needs care. In *Counseling Under the Cross*, Bob Kellemen shows how Martin Luther's biblical theology, fashioned on the anvil of his own desperate need, inevitably shaped him to be a lover of souls who longed to see gospel truth bring freedom to fellow sufferers. We do well to sit with him at Jesus's feet and learn, along with Bob Kellemen, what he meant when he called us to love one another. *Counseling Under the Cross* is accessible, insightful, instructive, encouraging, and it has been a means for me to worship God as Bob has masterfully portrayed his faithfulness to build his church one needy soul at a time."

    Betty-Anne Van Rees, Council Board Member of the BCC; Founding Member of the Canadian BCC

"With the flood of Reformation 500 books coming out, Bob Kellemen offers a unique contribution and perspective with *Counseling Under the Cross*. Like pulling up to Luther's famous dinner table in Wittenberg for a table talk, Kellemen guides us through the pastoral care of one of the heroes of the faith. Luther's counsel on suffering is particularly needed in our contemporary church. I'm happy to commend Dr. Kellemen's book to any Christian wanting to know Luther and the God Luther served."

    Steve DeWitt, Sr. Pastor, Bethel Church; author of *Eyes Wide Open*

"While movements may bear a leader's name, we must never forget the source of a leader's fame—grace alone. Dr. Bob Kellemen, practically, powerfully, and beautifully illustrates how God ministers his grace to and through sinful and broken vessels—like Martin Luther and us! It is refreshing and encouraging to see our weaknesses and the all-sufficient grace of God mirrored through Martin Luther's discovery and application of God's grace to himself and others. Dr. Kellemen's excellent work and writing in *Counseling Under the Cross* motivates us to thank God that our counseling does not lead to ourselves or any other human being but rather to the victory won at the cross!"

A. Charles Ware, President of Crossroads Bible College; Council Member, Biblical Counseling Coalition

"We know Martin Luther as the father of the Reformation, not as a counselor. But as you read Luther in *Counseling Under the Cross*, what you find is a theologian who cared deeply for God's people: Luther's cross-centered theology translated to gospel-centered counseling. Kellemen's *Counseling Under the Cross* is a rich collection of Luther's stories, quotes, and lively vignettes that trace out how Luther's care of souls puts Christ squarely at the center of everything!"

Deepak Reju, Pastor of Biblical Counseling and Family Ministry, Capitol Hill Baptist Church, Washington, DC; author of *The Pastor and Counseling*

"When he nailed his Ninety-Five Theses to the door of the church in Wittenberg 500 years ago, Martin Luther didn't just spark a church reformation, he started a personal revival for soul care. Bob Kellemen's insightful book, *Counseling Under the Cross*, keeps the Reformation alive. When it comes to the cure of souls, Dr. Kellemen writes like few others. Now we know why. He has been deeply influenced by the suffering and victory of Martin Luther, a man once under a hopeless works theology. Luther's deliverance is ours too. Grace-saturated and gospel-focused, *Counseling Under the Cross* will change the way you counsel yourself and others. I highly recommend it."

Garrett Higbee, President of Soul Care Consulting

COUNSELING UNDER THE CROSS

HOW MARTIN LUTHER APPLIED THE GOSPEL TO DAILY LIFE

Bob Kellemen

New
Growth
Press

www.newgrowthpress.com

New Growth Press, Greensboro, NC 27404
Copyright © 2017 by Bob Kellemen.

Cover Design: Faceout Books, faceoutstudio.com

ISBN 978-1-945270-21-5 (Print)
ISBN 978-1-945270-22-2 (eBook)

Library of Congress Cataloging-in-Publication Data on file

Printed in the United States of America

24 23 22 21 20 19 18 17   1 2 3 4 5

CONTENTS

ACKNOWLEDGMENTS

THERE'S SOMEONE in my life who reminds me a great deal of Martin Luther—my daughter, Marie. As I write this, Marie is in her late twenties, and like Luther at that age, she persistently seeks peace with God through tenaciously clinging to Christ's gospel of grace.

As I crafted *Counseling Under the Cross*, I would email or text Luther quote after Luther quote to Marie. I'd often share, "This is *so you!*" Or, "Isn't this exactly what we were talking about last week in our own walk with Christ?"

Marie, you have been my motivation for sharing the heartbeat of Luther's pastoral counseling with the larger world. Our talks about Luther have so richly and deeply impacted both of us that I knew I had to share his grace-filled and gospel-centered wisdom with others.

Marie and I would both point to another person who is very Luther-like: my wife and Marie's mom—Shirley. No one in our lives has lived gospel truth in love more than you, Shirley. Thank you for your Christlike model of grace relationships.

I'd like to thank the team at New Growth Press. Your passion for this project has been an encouragement each step of the way.

Finally, eternal thankfulness to the Father of compassion and the God of all comfort—it's all about him. And eternal praise to his Son and our Savior through whom we have peace with God—in Christ alone.

INTRODUCTION:
MARTIN LUTHER REFORMED MY LIFE AND MINISTRY

I ADMIT it. This is an unusual title for an introduction: "Martin Luther Reformed My Life and Ministry." It is, of course, something of a play on words, since we know Martin Luther as a Reformer—the man who launched the Protestant Reformation. It is a title you might expect in the Acknowledgments—acknowledging people who influenced me or motivated me to write this book. More than a play on words, this is an honest confession. Martin Luther reformed my Christian life and my counseling ministry.

Martin Luther Reformed My Christian Life

I had been a Christian for over two decades when I first started studying Martin Luther. I was a graduate of an evangelical Bible college and of an evangelical seminary. I had been Counseling Pastor at an evangelical mega-church, and I had been Senior Pastor at an evangelical church. I was teaching at an evangelical seminary. And yet, before Luther, I only applied half the picture of my salvation.

Before studying Luther, I pictured my salvation like this: God is a holy and righteous judge, and I am on trial before him because of my sins. God is about to pronounce me guilty when Christ steps up and says, "Charge me instead. Put Bob's sins on me, and put my righteousness on Bob." God the judge accepts his holy Son's payment on my behalf and declares me, "Not guilty. Pardoned. Forgiven."

That's pretty amazing. But before Luther, my picture used to stop there. God is the judge; he forgives me; then he sends me away on my own and says, "Next case."

But that's not the full picture of salvation. Luther paints a more beautiful, more biblical picture—Christ takes me from the courtroom by the hand and leads me into the Father's house, walking me into God's presence. When we enter the living room, the Father, my Father, is not in his judge's robes. He's in his family attire. When he sees me, it is just like the portrait in Luke 15 of the prodigal son. My Father runs to me, throws his arms around me, and kisses me. He puts the family ring on my finger, ushers me back home, and celebrates with me!

Martin Luther reformed and transformed my Christian life by showing me that through Christ, God is not only the judge who forgives me; he is my Father who welcomes me. Out of his grace-love, God the Father sent his Son to die for me. With the barrier of sin demolished, nothing stands between me and my loving heavenly Father. I can fellowship with God person-to-person and son-to-Father.

I could have told you the theology of all of this before I read Martin Luther, but I was not experiencing the reality of it. In Ephesians 3:18–19, Paul tells us how we come to truly understand the love of God in Christ: "we grasp it together with all the saints." As I read Luther, he helped me grasp how wide and long and high and deep is the love of Christ, and I came to know this love that surpasses knowledge.

I am praying for you as you read *Counseling Under the Cross*. My prayer is that you will grasp together with Martin Luther, Bob Kellemen, and God's people how wide and long and high and deep is the love of Christ and come to know in a richer way this love that surpasses knowledge.

Martin Luther Reformed My Counseling Ministry

People frequently ask me, "Who has been the greatest influence on your approach to biblical counseling?" Some of the names I mention include modern authors and counselors such as David Powlison, Steve Viars, and Ron Allchin. However, people are often surprised to hear me respond, "The person who has most impacted my understanding and practice of counseling is Martin Luther."

I had been counseling for a decade when I first started examining Martin Luther's pastoral counseling. For that entire time, I had been seeking to ask and answer one fundamental question: "What would a model of counseling look like that was built solely on Christ's gospel of grace?"

As the title of this book suggests, Martin Luther's counseling is gospel-centered and cross-focused. It is grace-filled and gospel-rich. But that does not mean that when Luther encountered a suffering saint, he simply shouted, "Gospel!" It does not mean that when Luther counseled a saint struggling against a besetting sin, that he simply yelled, "Gospel!" In *Counseling Under the Cross*, you will read firsthand accounts and real-life vignettes of Martin Luther's pastoral counseling. In a hundred different ways you will see what I saw—Luther richly, relevantly, robustly, relationally applying the gospel to suffering, sin, sanctification, and people's search for peace with God.

As you read *Counseling Under the Cross*, I am praying that your counseling—your personal ministry of the Word, your one-another ministry—will be enriched with the gospel of Christ's grace. That's what is happening in my ministry, by God's grace, as I learn from Martin Luther, the master pastoral counselor.

Luther is teaching me how to apply the apostle Paul's counseling focus from Colossians 1—2. When Paul ministered to saints struggling against sin and enduring suffering, he pointed people to Christ alone—the hope of glory (Colossians 1:27). With all of God's energy powerfully working within Paul (Colossians 1:29), he proclaimed Christ alone (Colossians 1:28). To people receiving all sorts of counsel from a myriad of sources, Paul pointed people to the one in whom are hidden all the treasures of wisdom and knowledge—Christ alone

(Colossians 2:4, 8). Martin Luther is equipping me to counsel like Paul by pointing me to the counsel of the cross, to the sufficiency of the gospel of Christ's grace. I pray that as you read *Counseling Under the Cross* you will be further equipped to counsel in Christ alone.

What Formed and Reformed Martin Luther's Counseling?

For Luther's counseling to reform us, it will help us to ponder what formed and reformed Martin Luther's counseling. In Section 1 of *Counseling Under the Cross*, we will learn together two shaping factors that formed Luther's counseling. The first shaping factor (chapter 1) was incredibly personal—Luther's own spiritual trials—his doubts about ever being able to find a gracious God. In turn, this factor became incredibly pastoral—Luther's desire to help others to find peace with God.

The second shaping factor (chapter 2) was richly theological. Luther's search for gospel grace and gospel peace led him to his cross-shaped theology which led to his cross-centric counseling. To understand Luther and his pastoral counseling, we must understand these shaping influences on his life and ministry.

We not only want to understand what formed Luther's pastoral counseling. We also want to understand the form or the shape of Luther's counseling. Chapter 3 introduces this form and chapters 4–11 explore it—how Luther followed a four-fold historic Christian approach to pastoral care—sustaining, healing, reconciling, and guiding. These four counseling compass points will be our GPS as we discover how Luther took this historic approach and infused it with the gospel—demonstrating the rich relevance of the gospel for daily life.

SECTION ONE
WHAT SHAPED MARTIN LUTHER'S PASTORAL COUNSELING?

NO APPROACH to ministry develops in a vacuum. Two primary factors shaped Martin Luther's pastoral counseling ministry.

First, Luther was shaped by his spiritual trials—his spiritual separation anxiety. Chapter 1 narrates how Luther lived his life terrified that he would never find peace with God. During the first chapter of his life story, Luther sought that peace through works. He tried to address spiritual trials through self-sufficient, self-counsel. Chapter 1 ends where Luther's early life ended—in despair.

Second, Luther's counseling ministry was fashioned by his cross-shaped theology. Luther faced his spiritual trials face-to-face with Christ alone. Chapter 2 travels with Luther on his reformation journey to salvation by faith alone through grace alone. It tells the story of salvation as a justification-reconciliation journey back to the heart of a God who is a loving Father—not an angry judge. The cross of Christ displays God's gracious heart, and it became the heart of Luther's pastoral counseling ministry.

CHAPTER ONE
TERRIFIED BEFORE GOD:
LUTHER'S SPIRITUAL TRIALS

COMPELLED BY intense pastoral concern, on October 31, 1517, Martin Luther nailed his Ninety-Five Theses to the door of the Castle Church in Wittenberg. The same day, Luther dispatched a cover letter to Cardinal Albrecht, Archbishop of Mainz, outlining his soul care concern that motivated his Reformation ministry. Luther began his letter by expressing alarm for his flock—many of whom were journeying to the Dominican, John Tetzel, in an attempt to purchase their freedom from guilt: "I bewail the gross misunderstanding among the people which comes from these preachers and which they spread everywhere among common men. Evidently the poor souls believe that when they have bought indulgence letters they are then assured of their salvation."[1]

The Reformer then directly addresses the Cardinal, "O great God! The souls committed to your care, excellent Father, are thus directed to death. For all these souls you have the heaviest and a constantly increasing responsibility. Therefore, I can no longer be silent on this subject."[2] Luther, the pastor and shepherd, inspired Luther the Reformer.

Luther's Pastoral and Personal Motivation
McNeil rightly observes, "in matters concerning the cure of souls the German Reformation had its inception."[3] Sproul concurs, "To be sure, the Ninety-Five Theses posted on the church door at Wittenberg were penned in Latin as a request for theological discussion among the faculty members of the university. But what provoked Luther to request

such a discussion? Simply put, it was pastoral concern."[4] Tappert further explains:

> Martin Luther is usually thought of as a world-shaking figure who defied papacy and empire to introduce a reformation in the teaching, worship, organization, and life of the Church and to leave a lasting impression on Western civilization. It is sometimes forgotten that he was also—*and above all else*—a pastor and shepherd of souls. It is therefore well to remind ourselves that the Reformation began in Germany when Luther became concerned about his own parishioners who believed that if they had purchased letters of indulgence they were sure of their salvation.[5]

Luther empathized deeply with his flock's fears because long before he nailed his Theses, he wrestled personally with the demons of doubt about the grace and forgiveness of God: "Though I lived as a monk without reproach, I felt that I was a sinner before God with an extremely disturbed conscience. I could not believe that anything that I thought or did or prayed satisfied God."[6] The thought of standing face-to-face with a holy God created in Luther a lifelong dread and constant apprehension that he would never find peace with God.

In the Ninety-Five Theses, Luther's agonizing personal search for a gracious God merged with his pastoral care for his confused flock: "It is crucial to realize that Luther became a reformer who was widely heard and understood by transforming the abstract question of a just God into an existential quest that concerned the whole human being, encompassing thought and action, soul and body, love, and suffering."[7] For Luther, theology is for life. It provides the answer to life's ultimate question, *How do we find peace with a holy God?*

We can best grasp Luther, the pastoral counselor, from an autobiographical viewpoint. His personal struggle for perfection and acceptance before God was an elemental spiritual one in which he searched for the assurance that God was gracious to him even though he was a sinner. Luther's personal quest for God's grace not only animated his personal religious experience, it also motivated his Reformation agenda and his pastoral work.

As a soul physician, "with all of Germany for his parish,"[8] Luther guided his flock toward the ultimate Soul Physician on a journey to grasp the grace of God. As a fellow pilgrim, Luther journeyed with the Soul Physician on his personal search for peace with God.

Kittleson succinctly captures Luther's focus: "Luther's sole compulsion was to discover how a Christian could live with a righteous God whom he could never possibly satisfy."[9] *Where do we find the grace of God and peace with God?* This was Luther's primary soul care question. He asked and answered this question in his letter to Cardinal Albrecht. Even at this early stage of his reforming career, Luther insisted that the pure gospel of grace be preached because it was the sole hope for peace with God: "The first and only duty of the bishops, however, is to see that the people learn the gospel and the love of Christ. For on no occasion has Christ ordered that indulgences should be preached, but he forcefully commanded the gospel to be preached."[10]

Three years later, Luther wrote another letter to the Cardinal. His Christ-alone (*solus Christus*) conviction had only strengthened, as had his rhetoric: "My humble supplication to Your Electoral Grace is, therefore, that Your Electoral Grace refrain from leading the poor people astray and from robbing them, and present yourself as a bishop and not as a wolf. It is sufficiently well known that indulgences are nothing else but knavery and fraud and that Christ alone should be preached to the people."[11]

Luther was not only a theologian, not only a writer, not only a preacher; Luther was a pastoral counselor who engaged in the personal ministry of the Word. Luther not only reformed theology; he reformed the art of pastoral counseling—under the cross. Luther is the father of cross-centered counseling that applies Christ's gospel of grace richly, relevantly, and robustly to suffering, sin, sanctification, and the search for peace with God. As his sons and daughters in the faith, we have much to learn from his life and ministry.

Luther's Spiritual Separation Anxiety

Before Luther could teach us about grace-based counseling, he had to learn a new view of Christ—a view that was a universe apart from the religious culture of his day. A man of his times, Luther viewed God as his vindictive enemy and merciless judge: "I lost hold of Christ the Savior and comforter and made of him a stock-master and hangman over my poor soul."[12] Luther was not alone. He inhabited a world where people "thought a threatening God kept a suspicious eye on every human act" and where "their religious ventures taught them to be consumed by the threat of damnation."[13] And if this God was angry with Luther, then Luther was plenty angry with him:

> I did not love, yes, I hated the righteous God who punishes sinners, and secretly, if not blasphemously, certainly murmuring greatly, I was angry with God, and said, "As if, indeed, it is not enough that miserable sinners, eternally lost through original sin, are crushed by every kind of calamity by the law of the Decalogue, without having God add pain to pain by the gospel and also by the gospel threatening us with his righteousness and wrath!" Thus I raged with a fierce and troubled conscience.[14]

An Anxious Pilgrim in a Vale of Tears

The spiritual milieu of Luther's day helps us identify with Luther's sense of foreboding in the face of an angry God. Shortly before midnight on November 10, 1483, in Eisleben, Margarethe Lindemann Luder gave birth to a son. Martin was named after St. Martins of Tours, whose feast day was November 11. Luther's father, Hans, moved to Eisleben to work in the copper mines, eventually becoming a leaseholder of mines. In 1484, Luther's parents moved to Mansfield where they stayed for the rest of their lives.

Life was hard and the people were harder. Years later, in a table talk shared during the winter of 1533, Luther reflected upon the evil that lurked around the edge of everything in Mansfield: "Luther said many things about witchcraft and nightmares, and how his mother had been tormented by a neighbor woman who was a witch."[15] Spells, poison, and death inhabited the air they breathed.

In our relatively safer society, it can be challenging for us to relate to a world where death marched around every corner. In the summer of 1505, just before entering his final course of studies, Martin visited his family. It was a difficult time for the region. Erfurt had been struck by the plague that had killed so many people that entire cities were left empty, and some of Luther's friends and teachers had died.

Because this life was so difficult, people hoped at least for a better eternal life after their earthly vale of tears. However, Luther, like the people of his day, worried about death because he feared he had not done enough to please God. He was terrified of the *jungsten Tag*—the day of final reckoning when Christ would return to judge the world. It seemed impossible to him that even his best efforts in cooperation with grace could ever prove anything but inadequate. No one could love God as the Bible required, and God stood ready to condemn and destroy in that last day of judgment.[16]

Just as they struggled to achieve physical and material security in their daily lives, so Luther and the people of his day searched for and struggled to achieve spiritual security. Salvation was something to be earned; theirs was a religion of works; and their God was a God of wrath. Christ was commonly pictured seated on his throne, from one side of his head came a lily (symbolizing the resurrection), and from the other side came a sword. The burning question was, "How can I avoid the sword and earn the lily?"[17]

In a December 1531 table talk, Luther depicted how his religious environment had impacted him personally: "It's very difficult for a man to believe that God is gracious to him. The human heart can't grasp this." In the same table talk, Luther illustrated his sub-biblical view of God from an event from his student days:

> This is the way we are. Christ offers himself to us together with the forgiveness of sins, and yet we flee from his face. This also happened to me as a boy in my homeland when we sang in order to gather sausages. A townsman jokingly cried out, "What are you boys up to? May this or that evil overtake you!" At the same time he ran toward us with two sausages. With my companion I took to my feet and ran away from the man who was offering his gift. This is precisely what happens to us in our relation to God. *He gave us Christ with all his gifts, and yet we flee from him and regard him as our judge.*[18]

Luther, like the men and women of his day, lived in ultimate fear of God and terror of eternal separation from God—spiritual separation anxiety. Martin experienced incessant torment in his soul because he believed that no matter what he did, he could never obtain the love of God. Luther's every human effort only made matters worse: "For I had hoped I might find peace of conscience with fasts, prayer, and the vigils with which I miserably afflicted my body, but the more I sweated it out like this, the less peace and tranquility I knew."[19]

Before he came under the influence of the cross, Luther lived life as a man terrified that he would never find peace with God because his God was not a God of peace. Luther lived with a constant sense of guilt and dread in the face of a terrifying, angry, and unforgiving God.

A Hopeless Sinner in the Hands of an Angry God: Luther's *Anfechtungen*

Always the astute soul physician, Luther even supplied a spiritual diagnostic label for his spiritual trials: *anfechtungen* (the plural form of the German word *anfechtung*). No single English word can translate *anfechtung*, but an image captures the idea: an angry, finger-wagging, judgmental, harsh, condemning, aloof, holy God. *Anfechtungen* paint the image of a hopeless sinner in the hands of an angry God.

With *anfechtung*, Luther pictured the opposite of the father in the parable of the prodigal son: "But while he was still a long way off, his father saw him and was filled with compassion for him; he ran to his son, threw his arms around him and kissed him" (Luke 15:20). *Anfechtungen* are spiritual doubts that we could ever be forgiven and welcomed home as the Father's son or daughter. They are spiritual doubts that we could ever find peace with God, ever have a relationship with a forgiving Father. Luther used *anfechtung* to picture God as angry with and incensed against him: "When I was in spiritual distress [*anfechtung*] a gentle word would restore my spirit. Sometimes my confessor said to me when I repeatedly discussed silly sins with him, 'You are a fool. God is not incensed against you, but you are incensed against God. God is not angry with you, but you are angry with God.'"[20]

Luther obsessed about how to calm his terrified conscience and was desperate to know how he could find rest for his soul. The Reformer felt hopeless as he faced the eternal dilemma of not being able to satisfy God at any point. He asked, *How can I face the terror of the Holy?* "The words 'righteous' and 'righteousness of God' struck my conscience like lightning. When I heard them I was exceedingly terrified. If God is righteous, I thought, he must punish me."[21]

Bainton emphasizes the importance of *anfechtung* in Luther's life and ministry, while also providing a working definition:

> Toward God he was at once attracted and repelled. Only in harmony with the Ultimate could he find peace. But how could a pygmy stand before divine Majesty; how could a transgressor confront divine Holiness? Before God the high and holy Luther was stupefied. For such an experience he had a word. The word he used was *Anfechtung*, for which there is

no English equivalent. It may be a trial sent from God to test man, or an assault by the Devil to destroy man. It is all the doubt, turmoil, pang, terror, panic, despair, desolation, and desperation which invade the spirit of man.[22]

Anfechtung was Luther's label for his "grinding sense of being utterly lost. By it he intended the idea of swarming attacks of doubt that could convince people that God's love was not for them."[23] *Anfechtung* is the experience of always falling short and never measuring up because our human balance sheet always shows a deficit before a perfect God.

Martin Marty links Martin Luther's personal spiritual struggle to the cultural milieu of his day: "He makes the most sense as a wrestler with God, indeed, as a God-obsessed seeker of certainty and assurance in a time of social trauma and personal anxiety, beginning with his own."[24] Luther, as a man of his times, was always asking the question, *Where can I find peace with God?* Despairing of any hope for finding peace, Luther lived constantly haunted by the ultimate fear of estrangement from God—spiritual separation anxiety.

To read Luther is to come to know a person who saw his soul and the souls of others in despair. His pastoral care of his own soul and of others, therefore, focused upon *anfechtungen*—spiritual doubts about acceptance by God, spiritual depression because of feelings of rejection by God, spiritual despair over ever pleasing God—all caused by a sense of alienation from God.

But what was Luther to do? Before he discovered Christ's gospel of grace, he did what everyone in his day did: he sought peace through works. During the early chapters of his life story, Luther strove to address his spiritual trials—his *anfechtungen*—through self-sufficient self-counsel.

Luther's Story of Self-Sufficient Self-Counsel

In his dread and despair, Luther trusted in his own human wisdom and his own human works. Instead of clinging to the sufficiency of Christ and Scripture, Luther attempted to cure his soul through the self-sufficient methods common in the medieval church of his day.

In Sheer Terror, Luther Made a Vow

A fearful external storm and an even more tumultuous internal soul storm led Luther to enter the Augustinian Monastery in Erfurt. Fear of physical death, terror of spiritual death, and horror at eternal separation from God led Luther to make a vow. Bainton offers the classic account of Luther's vow to become a monk:

> On a sultry day in July of the year 1505 a lonely traveler was trudging over a parched road on the outskirts of the Saxon village of Stotternheim. He was a young man, short but sturdy, and wore the dress of a university student. As he approached the village, the sky became overcast. Suddenly there was a shower, then a crashing storm. A bolt of lightning rived the gloom and knocked the man to the ground. Struggling to rise, he cried in terror, "St. Anne help me! I will become a monk." The man who thus called upon a saint was later to repudiate the cult of the saints. He who vowed to become a monk was later to renounce monasticism. A loyal son of the Catholic Church, he was later to shatter the structure of medieval Catholicism. A devote servant of the pope, he was later to identify the popes with Antichrist. For this young man was Martin Luther.[25]

Miners prayed to their popular protector, St. Anne, known to them as the mother of the Virgin Mary: "The pious, hoping such saints would shield them, feared a God who judged and punished them." Luther, the son of a miner and the son of his times, terrified of God, did not seek the solace of a Savior, but the succor of St. Anne.[26]

In a letter to his father, Luther explains, "I told you that I had been called by terrors from heaven and that I did not become a monk of my own free will and desire, still less to gain any gratification of the flesh, but that I was walled in by the terror and the agony of sudden death and forced by necessity to take the vow."[27] Like his contemporaries, Luther believed what the church taught. And the church taught that sensible people would not wait until their deathbed to make an act of contrition and plead for grace. Rather, from beginning to end, the only secure course was to lay hold of every help the church had to offer: confession, spiritual disciplines, sacraments, pilgrimages, indulgences, and the saints' intercession and merits. These were ideas on which Luther and his peers were nurtured. There was nothing peculiar in Martin's beliefs or his responses save their intensity.

In Superhuman Effort, Luther Sought a Holy Standing before a Holy God

Luther entered the monastery to quiet his soul and to find peace with God. It did not work. The occasion of saying his first mass was like another thunderstorm—this one in his spirit: "When at length I stood before the altar and was to consecrate, I was so terrified of the words *aeterno vivo vero Deo* [to Thee the eternal, living, and true God] that I thought of running away from the altar and said to my prior, 'Reverend Father, I'm afraid I must leave the altar.' He shouted to me, 'Go ahead, faster, faster!' So terrified was I by those words!"[28]

Luther reported that at these words (to Thee the eternal, living, and true God), he was utterly stupefied and terror-stricken. He thought to himself:

> With what tongue shall I address such Majesty, seeing that all men ought to tremble in the presence of even an earthly prince? Who am I, that I should lift up mine eyes or raise my hands to the divine Majesty? The angels surround him. At his nod the earth trembles. And shall I, a miserable little pygmy, say "I want this, I ask for that?" For I am dust and ashes and

full of sin and I am speaking to the living, eternal and the true God.[29]

Since Luther did not believe that he could appear before the tribunal of a holy God with an impure heart; he must become holy. Thus he had a great thirst for spiritual purity but unanswered questions about where he could find it. Luther's quest for a fellowship-through-holiness took him through the path of the spiritual disciplines.

In the religious atmosphere of his day, where better to stalk holiness than in the monastery? As Luther preached in a sermon on June 24, 1524, "The greatest holiness one could imagine drew us into the cloister. . . . We fasted and prayed repeatedly, wore hair shirts under woolen cowls, led a strict and austere life. In short, we took on a monkish holiness. We were so deeply involved in that pretentious business that we considered ourselves holy from head to toe."[30]

In the monastery, one found heroic, spiritual athletes who rigorously attempted to take heaven by storm. One of the privileges of monastic life was that it freed the sinner from distractions and allowed the monk to strive to save his soul by practicing the spiritual disciplines: charity, sobriety, love, chastity, poverty, obedience, fasting, vigils, and mortifications of the flesh. Luther became a monk among monks: "Whatever good works a man might do to save himself, these Luther was resolved to perform."[31] Luther's own words highlighted his obsessive dedication. If the apostle Paul could say that he was a Hebrew among Hebrews, then Luther could certainly proclaim that he was a monk among monks:

> I was a good monk, and I kept the rules of my order so strictly that I may say that if ever a monk got to heaven by his monkery it was I. All my brothers in the monastery who knew me will bear me out. If I had kept on any longer, I should have killed myself with vigils, prayers, reading, and other work.[32]

Luther later reflected on how "I almost fasted myself to death, for again and again I went for three days without taking a drop of water or a morsel of food. I was very serious about it."[33] He was equally vigilant in his routine of prayers:

> When I was a monk I was unwilling to omit any of the prayers, but when I was busy with public lecturing and writing I often accumulated my appointed prayers for a whole week, or even two or three weeks. Then I would take a Saturday off, or shut myself in for as long as three days without food and drink, until I had said the prescribed prayers. This made my head split, and as a consequence I could not close my eyes for five nights, lay sick unto death, and went out of my senses. Even after I had quickly recovered and I tried again to read, my head went 'round and 'round. Thus our Lord God drew me, as if by force, from that torment of prayers. To such an extent had I been captive to human traditions![34]

Despite Luther's desire to find peace with God, all the rigors of the ascetic life could not quiet his conscience: "I was very pious in the monastery, yet I was sad because I thought God was not gracious to me. I said mass and prayed and hardly ever saw or heard a woman as long as I was in the order."[35] Luther could not satisfy God at any point.

In Abject Failure, Luther Turned to the Merits of the Saints

For Luther, no amount of human effort worked: "I saw that I was a great sinner in the eyes of God and I did not think it possible for me to propitiate him by my own merits."[36] Since his own merits would not suffice, Luther the monk fled to the merits of the saints.

Luther, who had prayed to St. Anne for her protection before he entered the monastery, exponentially expanded the list of saints he clung to once he arrived at Erfurt: "I chose twenty-one saints and prayed to three every day when I celebrated mass; this I completed the number every week. I prayed especially to the Blessed Virgin, who with her womanly heart would compassionately appease her Son."[37] Notice Luther's goal: that the merit and mercy of Mary would mollify the Messiah.

Alas, for meticulous Martin, even the merits of twenty-one saints would not be enough. So, wanting to take full benefit of the transfer of merits (indulgences), Luther felt himself highly privileged when an opportunity arose for him to go to Rome. Rome, like no city on earth, was richly endowed with spiritual indulgences so Luther could seek to appropriate for himself and his relatives all the enormous benefits available.

After a lengthy pilgrimage to Rome, Luther finally began to ascend the *Scala Sancta*—the twenty-eight marble steps thought to be those Jesus walked on the way to his trial before Pilate. Luther climbed Pilate's stairs on his hands and knees repeating a *Pater Noster* for each stair and kissing each step in the hope of obtaining grace from the merit of the saints.

But doubts assailed him. At the top, Luther raised himself up and exclaimed, "Who knows whether it is so?" He later described that he had gone to Rome with onions and returned with garlic.[38] Now another tenet of hope was shattered. Luther did not receive the merit necessary to earn God's grace, nor did the church have the means to quell his conscience and free his soul.

In Obsessive Scrupulosity, Luther Confessed Meticulously

Luther thought that if he could not acquire heaven by becoming a saint or by the merits of the saints, then perhaps he could do so by the confession of every known sin. Even Luther's pilgrimage to Rome focused on scrupulous confession: "My chief concern when I departed for Rome was that I might make a full confession of my sins from my youth up and might become pious, although I had twice made such a confession in Erfurt."[39] This too became a futile remedy for Luther, as his own words attest: "While I was a monk, I no sooner felt assailed by any temptation than I cried out—'I am lost!' Immediately I had recourse to a thousand methods to stifle the cries of my conscience. I went everyday to confession, but that was of no use to me."[40]

For a Christian of Luther's time and place, the whole sacramental system was designed to mediate God's help to sinners. Luther, seeing himself as the chief of sinners, made frequent use of this means of forgiveness. He "quickly became a virtuoso self-examiner, boring his mentor during six-hour confession sessions."[41] He believed that every sin, in order to be absolved, had to be confessed. Truly penitent sinners were expected to search their hearts for sins of action and of motivation. Therefore, Luther would review his entire life, to be sure of remembering everything, until his confessor grew weary:

> I often made confession to Staupitz, not about women but about really serious sins. He said, "I don't understand you." This was real consolation! Afterward when I went to another confessor I had the same experience. In short, no confessor wanted to have anything to do with me. Then I thought, "Nobody has this same temptation except you," and I became as dead as a corpse. Finally, when I was sad and downcast, Staupitz started to talk to me at table and asked, "Why are you so sad?" I replied, "Alas, what am I to do!"[42]

Assurance still escaped Luther. His soul would recoil in horror when, after six hours of confession, a new sin would come to mind which he had not remembered. Even more frightening was the realization that some sins were not even recognized as such by sinners. Luther's despair only escalated:

> I tried to live according to the Rule with all diligence, and I used to be contrite, to confess and number off my sins, and often repeated my confession, and sedulously performed my allotted penance. And yet my conscience could never give me certainty, but I always doubted and said, "You did not perform that correctly. You were not contrite enough. You left

that out of your confession." The more I tried to remedy an uncertain, weak, and afflicted conscience with the traditions of men, the more each day found it more uncertain, weaker, and more troubled.[43]

Feel the hopelessness.

In Human Hopelessness, Luther Stood Naked before a Holy God

A hopeless Luther had availed himself of every resource of the medieval church for assuaging the anguish of a spirit alienated from God. When Staupitz met Luther, he met a man in the midst of the most frightful insecurities. Panic had invaded Luther's spirit. His soul was tortured by despair because his sin left him alienated from God.

Luther entered the monastery to find peace with God. Though driven there for rest for his soul, monastic life failed to ease his guilt: "Then, bowed down by sorrow, I tortured myself by the multitude of my thoughts. 'Look,' exclaimed I, 'thou art still envious, impatient, passionate! It profiteth thee nothing, O wretched man, to have entered this sacred order.'"[44]

Luther failed to find peace for his anxious soul in his works of righteousness, for all his strivings simply increased his despair. The purpose of his good works was to compensate for his sins, but he could never believe that the ledger was perfectly balanced. He could not satisfy a holy God at any point. None of Luther's good works worked. At this stage of his life, Luther finds himself standing stark naked and emptyhanded before the God who is "Holy, Holy, Holy." What now? What next?

Timeless Truth for Life and Ministry Today

The first chapter of Luther's life story ends like the Old Testament—begging for more; pleading for hope; despairing for grace; hoping for the good news, for the gospel; longing for the Christ of the cross.

Luther's life story mirrors Israel's story in Jeremiah where the Israelites have committed two sins: they forsook God—the spring of living water, and they dug their own cisterns—broken cisterns that cannot hold water (Jeremiah 2:13). In this passage, the ultimate Soul Physician diagnoses why God's people choose empty, broken cisterns over living spring water: they find fault with God and hold onto faulty views of God (Jeremiah 2:5). They forsake the Lord their God because they have lost their awe of God (Jeremiah 2:19).

In the beginning, the Israelites were devoted like a bride who loved God and followed him through the desert (Jeremiah 2:2). But now, rather than follow God in the desert, they see him as a desert, as a land of great darkness (Jeremiah 2:31). Because they have lost their awe of God, their faulty, foolish, and unbiblical view of God leads them to flee from God (Jeremiah 2:31) and trust in anyone and anything but God (Jeremiah 2:13, 36–37).

Luther follows a similar path. Every works-righteousness cistern that Luther dug was broken beyond repair. But why keep turning to broken cisterns when God, the spring of living water, is inviting Luther to drink? At this point of his life, Luther had a faulty, non-Christ, non-cross, non-gospel, non-grace view of God.

Reflecting upon this time in his life, Luther told his students of Satan's bewitching deceptions. Referencing Galatians 3:1, Luther explains, "To tell the truth, he [Satan] sometimes assails me so mightily and oppresses me with such heavy cogitations, that he utterly shadows my Savior Christ from me and, in a manner, takes Him out of my sight."[45] Satan was cropping the Christ of the cross out of Luther's picture.

What's missing throughout the first chapter of Luther's story? The Christ of the cross is missing. In fact, we can encapsulate the primary gospel-centered counseling lesson of chapter 1 with this tweet-size summary:

> We desperately need counseling under the cross because Satan
> seeks to crop the Christ of the cross out of our salvation picture
> so we'll flee from the Father and entrust ourselves to anyone
> but God.

Think back on Luther's spiritual journey from chapter 1. Imagine that you could time travel back 500 years to counsel Luther when he is crying out, "Alas, what am I to do!"

Would our counsel be works-centered? Would we tell Luther what to do? Or, would our counseling be cross-centered. Would we invite Martin Luther into a gospel conversation about what Christ has already and eternally done? In chapter 2, we discover what biblical counsel Luther uncovers in the second stage of his spiritual journey.

CHAPTER TWO
PEACE WITH GOD:
LUTHER'S CROSS-SHAPED THEOLOGY

LUTHER WROTE to his fellow Augustinian friar, George Splenein, on April 8, 1516. After just one paragraph, Luther abruptly inquires about the state of his friend's soul: "Now I should like to know whether your soul, tired of its own righteousness, is learning to be revived by and to trust in the righteousness of Christ."[1] Not only is this an abrupt transition in his letter, it is an abrupt transition in our book—considering that we when we last left Luther he was hopelessly clinging to his own righteousness.

But we have barely scratched the surface of Luther's gospel-focused missive, which continues for several pages—all with a remarkable emphasis on salvation by faith alone through grace alone in Christ alone:

> For in our age the temptation to presumption besets many, especially those who try with all their might to be just and good without knowing the righteousness of God, which is most bountifully and freely given us in Christ. They try to do good of themselves in order that they might stand before God clothed in their own virtues and merits. But this is impossible. While you were here, you were one who held this opinion, or rather, error. So was I.[2]

Having pointedly contrasted righteousness through Christ's grace with false and futile attempts at righteousness through our works, Luther now invites Spenlein to embrace the Christ of the cross: "Therefore, my dear Friar, learn Christ and him crucified. Learn to praise him and, despairing of yourself, say, 'Lord Jesus, you are my righteousness, just as I am your sin. You have taken upon yourself what is mine and have given to me what is yours. You have taken upon yourself what you were not and have given to me what I was not.'"[3]

Given Luther's tormented conscience, his struggles with *anfechtungen*, and his past view of God as terrifying, angry, and judgmental, his words to Spenlein are astonishing:

> Meditate on this love of his and you will see his sweet consolation. For why was it necessary for him to die if we can obtain a good conscience by our works and afflictions. Accordingly, you will find peace only in him when you despair of yourself and your own works. Besides, you will learn from him that just as he has received you, so he has made your sins his own and has made his righteousness yours.[4]

In the first chapter of his life story, Luther had seen himself as a prodigal son who was light-years away from God. He had attempted to find his way home to the Father by playing the part of the self-righteous, elder son. Luther had seen God as an impossible-to-please, angry, perfectionistic, damning judge. He longed to be welcomed back home as God's son, but he could not become a son of God apart from the Son of God. Luther's image of the Father changed when he began to view him through the cross-focused lens of the loving, sweet consolation of Christ the Savior.

Having been a gospel-centered soul physician for Spenlein, Luther concludes his letter by exhorting Spenlein to counsel others patiently with the counsel of the cross: "If you firmly believe this as you ought (and he is damned who does not believe it), receive your untaught and hitherto erring brothers, patiently help them."[5] Luther's concluding words to Spenlein summarize the essence of Luther's life-long ministry of faith active in love: "Only keep your eyes fixed on what he has done for you and for all men in order that you may learn what you should do for others."[6]

Ponder the historical timeline. In 1510, Luther had just returned home from his trip to Rome, where, instead of finding God's righteousness, he found the great shamelessness, godlessness, and wickedness of the people there, himself included.[7] Luther was a man terrified before God. Now, just six short years later, Luther composes a letter of spiritual counsel, fixated on Christ's righteousness alone. Luther is now a man at peace with God. Something drastic occurred during the six years from Luther's return from Rome to the writing of his letter to Spenlein: God's good heart, as seen through the grace heart of Christ, became the heart of Luther's pastoral counseling ministry.

Turning to the Great Soul Physician

In his study of Luther as a spiritual advisor, Nebe applies Luke 4:23 ("physician, heal thyself") to Luther: "This old proverb is and remains ever true in regard to pastoral care. No one can properly advise and care for another, unless he has beforehand advised and cared for himself. He who wishes to help others as a physician of souls, must first of all have conscientiously used the true remedy. Therefore, Luther as a spiritual advisor, had first to care for his own soul."[8]

I recommend a slight but significant change in the wording from *caring for his own soul* to *surrendering to Christ's care* for his soul. Luther had attempted to care for his soul through his own wisdom and it earned him nothing but despair. Only as Luther clung to the sufficiency of Christ and Scripture did he find peace for his troubled soul. Luther, the soul physician, first had to turn to Christ, the great Soul Physician.

Luther needed a soul physician to prescribe a remedy for his *anfechtungen*—his terrifying experience of separation from a holy God. In a table talk focused on Satan tempting us to doubt God's graciousness, Luther spoke to the value of *anfechtungen*: "I didn't learn my theology all at once. I had to ponder over it ever more deeply, and my spiritual trials [*anfechtungen*] were of help to me in this, for one does not learn anything without practice. What kind of physician would that be who stayed in school all the time. . . . Why shouldn't this be so in the case of the Holy Scriptures, too?"[9]

The effective soul physician is the person who has wrestled with doubts and turned to Christ for assurance of God's grace. As Luther explained, "If I live longer, I would like to write a book about *anfechtungen*, for without them no person is able to know Holy Scripture, nor faith, the fear or the love of God. He does not know the meaning of hope who was never subject to temptations."[10] *Anfechtung* was the existential place from which Luther thought, wrote, pastored, and counseled. It was the place, far from tranquil, where he encountered God. Speaking of his battle with *anfechtungen*, Luther writes, "living, dying and being damned make the real theologian."[11]

Luther's essential motivating concern was to find a way to be received home by God. His entire theology developed in response to this quest, and his pastoral care ministry was the outworking of his theological answer to this existential question. Luther's personal knowledge and experience of the terrors of distance from God shaped his view of spirituality. In turn, he provided pastoral care through the eyes of his *anfechtungen*: "The words he shares pastorally are drawn from the Scripture, tempered by his own deep and varied experiences with the *anfechtungen*. In his dialogues with others, he offers essentially what he has found helpful himself."[12]

Years of a terrified conscience led to a humbled sinner who focused on knowing a God of justification (forgiveness in Christ) and reconciliation (acceptance by the Father), a God who was no longer angry with sinners but rather accepted and welcomed sinners freely because of Christ. Justification/reconciliation by grace through faith was the core of Luther's pastoral cure—not only for salvation—but for daily Christian living. And the fear of rejection by God was the context of Luther's pastoral care. He saw every person he ministered to as a soul desperately needing to hear from the Father, "Forgiven! Welcome home!"

Finding Spiritual Peace with God

How did Luther move from spiritual separation anxiety to spiritual peace with God? When we left off telling Luther's story, Martin was an anxious pilgrim in a vale of tears and a hopeless sinner in the hands of an angry God. When we last journeyed with Luther, we witnessed his self-sufficient self-counsel. In sheer terror, he made a vow. In superhuman effort, he sought a holy standing before a holy God. In abject failure, he turned to the merits of the saints. In obsessive scrupulosity, he confessed meticulously. In human hopelessness, he stood naked before a holy God, crying out, "Alas, what am I to do!"

Luther came to believe that he could never satisfy God through himself or through the church. As Luther came to the end of his rope, God sent him a rope of hope in the form of Johann von Staupitz.

In Sheer Joy of Discovery, Luther Launched a Reformation

Upon his return from Rome, Luther was transferred from Erfurt to Wittenberg, where he lived in the Augustinian cloister at the opposite end from the Castle Church. The chief glory of the village was the university. In 1511, Luther was invited to be one of the new professors, and a very important figure entered Luther's life: the vicar of the Augustinian order, Johann von Staupitz. A decade later, in 1523, Luther expressed his eternal appreciation to Staupitz: "it was through you that the light of the gospel first began to shine out of the darkness into my heart."[13]

The anguish of soul and internal struggles to which Luther had fallen prey were evident to Staupitz upon their first introduction. D'Aubigne describes Luther when Staupitz initially encountered him:

He was a young man of middle height, whom study, fasting, and prolonged vigils had so wasted away that all his bones might be counted. His eyes, that were in later years compared to a falcon's, were sunken; his manner was dejected; his countenance betrayed an agitated mind, the prey of a thousand struggles, but yet strong and resolute. His whole appearance was grave, melancholy, and solemn.[14]

During the period when Staupitz was Luther's confessor, he pointed Luther away from the idea of confessing individual sins, and taught Luther that focusing on particular offenses was a counsel of despair. Luther discovered that there was something more drastically wrong with people than any particular list of offenses that could be enumerated, confessed, and forgiven. The very nature of a person was corrupt; the whole nature needed to be changed. For Luther, the penitential system failed because it was directed to particular lapses. Luther had perceived that the entire person was in need of forgiveness. Thus confession was no solution; it only exacerbated the already insecure conscience.[15]

As Luther's whole person stood exposed before a holy God, he became obsessed with the picture of Christ the avenger. Staupitz searched to find some way to console Luther. Clearly reasoning and comfort were ineffectual; some other approach had to be unearthed.

The solution was paradoxical. Luther would study for his doctor's degree so that he could undertake preaching and assume the chair of Bible at the university. Bainton noted the audacity of such a move, saying, "A young man on the verge of a nervous collapse over religious problems was to be commissioned as a teacher, preacher, and counselor to sick souls. Staupitz was practically saying, 'Physician, cure thyself by curing others.'" Staupitz thought that if Luther "was entrusted with the cure of souls he would be disposed for their sakes to turn from threats to promises, and some of the grace which he would claim for them might fall also to himself."[16]

The solution was also practical. Luther committed himself to learn and expound the Scriptures. On August 1, 1513, he began to lecture on the Psalms; in 1515, he started his lectures on Romans; and he taught Galatians from 1516 to 1517.

Through these studies, Luther began to see God in a drastically different light. His image of God was radically altered as the grace of Christ was cropped back into the picture. Where God had been an angry enemy, he now is a loving Father. Where Christ had been an avenging judge, he now is a gracious Savior. This change in Luther's image of God-in-Christ is the soul experience that changed Luther. How does a prodigal child find peace with a holy Father? Is it by doing the good works of a self-righteous son? No! It is through receiving by faith the amazing grace of the perfect Son.

While Luther worked on the Psalms, Staupitz summarized the dilemma in Martin's soul with these words: "There is a great mountain. 'You must cross it'—says the Law. 'I will cross it,'—says presumption. 'You cannot,'—says the conscience. 'Then I won't attempt it,'—says despair." Luther would never forget those words. Instead of allowing the voices of the Law, presumption, the conscience, or despair to dominate, Staupitz encouraged Luther by sharing a new vision of Christ, "Christ does not alarm, but comforts." Staupitz exhorted Luther to, "Look at the wounds of Christ and at his blood shed for you." These words of exhortation hit their mark, becoming like a neon light emblazoned on Luther's soul, as Luther himself expressed, "sticking like the sharp arrow of a warrior in his soul."[17]

Through "his Staupitz," as Luther afterwards liked to call him, the Reformer was further liberated from his morbid consciousness of sin by the statement, "You want to be an imaginary sinner and to regard Christ as an imaginary Saviour. You must accustom yourself to think that Christ is a real Saviour and that you are a real sinner. God does nothing for fun nor for show, and he is not joking when he sends his Son and delivers him up for us."[18]

Staupitz also impacted Luther's view of the penitential system of his day. In 1518, Luther wrote to Staupitz to thank him for his wonderful consolation: "Reverend Father: I remember that during your most delightful and helpful talks, through which the Lord Jesus wonderfully consoled me, you sometimes mentioned the term '*poenitentia*.'"[19] Luther's new understanding of *poenitentia* became a core concept in Luther's personal spiritual transformation.

Poenitentia can mean either the remorse of the sinner or the penance imposed on the sinner by the church. The penitential system of the medieval church fused both meanings into the term "do penance" which meant both a contrite heart and the fulfillment of satisfactions. This understanding partially caused Luther's desperation in the monastery. On the one hand, he realized that he could never completely atone for his sins despite his constant struggle to do penance properly. On the other hand, he believed that without *poenitentia*, no one could stand before God free of guilt. Luther praised Staupitz for relieving him of the distress of his tortured conscience: "Therefore, I accepted you as a messenger from heaven when you said that *poenitentia* is genuine only if it begins with love for justice and for God."[20]

Thus, under Staupitz, Luther learned that *poenitentia* began with love for God, that is, with a heart turned to God. Luther was learning that a heart is brought to this love and repentance only by the God of grace and love, who reveals himself in Jesus Christ. Servile fear and guilt cannot produce love and repentance. Luther summarized the essence of his discovery: the change in our relationship to God is accomplished not by our works of penance, but by "the grace of God."[21]

Upon coming to this understanding, Luther shared with Staupitz the joy of his discovery: "Biblical words came leaping toward me from all sides, clearly smiling and nodding assent to your statement. They so supported your opinion that while formerly no word in the whole Scripture was more bitter to me than *poenitentia* . . . now no word sounds sweeter or more pleasant to me than *poenitentia*." Notice what was central to this heart change for Luther: his new view of God-in-Christ. Luther explains, "The commandments of God become sweet when they are read not only in books but also in the wounds of the sweetest Savior."[22] The pastoral cure for Luther's guilt-ridden soul came through the pastoral care of cropping the Christ of the cross back into Luther's picture.

Through Staupitz's ministry, Luther came to grasp "together with all the saints" (Ephesians 3:18) the infinite grace and multifaceted love of God-in-Christ. Luther began to see justification and forgiveness as the mechanism for reconciliation and relationship. Justification is Christ's sledgehammer that knocks down the door separating the prodigal from the Father. Reconciliation is the bridge that paves the way for the Father to race to the prodigal and throw his loving arms around him.

The Reformer concluded his letter to Staupitz by connecting these discoveries to the writing of the Ninety-Five Theses. While he was still pondering his new understanding of salvation by grace, "behold, suddenly around us the new war trumpets of indulgences and the bugles of pardon started to sound, even to blast." So what did Luther do? "Since I was not able to counteract the furor of these men, I determined modestly to take issue with them and to pronounce their teachings as open to debate."[23] What Luther considered "modest," was none other than the Ninety-Five Theses which began the Reformation movement. The Ninety-Five Theses blossomed out of Luther's joyful and sweet discovery that he was at peace with God because God was at peace with him through his faith in Christ's grace. In sheer joy of discovery, Luther launched a Reformation!

In Daring Confidence in God's Grace, Luther Staked His Life on Christ

Christ was at work in Luther's heart from numerous directions. The Spirit used not only the people of God, like Staupitz, but also the Word of God. Confident in the sufficiency and efficacy of the Scriptures, Luther brought the questions that troubled his soul to them, expecting answers. God's Word was his daily bread: "No other study pleased me like that of the Holy Scripture. I read in it diligently and imprinted it upon my memory. Often a single passage of weighty import occupied my thoughts the whole day. . . . I want only the Word of God and do not ask for any miracle, nor desire any vision, nor will I believe an angel that teaches me anything different from the Word of God."[24]

The *Anfechtungen* of Christ on the Cross

While studying Psalm 22, Luther was stunned by the realization that Christ had experienced *anfechtungen*. On the cross, Christ cried out the words, "My God, My God, why have you forsaken me?" (Psalm 22:1). Christ had suffered what Luther had suffered—the cry of forsakenness, of abandonment, of separation. Luther wanted to know how this could be, for he did not understand why the sinless Christ should have known such desolation. Christ was neither weak, nor sinful. Luther, yes. Christ, no.

A new picture of Christ was emerging for Luther. As he focused on the cross, Luther concluded that the only explanation must be that Christ took to himself the iniquity of the human race. He who was without sin, for our sake became sin for us and so identified himself with us as to participate in our alienation.

A new view of the Father was also developing. The All Terrible was now the All Merciful. Wrath and love mingled on the cross of Christ. Somehow, in the utter desolation of the forsaken Christ, God the Father was able to reconcile sinners to himself.[25] This would become a constant theme of Luther's pastoral care—seeing, perceiving, imagining, and viewing God through the lens of the Christ of the cross.

The contemplation of the cross had convinced Luther that God was not malicious; however, the problem of the justice of God still remained. Bainton depicts the dilemma now facing Luther, "Wrath can melt into mercy, and God will be all the more the Christian God; but if justice be dissolved in leniency, how can he be the just God whom Scripture describes?"[26]

Our Righteousness from Christ

The study of Romans proved to be of inestimable value to Luther in answering this final question. In the fall of 1515, Dr. Martin Luther, now professor of Sacred Theology at the University of Wittenberg, began to expound Romans to his students. As Luther prepared his lectures, he gradually came to a clear knowledge of what he saw as the central teaching of Scripture—the doctrine of justification by grace through faith in Christ apart from works. In his preface to the written edition of his lecture notes on Romans, Luther writes, "This Epistle is really the chief part of the New Testament and the very purest Gospel, and is worthy not only that every Christian should know it word for word, by heart, but occupy himself with it every day, as the daily bread of the soul."[27]

In Romans, Luther found the answers that he had been searching after for so long. Most importantly for Luther's struggle and for the development of his Reformation theology, it was in Romans that Luther uncovered the meaning of righteousness. After searching for three decades, in the winter of 1542–1543, Luther offered a clear contrast between his understanding of righteousness when he was a monk and his understanding of righteousness from his study of Romans:

> For a long time I went astray in the monastery and didn't know what I was about. To be sure, I knew something, but I didn't know what it was until I came to the text in Romans 1, 'He who through faith is righteous shall live.' That text helped me. There I saw what righteousness Paul was talking about. Earlier in the text I read 'righteousness.' I related the abstract "righteousness" with the concrete "the righteous One" and became sure of my cause. I learned to distinguish between the righteousness of the law and the righteousness of the gospel.

I lacked nothing before this except that I made no distinction between the law and the gospel. I regarded both as the same thing and held that there was no difference between Christ and Moses except the times in which they lived and their degrees of perfection. But when I discovered the proper distinction—namely, that the law is one thing and the gospel is another—I made myself free.[28]

Luther had previously interpreted righteousness as the active righteousness of God—his attribute that rightly and justly condemns the guilty sinner. Now Luther began to understand righteousness as passive righteousness from God—his gift of righteousness that justifies the ungodly through faith alone by grace alone.

Righteousness by Faith, Not by Works

In Romans, Luther found that the route to God led through the path of faith: "Hence it comes that faith alone makes righteous and fulfills the law."[29] Going yet further, Luther discovered that the essence of sin is unbelief or lack of faith: "Hence, Christ calls unbelief the only sin, when He says, 'The Spirit will rebuke the world for sin, because they believe not on me.' For this reason, too, before good or bad works are done, which are the fruits, there must first be in the heart faith or unbelief, which is the root, the sap, the chief power of all sin.'"[30]

Luther also uncovered the meaning of faith through his study of Romans. In that meaning he found the implication of faith—life lived freely and powerfully for God and others—faith active in love: "Faith is a living, daring confidence in God's grace, so sure and certain that a man would stake his life on it a thousand times. This confidence in God's grace and knowledge of it makes all men glad and bold and happy in dealing with God and all His creatures; and this is the work of the Holy Ghost in faith."[31]

Lecturing to his students on Galatians 3:13, Luther powerfully pictures the amazing nature of this grace:

Hereby it appears that the doctrine of the gospel (which of all others is most sweet and full of most singular consolation) speaks nothing of our works or of the works of the law, but of the inscrutable mercy and love of God towards most wretched and miserable sinners. Our most merciful Father, seeing us to be oppressed and overwhelmed with the curse of the law, and that we could never be delivered from it of our own power, sent His only Son into the world and laid upon Him all the sins of all men, saying, be Thou Peter that denier; Paul that persecutor and cruel oppressor; David that adulterer; that sinner who did eat the fruit in Eden; that thief who hanged upon the cross, and be Thou that person who has committed the sins of all men: see therefore, that Thou pay and satisfy for them.[32]

For Luther, none of these theological discoveries were abstract, esoteric, academic, or unrelated to life. His discoveries in Romans directly related to his search for peace with God. Speaking of Romans 5:1, Luther lectured his students, "With 'peace' the Apostle here means that peace of which all prophets speak, namely, spiritual peace as he indicates this by the phrase 'peace with God.' This peace consists properly in an appeased conscience and in confidence in God, just as conversely the lack of peace means spiritual anxiety, a disturbed conscience and mistrust over against God."[33] The gospel grace of justification/reconciliation is Christ's answer to our *anfechtungen*—an answer that calms our conscience with the assurance of forgiveness and welcome home.

In Christ Alone, Luther Found the Door to the Father's Home

Luther's tower experience is so called because it occurred in the tower of the Black Cloister in Wittenberg (later Luther's home) at an undetermined date between 1508 and 1518. In later years, Luther often reflected on this experience and saw it as the breakthrough for which he had been searching:

> The words "righteous" and "righteousness of God" struck my conscience like lightning. When I heard them I was exceedingly terrified. If God is righteous (I thought), he must punish. But when by God's grace I pondered, in the tower and heated room of this building, over the words, "He who through faith is righteous shall live" (Rom. 1:17) and "the righteousness of God" (Rom. 3:21), I soon came to the conclusion that if we, as righteous men, ought to live from faith and if the righteousness of God should contribute to the salvation of all who believe, then salvation won't be our merit but God's mercy.[34]

This was a soul-freeing, joy-filled encounter for Luther: "My spirit was thereby cheered. For it's by the righteousness of God that we're justified and saved through Christ. These words (which had before terrified me) became more pleasing to me. The Holy Spirit unveiled the Scriptures for me in this tower."[35]

Six years later, on September 12, 1538, Luther's thrill of discovery had only grown:

> The expression "righteousness of God" was like a thunderbolt in my heart. When under the papacy I read, "In thy righteousness deliver me" and "in thy truth," I thought at once that this righteousness was an avenging anger, namely, the wrath of God. I hated Paul with all my heart when I read that the righteousness of God is revealed in the gospel. Only afterward, when I saw the words that follow—namely, that it's written that the righteous shall live through faith—and in addition consulted Augustine, was I cheered, When I learned that the righteousness of God is his mercy, and that he makes us righteous through it, a remedy was offered to me in my affliction.[36]

The very expression at which Luther had trembled—the justice of God—now became his friend. Luther explains the results of this shift. "Thereupon I felt myself to be reborn and to have gone through open doors into paradise." Now, "the whole of Scripture took on a new meaning, and whereas before the 'justice of God' had filled me with hate, now it became to me inexpressibly sweet in greater love. This passage of Paul became to me a gate to heaven."[37]

Staupitz, Psalms, and Romans all converged to provide Luther with a new cross-centered view of Christ, God, and himself. He saw Christ as a gracious Savior instead of a wrathful enemy. Luther now viewed God as a loving Father instead of an avenging judge. He perceived himself as loved by God and freed to love others instead of being hated by God and consumed with hate. At the cross, Luther first saw the light. And the light triumphed over the darkness of his heart, and the burdens and *anfechtungen* of his heart rolled away.

Jesus the Open Door

Luther's quest for personal peace ended at the foot of the cross. Because Christ was nailed to the cross, Luther no longer found himself standing outside the door of his Father's home. So he nailed his theses to the door of the Castle Church in Wittenberg, proclaiming that Christ the great Shepherd is the only door to the Father's house. Having found personal spiritual peace, Luther shifted his focus from his own spiritual state to the spiritual state of the sheep he was called to shepherd. He did not want them to experience the tormented conscience he had so long endured.

Luther's Ninety-Five Theses are the theological, logical, historical, and practical bridges between Luther the troubled soul and Luther the pastor of souls. Picture again the religious situation. According to the officially sanctioned practice of the medieval church, absolution of sin was granted to sinners who had repented, upon their confession and penance (such as fasting, prayers, pilgrimages). Yet sinners who were reconciled to God through absolution still had to experience purgatory. Indulgences relaxed or even commuted the punishment that the penitent would have to undergo in purgatory. Indulgence letters were granted for certain religious works such as participation in a crusade, the visiting of certain shrines, praying in sanctuaries where relics of saints were kept, ordering and paying for the celebration of masses, or simply for the payment of money to the church, a practice which became extremely popular in Luther's day.

Since purgatory was to cleanse the sinner of any remaining guilt, people increasingly viewed indulgences as a means of canceling their guilt. This inflamed Luther as he had broken free from guilt and was concerned that others also find such freedom from guilt. Luther's pastoral and theological concerns merged at this point. He was convinced that indulgences were positively harmful to the recipients because they impeded salvation by diverting one from the grace of God in Christ received by faith. Indulgences further induced a false sense of security. Luther reasoned that since Christ came to save sinners, then people who feel all their sins atoned for by indulgences will no longer see themselves as a sinner. In this state of self-deception, the need for faith in the sacrifice of Christ for sin has vanished.

This understanding brings us full circle—back to Luther's motivation for the Ninety-Five Theses. As Peter Manns notes, Luther's religious experience canonized his pastoral work.[38] His conscience had been tortured by the theology of the religious culture of his day, and now he sought to warn others away from this agony. His first and highest task was to ease the conscience of the faithful by pointing them away from works and toward Christ's grace. He started on his path to reform when Tetzel's indulgence sale threatened his concerns as a pastor. The Ninety-Five Theses was a pastoral soul care ministry of consoling troubled consciences by pointing people to Christ's gospel of grace.

Timeless Truth for Life and Ministry Today

If the first chapter of Luther's life story ended like the Old Testament—desperate for grace, then the second chapter of Luther's personal narrative finds Dr. Martin drinking in Christ's grace as his only hope and his spring of living water. Chapter 1 of Luther's story ends with the cry, "Alas, what am I to do!" Chapter 2 of Luther's soul care narrative cries out, "Trust in Christ alone!" Luther's life teaches us that earthly life is a boot camp where we fight *anfechtungen* through the regular exercise of faith—absolute reliance on Christ alone.

By October 31, 1517, the gospel core of Luther's theological development was well established. The rest of Luther's life and ministry and all his letters of spiritual counsel are the application to life of the truth of justification/reconciliation by faith through grace. From 1517 to 1520, "Luther began to apply his faith to the practicalities of the Christian life." He launched his soul care work in earnest in 1520, "when he heard that Elector Frederick was ill, and wrote *Fourteen Consolations for Those Who Suffer*. There he pressed an image he borrowed from Carlstadt according to which Christ, and Christ alone, was the vessel in whom believers were borne to heaven."[39] For suffering and for sin, Luther's answer was Christ and Christ alone.

We capture the essence of how Christ's gospel story invaded Luther's life story with this tweet-size summary of chapter 2:

> The Christ of the cross transformed Luther the man terrified before God into Luther the man at peace with God.

Luther's spiritual trials—his *anfechtungen*—shaped his core pastoral care question. Luther's cross-focused theology—the Christ of the cross—shaped his soul cure remedy. But what is the shape of Luther's soul care? Chapter 3 provides the gospel-centered answer to that vital question.

SECTION TWO
WHAT IS THE SHAPE OF MARTIN LUTHER'S PASTORAL COUNSELING?

LUTHER'S COUNSELING reflects his theology—it is cross-shaped and gospel-centered. Section 2 unpacks the contours of Luther's gospel-centered counsel for saints who struggle with suffering and battle against sin.

In chapter 3, we see how Luther's counseling followed the historic focus of pastoral soul care and spiritual direction. Pastoral care always dealt both with the evils we have suffered in a fallen world and with the sins we have committed. From the time of Christ, to the church fathers, to the medieval church, up until Luther's day, spiritual care consistently addressed the four areas of sustaining and healing (*parakaletic* counseling for suffering) and reconciling and guiding (*nouthetic* counseling for sin).

Luther turned the counseling of his day back to the Christ of the cross. Satan insists that we cannot trust God's heart. The Christ of the cross is the one image, the one reality, the one truth that conquers the condemning lie of Satan.

Chapters 4–11 form the heart of this book. Each chapter uses vignettes, narratives, stories, and extended quotes from Luther's letters of spiritual counsel, table talks, and other writings to illustrate how Luther applied the heart of the gospel to the heart of his flock. Each chapter further discusses how we can apply Luther's gospel-centered counseling to our lives and ministries.

CHAPTER THREE
COUNSELING THROUGH THE LENS OF THE CROSS

MARTIN'S BROTHER, James, informed Luther that their mother, Mrs. Margaret Luther, was seriously ill. Immediately, on May 20, 1532, Martin wrote a letter of spiritual counsel and consolation to his mother.[1] Luther began with gospel-centered words that were common in his letter writing, "Grace and peace in Christ Jesus, our Lord and Savior, Amen." More than just a salutation, "grace and peace" were Luther's shorthand for justification ("Forgiven!") and reconciliation ("Welcome home!").

Tenderly, son Martin wrote, "My dearly beloved Mother! I have received my brother James's letter concerning your illness. Of course this grieves me deeply, especially because I cannot be with you in person, as I certainly would like to be." The whole family grieved: "All your children and my Katie pray for you; some weep."

Unable to be there in person, Luther wrote, "Yet I am coming to you personally through this letter, and I, together with all the members of my family, shall certainly not be absent from you in spirit." Luther assumed that what he shares in writing is already occurring naturally, as it should be, through the body of Christ: "I trust that you have long since been abundantly instructed, without any help from me, that (God be praised) you have taken God's comforting Word into your heart, and that you are adequately provided with preachers and comforters." It is Luther's basic presupposition that the people of God use the Word of God to bring comfort to a suffering child of God.

Having shared gospel sustaining with his mother by acknowledging the painfulness of her situation and by sharing in her sorrow and grief, Luther next brought gospel healing to his mother by pointing her to her heavenly hope in Christ: "Dear Mother, you also know the true center and foundation of your salvation from whom you are to seek comfort in this and all troubles, namely, Jesus Christ, the cornerstone." Luther does not point his mother to himself, but directed her to images of the ultimate Comforter—her Triune God. Mother Margaret can trust Christ's good heart: "He will not waver or fail us, nor allow us to sink or perish, for he is the Savior and is called the Savior of all poor sinners, and of all who are caught in tribulation and death, and rely on him, and call on his name." And she can trust the good heart of God the Father and God the Spirit: "The Father and God of all consolation grant you, through his holy Word and Spirit, a steadfast, joyful, and grateful faith blessedly to overcome this and all other trouble."

Luther's letter not only offered sustaining empathy and healing encouragement for Margaret's suffering, it also presents gospel reconciliation and gospel guidance for her sanctification. Luther raises the reality that this sickness, like all sickness, can be seen as part of "God's fatherly, gracious chastisement." Even sickness comes to us through the affectionate sovereignty of God, being "sent by God's grace" to help us to grow in grace as we cling to Christ's gospel of grace.

But how do we, along with Luther's mother, experience sanctification in suffering? Luther directed his beloved mother to God's Word, "Christ says, 'Be of good cheer; I have overcome the world.'" Nearly seventy-five percent of Luther's letter to his mother is a relevant, compassionate application of John 16:33 to her sickness. This is a constant theme in Luther's soul care—envisioning the victory of Christ over the schemes of Satan who seeks to use our suffering to cause us to doubt God's good heart. So Luther directed his mother's attention to "the dear Comforter" who "bids us to be of good cheer." She was to cast her cares on him because she can be confident that Christ cares for her.

This Jesus is not only caring; he is also in control. He is the Comforter Victor: "He is the victor, the true hero, who gives and appropriates to me his victory." Ever honest about the temptations to doubt,

Luther raised the possibility with his mother that the thought of sin and death would terrify her. If these fears arise, she was to practice gospel self-counsel: "Let us in opposition to this lift up our hearts and say: 'Behold, dear soul, what are you doing?'" Rather than listening to the terrorizing suggestions of the evil one, Margaret was to "listen to the comforting words of my Savior: 'Be of good cheer, be of good cheer; I have overcome the world.'"

Martin encourages his mother to preach the gospel to herself, saying to herself and saying against Satan, sin, and death:

> I shall cling to him, and to his words and comfort, I shall hold fast; regardless of whether I remain or go yonder, I shall live by this word, for he does not lie to me. You would like to deceive me with your terrors, and with your lying thoughts you would like to tear me away from such a victory and savior. But they are lies, as surely as it is true that he has overcome you and commanded us to be comforted.

To John 16:33, Luther adds 1 Corinthians 15:54: "Saint Paul also boasts likewise and defies the terrors of death: 'Death is swallowed up in victory. O death, where is thy victory. O hell, where is thy sting.'" Luther exhorted his mother toward confidence in Christ alone and in Scripture alone: "By such words and thoughts, and by none other, let your heart be moved, dear Mother."

Luther's counsel to his mother is gospel saturated. He rejoices with her that they are no longer captured by the deceiving image that sees Christ "not as a comforter but as a severe judge and tyrant, so that we had to flee from him to Mary and the saints, and not expect of him any grace or comfort." Gospel images of Christ make all the difference in how we do gospel-centered counseling. Son and mother face their grief with a God who "is not a judge, nor cruel," and with a Savior who "is not the man who accuses and threatens us, but rather the man who reconciles us with God, and intercedes for us with his own death and blood shed for us so that we should not fear him, but approach him with all assurance and call him dear Savior, sweet Comforter, faithful bishop of our souls."

Forty days after Martin wrote his mother about victory over death, Mrs. Margaret Luther passed from death to life through him who overcame death. She experienced what Luther wrote in the conclusion of his letter of gospel consolation: ". . . and finally to taste and experience that what he himself says is true: 'Be of good cheer; I have overcome the world.' And with this I commend your body and soul to his mercy. Amen. Your loving son, Martin Luther."

In this very personal letter, we find the contours of Martin Luther's pastoral counseling ministry. We see:

- Luther the pastor engaged in the personal ministry of the Word through letters of spiritual consolation and gospel conversations.
- Luther's commitment to the sufficiency of Scripture in addressing the human heart's most pressing struggles.
- Luther's practice of historic soul care through gospel-centered sustaining and healing for people struggling with suffering.
- Luther's practice of historic spiritual direction through gospel-centered reconciling and guiding for sin and sanctification.

Chapters 4–11 narrate, illustrate, and apply these themes. Chapter 3 addresses these major motifs through the lenses of the personal ministry of the Word, the sufficiency of Scripture, and historic gospel-centered counseling.

Luther the Pastor and the Personal Ministry of the Word

While we often see Luther as a theologian-reformer, he envisioned himself as a pastor-counselor. In this calling, Luther engaged both in the pulpit ministry of the Word—preaching, and in the personal ministry of the Word—counseling. Luther believed that every pastor should be a soul caregiver.

In his lectures to his students on Galatians, Luther specifically identified the pastor's calling, "If I am a minister of the Word, I preach, I comfort the brokenhearted, and I administer the sacraments."[2] Luther never dichotomized preaching and counseling. He saw both as gospel-centered, Word-based ministries. Luther had the same message in his letter to Lazarus Spengler, penned on August 15, 1528. Speaking of administering the sacraments, Luther then outlines the calling and role of God's minister: "This is the same as their obligation to preach, comfort, absolve, help the poor, and visit the sick, as often as these services are needed and demanded."[3] Luther expected pastors to be soul physicians—as he was.

Luther the Letter Writer and Table Talker

As part of Luther's active pastoral ministry, he wrote thousands of letters, similar to the one he sent his mother, comforting and counseling fellow Christians. Approximately 2,580 of Luther's letters are still in existence. Many were letters of spiritual consolation and counsel through which Luther practiced the soul physician art of the personal ministry of the Word. Krodel explains their relevance, "The letters originated in the complex situation in which Luther found himself; yet they reveal insights which speak to men of today."[4]

But why write so many letters? At various times, Luther was in hiding due to the threat of arrest or execution. At other times, geographical distance and the travel limitations of his day meant that the only way to minister personally was through letters.

Yet, whenever possible, Luther ministered personally. We find evidence of this in Luther's table talks. The Augustinian friars who had lived in the Black Cloister in Wittenberg abandoned their monastic life due to the Reformation. From the time of his marriage to Katherine von Bora in 1525 until his death in 1546, Luther's family resided in the Black Cloister, where he welcomed guests and housed those in need.

The relaxed atmosphere of the hospitable home was conducive to spiritual conversation, and John Mathesius, who was often present in 1540, left this description:

> Although our doctor [Martin Luther] often took weighty and profound thoughts to table with him and sometimes maintained the silence of the monastery during the entire meal, so that not a word was spoken, yet at appropriate times he spoke in a very jovial way. We used to call his conversation the condiments of the meal because we preferred it to all spices and dainty food. When he wished to get us to talk he would throw out a question . . . Often good questions were put to him from the Bible, and he provided expert and concise answers.[5]

Some of the men who listened to Luther's dinner conversation began to record these gospel conversations, and these times became known as table talks. As a teacher, Luther was accustomed to seeing open notebooks and poised pens before him. He often challenged the note takers to record statements with exhortations of *Write it down! Mark this well!*

Luther, the Word of God, and the People of God

Luther never saw the ministry of the Word as something reserved for a distinct class of people such as the clergy. He linked the Word of God and the people of God through the personal ministry of the Word: "No man should be alone when he opposes Satan. The church and the ministry of the Word were instituted for this purpose, that hands may be joined together and one may help another. If the prayer of one doesn't help, the prayer of another will."[6]

In a table talk recorded by Conrad Cordatus during the autumn of 1531, Luther urges every believer to engage in gospel conversations: "Those who are tempted by doubt and despair I should console in this fashion. First, by warning them to beware of solitude and *to converse constantly with others about the Psalms and Scriptures.*"[7]

The personal ministry of the Word was essential in the issue that was most central to Luther's soul, to his soul care ministry, and to the Reformation—salvation in Christ alone. A dispute had arisen as to whether confession and absolution of sin should only be done publicly through "the preaching of the holy gospel." On April 18, 1533, Luther writes to the council of the City of Nurnberg to insist that the personal ministry of the Word was also necessary:

> For one has to instruct consciences that the comfort of the gospel is directed to each individual particularly; therefore, as you people who understand these matters know, the gospel has to be applied through Word and sacrament to each individual particularly, so that each individual in his conscience is tossed about by the questions whether this great grace, which Christ offers to all men, belongs to him too. Under these circumstances it can easily be understood that one is not to abolish private absolution in favor or public absolution.[8]

Luther practiced what he preached by receiving the gospel when others ministered the Word to him: "I have often been refreshed by the words which John Bugenhagen once spoke to me: 'You ought not to despise my consolation because I am convinced that I speak words of God from heaven.'"[9]

We are ambassadors of gospel reconciliation for each other: "Often when I was troubled by something, Pomeranus or Philip or even my Katy would speak to me, and I was comforted as I realized that God was saying this because a brother was saying it either out of duty or out of love."[10]

Luther believed in the pulpit ministry of the Word—preaching and applying the gospel. He also believed in the personal ministry of the Word—sharing and applying the gospel with each other. And he believed in the private ministry of the Word—preaching the gospel to ourselves. Lecturing his students on Galatians 5:6 (we are sons of God who can cry out, "Abba, Father!"), Luther urges them to speak gospel truth to themselves:

> Let every man, then, so practice with himself, that his con-
> science may be fully assured that he is under grace, and that
> his person and his works do please God. And if he feel any
> wavering or doubting, let him exercise his faith, and wrestle
> against it, and labor to attain more strength and assurance
> of faith, and so be able to say: I know that I am accepted
> and have the Holy Ghost, not for my own worthiness, work,
> or merit, but for Christ's sake, who of His love towards us
> made Himself subject to the law and took away the sin of
> the world. In Him do I believe. If I am a sinner, and err, he is
> righteous and cannot err."[11]

Luther was committed to the ministry of the Word—in every form and fashion—because he was convinced of the sufficiency of Scripture.

Luther the Pastor and the Sufficiency of Scripture

For Luther, the sufficiency of Scripture equals the sufficiency of Christ's gospel victory narrative. He looked at Scripture and counseling through the lens of the cross. In *The Freedom of the Christian*—Luther's most focused writing on the application of the gospel to daily life—Luther offers a summary of how to apply the gospel:

> You may ask, however, "Which is the word that gives such
> abundant grace, and how shall I use it?" The answer:
>
> It is nothing but the preaching of Christ in accordance with
> the gospel, spoken in such a way that you heard your God
> speaking to you. It shows how your whole life and work are

nothing before God but must eternally perish with everything that is in you. When you truly believe that you are
guilty, then you must despair of yourself and confess that the
verse in Hosea is true, 'O Israel, in yourself you have nothing
but your destruction; it is in me alone that you have your
help.' So that you can come out of yourself and away from
yourself, that is, out of your perishing, God places the dear
Son, Jesus Christ, before you and allows you to be addressed
by this living and comforting Word. You are to surrender
yourself with steadfast faith in this Word and boldly trust
God. And for the sake of this selfsame faith, all your sins will
be forgiven, all your destruction will be overcome, and you
will be righteous, genuine, satisfied, upright, and fulfill all the
commandments and be free of all things.[12]

After Luther's work on Psalms, Romans, and Galatians, and after
his posting of the Ninety-Five Theses, the core of his theological development was complete. From that time forward, Luther focused his life,
ministry, and letters of spiritual counsel on applying to life the truth of
justification/reconciliation by faith through grace:

What remained was to spell out its impact on the daily conduct of the Christian life. In this regard the first and highest task was to ease the consciences of the faithful. His own
conscience had been tortured by the religious world in which
he became an adult, and now he sought to warn others away
from this agony. He started on the path to reform when Tetzel's
indulgence sale contradicted his teachings as a professor and
threatened his concerns as a pastor. Now these same concerns
thrust him back into the fray, even if from afar. By explaining
the practical consequences of his theology, he took responsibility for all he had earlier said and done.[13]

Tappert, who edited and translated *Luther: Letters of Spiritual Counsel*, maintains, "an examination of the collected works of Luther makes it clear that his spiritual counsel was not simply the applications of external techniques. It was part and parcel of his theology."[14] According to Tappert, Luther rejected the assumption of the medieval scholastics that wisdom for living in a broken world could be known by means of reason or logic. Luther also disavowed the theory of the medieval mystics that God and his will can be known by means of self-mortification or ecstasy.

What then is the sufficient source for scriptural care? Tappert explains, "In Luther's eyes, therefore, spiritual counsel is always concerned above all else with faith—nurturing, strengthening, establishing, practicing faith—and because 'faith cometh by hearing,' the Word of God (or the gospel) occupies a central place in it." Luther grounded his theology of counseling on the sufficiency of Christ's gospel of grace. Tappert captures it succinctly, "The ministry to troubled souls is a ministry of the gospel."[15]

Luther lived and breathed Scripture for his life. Nebe fittingly summarizes, "The Reformer used the Scriptures for edification as long as he lived. God's Word was his daily food, and his unfailing weapon of offence and defence."[16] This was Luther's testimony, "No other study pleased me like that of the Holy Scripture. I read in it diligently and imprinted it upon my memory. Often a single passage of weighty import occupied my thoughts the whole day."[17] What started in the monastery, continued lifelong: "For some years now I have read through the Bible twice every year. If you picture the Bible to be a mighty tree and every word a little branch, I have shaken every one of these branches because I wanted to know what it was and what it meant."[18]

What was true for Luther's life was also true for his counseling ministry. In a letter to Henning Teppen in 1522, Luther recommended the Holy Scriptures as the only true comfort in distress. Applauding Teppen's "great knowledge of Scripture," Luther directed

him to Paul: "You have the Apostle who shows to you a garden, or
paradise, which is full of comfort, when he says: 'Whatever was written, was written for our instruction, so that through patience and the
consolation of the Scriptures we might have hope.' Here he attributes
to Holy Scripture the function of comforting. Who may dare to seek
or ask for comfort anywhere else?"[19] Is there any clearer statement of
the sufficiency of Scripture for counseling?

Luther saw Scripture as sufficient for finding comfort and also
for fighting temptation. In *The Large Catechism*, he wrote, "Nothing
helps more powerfully against the devil, the world, the flesh, and all
evil thoughts than occupying oneself with God's word, having conversations about it, and contemplating it."[20]

The gospel is sufficient for comfort in suffering, for victory over
sin, and for assuaging spiritual doubts. This is true for self-counsel:
"Let us learn, therefore, in great and horrible terrors, when our conscience feels nothing but sin and judges that God is angry with us, and
that Christ has turned His face from us, not to follow the sense and
feeling of our own heart, but to stick to the Word of God." It is true
also for counseling others: "So we also labor by the Word of God that
we may set at liberty those that are entangled, and bring them to the
pure doctrine of faith, and hold them there."[21]

Luther's doctrine of sufficiency was robust enough to make room
for the appropriate role of reason-redeemed-by-faith. In a table talk,
Luther was asked whether reason had any value for the Christian. Luther answered, "Prior to faith and a knowledge of God, reason is darkness, but in believers it's an excellent instrument. Just as all gifts and
instruments of nature are evil in godless men, so they are good in believers." Luther understood the destructive noetic (mental/reasoning)
effect of sin on unregenerate reason. He also understood the impact
of regeneration on the redeemed mind: "Faith is now furthered by
reason, speech, and eloquence, whereas these were only impediments

prior to faith. Enlightened reason, taken captive by faith, receives life from faith, for it is slain and given life again."[22] Faith redeems reason.

Luther's doctrine of sufficiency was also robust enough to make room for the appropriate use of medication:

> Accordingly a physician is our Lord God's mender of the body, as we theologians are his healers of the spirit; we are to restore what the devil has damaged. So a physician administers theriaca (an antidote for poison) when Satan gives poison. Healing comes from the application of nature to the creature. . . . It's our Lord God who created all things, and they are good. Wherefore it's permissible to use medicine, for it is a creature of God. Thus I replied to Hohndorf, who inquired of me when he heard from Karlstadt that it's not permissible to make use of medicine. I said to him, "Do you eat when you're hungry?"[23]

God graces us with soul physicians who prescribe the medicine of Scripture for the soul, and God graces us with physicians who prescribe medicine for the body.

Luther the Pastor and Historic Gospel-Centered Counseling

Luther did not invent pastoral counseling; he reformed it. The church has always been about the business of helping hurting and hardened people. The contours of Luther's counsel followed the historic focus of pastoral counseling from the time of Christ, to the church fathers, to the medieval church, up until his day. Pastoral care always dealt both with the evils we have suffered and with the sins we have committed. It always addressed four areas: sustaining, healing, reconciling, and guiding. Sustaining and healing, or *parakaletic* counseling, apply the gospel to suffering with the goal of sanctification. Reconciling and guiding, or *nouthetic* counseling, apply the gospel to sin with the goal of sanctification.

Luther returned the pastoral counseling of his day to its historic gospel moorings by focusing on the Christ of the cross—an image which became a theme, a picture, a controlling vision for Luther's counseling ministry. Luther's cross-shaped counseling applied the gospel to suffering—directing people to the Christ of the cross to see that God is good even when life is bad. Luther's Christ-focused lens applied the gospel to sin—directing people to the cross of Christ to see that God is gracious even when we are sinful. Sustaining, healing, reconciling, and guiding encompass a four-directional, historical map. These four compass points are the traditional, time-tested, and widely-recognized model for understanding Christian spiritual care.

Too often, we build personal ministry models without the wisdom of the historic voices of the church. Clebsch and Jaekle present a convincing explanation for our lack of connection with the history of Christian mutual care:

> Faced with an urgency for some system by which to conceptualize the human condition and to deal with the modern grandeurs and terrors of the human spirit, theoreticians of the cure of souls have too readily adopted the leading academic psychologies. Having no pastoral theology to inform our psychology or even to identify the cure of souls as a mode of human helping, we have allowed psychoanalytic thought, for example, to dominate the vocabulary of the spirit.[24]

Today's crying needs drown out yesterday's relevant answers. Why? We lack a sufficient awareness of the victorious ways in which people have faced life issues in centuries past. In particular, we lack awareness of how the Reformers, led by Luther, assumed the ancient roles of soul physicians and spiritual friends and modeled the ancient arts of soul care and spiritual direction.

Imagine that we stumbled upon a treasure map directing us to the riches of biblical insights for living found in Luther's reforming ministry. Using our map and arriving at our destination, we find an immeasurable treasure. In fact, we find so much truth for life that we are overwhelmed. How do we sort it all out, decode it, translate it? How do we incorporate the changing with the changeless and balance today's demands with yesterday's treasures?

We require a model, map, or grid that can alert us to currently forgotten but time-tested modes for meeting people's spiritual needs. We have chosen to use the traditional model of soul care (sustaining and healing) and spiritual direction (reconciling and guiding) as a guide into the past beliefs and practices of our ancestor in the faith—Martin Luther.

We need to define our terms in order to use sustaining, healing, reconciling, and guiding to explore Luther's one-another ministry. Once we understand these specific definitions, we can use them to ask concrete questions when reading Luther's letters of spiritual counsel, table talks, personal narratives, commentaries, and other primary historical documents. This aids us in uncovering the richness and diversity of Luther's soul care and in distilling relevant applications for our practice of Christian care giving.

Plotting the Map of Soul Care and Spiritual Direction: The Twin Themes

Experts who examine the history of spiritual care have consistently identified the twin historical themes of soul care and spiritual direction. McNeil's *A History of the Cure of Souls* traces the art of soul care throughout history and various cultures: "Lying deep in the experience and culture of the early Christian communities are the closely related practices of mutual edification and fraternal correction." Speaking of the apostle Paul, McNeil notes, "In such passages we cannot fail to see the Apostle's design to create an atmosphere in which the intimate exchange of spiritual help, the mutual guidance of souls, would be a normal feature of Christian behavior."[25]

Throughout his historical survey, McNeil explains that mutual edification involves soul care through the provision of sustaining (consolation, support, and comfort) and healing (encouragement and enlightenment). Fraternal correction includes spiritual direction through the provision of reconciling (discipline, confession, and forgiveness) and guiding (direction and counsel).

In *Clinical Theology*, Lake clarifies that historically soul care deals with suffering while spiritual direction deals with sin. He summarizes his classification, explaining how "pastoral care is defective unless it can deal *thoroughly* with these evils we have suffered as well as with the sins we have committed."[26] Throughout church history, biblical caregivers have practiced *parakaletic* counseling by providing sustaining and healing soul care that addresses suffering, deprivation, and hurting hearts. They have also practiced *nouthetic* counseling by providing reconciling and guiding spiritual direction that deals with sin, depravity, and hardened hearts.

Plotting the Map of Sustaining, Healing, Reconciling, and Guiding: The Four Tasks

Clebsch and Jaekle offer the classic description of traditional spiritual care. The care of souls has historically involved "helping acts, done by *representative Christian persons*, directed toward the *healing, sustaining, guiding, and reconciling of troubled persons* whose troubles arise *in the context of ultimate meanings and concerns.*"[27]

Oden suggests that the four tasks of sustaining, healing, reconciling, and guiding "try to absorb and work seriously with a wide variety of confessional and denominational viewpoints on ministry." They try to "reasonably bring all these voices into a centric, historically sensitive integration, with special attention to historical consensus."[28]

In 1538, a follower of Luther, Martin Bucer, wrote a pastoral care manual, *Concerning the True Care of Souls*. Bucer's summary of spiritual care included the categories of sustaining (strengthening weak Christians), healing (offering hope to hurting Christians), reconciling (drawing to Christ those who are alienated), and guiding (discipling and urging Christians forward in all good).[29]

The framework of the two themes and four tasks provides a perspective—a historical way of viewing and thinking about biblical counseling, the personal ministry of the Word, spiritual friendship, pastoral care, and one-another ministry. Combining the two themes and the four tasks creates the following profile of historic spiritual care.

- Soul Care: Comfort for Suffering
  » Sustaining
  » Healing

- Spiritual Direction: Confrontation for Sinning
  » Reconciling
  » Guiding

Figure 3-1 expands this outline. The rest of this chapter explains how I use the terms throughout this book to distill personal applications and ministry implications from Luther's ministry.

FIGURE 3-1

4 BIBLICAL COMPASS POINTS FOR GOSPEL-CENTERED COUNSELING

Gospel Conversations for the Evils We Have Suffered
Parakaletic Biblical Counseling
"God Is Good Even When Life Is Bad"

Gospel Compass Point #1: Sustaining and the Troubling Story—"It's Normal to Hurt"
- Gospel Foundation: The Christ of the Cross Understands Our Suffering
- Gospel Focus: Sense Their Earthly Story of Despair/Empathize with and Embrace Them

Gospel Compass Point #2: Healing and the Faith Story—"It's Possible to Hope"
- Gospel Foundation: The Resurrected Christ Provides Eternal Hope in Our Suffering
- Gospel Focus: Stretch Them to God's Eternal Story of Hope/Encourage Them to Embrace God

Gospel Conversations for the Sins We Have Committed
Nouthetic Biblical Counseling
"God Is Gracious Even When I Am Sinful"

Gospel Compass Point #3: Reconciling and the Redemptive Story—"It's Horrible to Sin, but Wonderful to Be Forgiven"
- Gospel Foundation: Christ's Grace Superabounds Over Our Sin
- Gospel Focus: Shed Their Enslaving Story of Death and Expose Their Sin and Christ's Grace

Gospel Compass Point #4: Guiding and the Growth-in-Grace Story—"It's Supernatural to Mature"
- Gospel Foundation: The Grace That Saves Is the Grace That Sanctifies
- Gospel Focus: Strengthen Them with Christ's Story of Life/Empower Them to Christlike Love

Gospel Compass Point #1: Sustaining

For over two thousand years, Christian sustaining has emphasized consolation and compassionate commiseration believing that shared sorrow is endurable sorrow. In sustaining, we offer empathy—feeling deeply the feelings of another, weeping with those who weep. We join with people in their grief and pain in their troubling story by communicating that *it's normal to hurt*. When the fallen world falls on our spiritual friends, we connect with them by acknowledging that *life is bad*. When our friends, like the apostle Paul in 2 Corinthians 1:8–9, feel the sentence of death and despair even of life, we climb in the casket with them, identifying with their feelings of despair.

Historic sustaining provides comfort in the original sense of the word—offering co-fortitude by coming alongside to lend support and to instill courage in a hurting heart. Through sustaining care, we help hurting people to endure and transcend irretrievable loss. When we are with those who are facing such loss and grief, we offer wise pilotage for souls in danger of floundering in external distress and inner doubt. We draw a line in the sand of the soul finding a stopping place against retreat from God. Unlike Job's miserable counselors, we comfort others with the comfort we have received from the God of all comfort.

Gospel Compass Point #2: Healing

For over two thousand years, Christian healing has underscored the encouragement that comes through enlightened eyes that see God at work behind life's miseries and mysteries. In healing, we understand that *when life stinks, our perspective shrinks*. Therefore, we embark on a journey with our hurting friends to listen together for God's eternal story of deliverance. In scores of ways we ask, in the midst of messes, *What is God up to in this? What are you doing with Christ in this?* We work with suffering people to co-create faith stories and cross-and-resurrection narratives so people can rejoice in the truth that in Christ, *it's possible to hope*.

When all seems dark and hopeless, we direct people to Christ and pray that the eyes of their hearts will be enlightened to the truth that *God is good. He's good all the time!* As healing soul physicians, we encourage our spiritual friends to say with the apostle Paul, "But this happened that we might not rely on ourselves but on God, who raises the dead" (2 Corinthians 1:9b). We celebrate the resurrection and rejoice because of the empty tomb.

Historic healing also emphasizes faith eyes, spiritual eyes, or cross-eyes by using gospel conversations to enlighten people to how Christ's victory narrative can invade their life story. If sustaining brings surviving, then healing produces thriving. Even when situations cannot change, attitudes and character can. We help people to find Christ even when they cannot find answers or relief. We follow a biblical theology of suffering that teaches that crisis provides a door of opportunity that can produce forward movement from victim to victor. Through creative suffering, we place ourselves and our spiritual friends on God's anvil to be master-crafted according to his perfect will and good heart.

Gospel Compass Point #3: Reconciling

For over two thousand years, Christian reconciling has focused upon guilt and grace, sin and forgiveness, repentance and mercy, shame and shalom. As ambassadors of reconciliation, we understand that reconciliation with God requires a personal awareness of the truth that, *it's horrible to sin, but wonderful to be forgiven.* Like the Puritans, we practice the twin arts of loading the conscience with guilt and lightening the conscience with grace—always reminding people that where sin abounds, grace superabounds. Through gospel conversations we seek to enlighten people to see that *God is gracious even when they are sinful.* We see ourselves as dispensers of grace.

As ambassadors of reconciliation, we understand the creation, fall, redemption narrative. In helping people to find victory over sin, we emphasize God's original creation of humanity in his image, humanity's fall into sin, and believers' redemption through Christ's grace. We also focus on a three-fold need for reconciliation—with God (due to alienation), with others (due to separation), and with self (due to dis-integration). We seek to restore people to a right relationship with God, others, and self through applying the redemptive story to their daily relationships.

Gospel Compass Point #4: Guiding

For over two thousand years, Christian guiding has concentrated on the wisdom necessary to apply God's Word in trying situations in order to promote growth in grace—Christlikeness. In guiding, we focus first on the prerequisite for wise, specific choices—a redeemed, maturing, God-dependent heart and mind (heart change). Rather than presenting self-sufficient sources for wisdom for living, we seek to communicate, *it's supernatural to mature.* We do this by stirring up the gift of God that already resides within the Christian as a new creation in Christ. We teach about our new nurture (justification, reconciliation) and our new nature (regeneration, redemption).

Building upon these foundations, we practice devil craft—Luther's name for the shared discovery of biblical principles for spiritual victory over Satan. We also engage in the mutual exploration of scriptural principles to help perplexed people make confident choices in matters of the soul. Together, as guide and disciple, we discover practical, proverbial, gospel-centered wisdom that equips our disciples to love God and others in increasingly mature ways.

Timeless Truth for Life and Ministry Today

Counseling has many names and labels: biblical counseling, pastoral counseling, one-another ministry, the personal ministry of the Word, mutual discipleship, mentoring, soul care, spiritual direction, et cetera. While we could list scores of descriptors, there are really only two ways to do counseling. We can view counseling through the lens of the cross, or we can view counseling through the lens of works.

When we view counseling through the lens of works, it is ultimately all about us—our effort, our self-sufficiency, our happiness, our situation improving. Works-based counseling becomes solution-focused counseling. We find temporary fixes for shallow external problems. Works-based counseling is ultimately always world-based counseling—our source of wisdom for life in a broken world is that identical broken world. Human reason unredeemed by grace seeks to fix human problems with human strength.

When we view counseling through the lens of the cross, it is ultimately all about him—Christ's work, Christ-sufficiency, Christ's glory—our souls becoming more like Christ. Grace-based counseling becomes soul-u-tion-focused counseling. Through Christ, we find eternal redemption for deep internal problems. Grace-based counseling is Word-based counseling—our source of wisdom for life in a broken world is the author of life and creator of that world. Reason redeemed by grace surrenders to Christ's resurrection power to cure human problems with Christ's strength and wisdom.

For the next eight chapters, we will look over Luther's shoulder as he offers grace-based sustaining, healing, reconciling, and guiding. Using these four compass points, we will discover Luther's theological GPS in one chapter, and then we will explore his methodological GPS in the next. Combined, we will learn how the gospel makes a difference in how we view and use the Bible to sustain, heal, reconcile, and guide God's people for God's glory through Christ's grace.

But before you turn that page, take a look at this tweet-size summary of the main message of chapter 3:

> In order to comprehensively view and competently use the Bible in counseling, we must view life through the lens of Christ's gospel victory narrative.

CHAPTER FOUR

SUFFERING AND THE TRIAL OF FAITH: LUTHER'S THEOLOGY OF SUSTAINING

IN EARLY May 1519, Luther's friend George Spalatin asked him to counsel Mark Schart who was experiencing distressing thoughts about death. Luther sent Schart his letter of spiritual counsel entitled, *A Sermon on Preparing to Die*. Martin Bertram, the modern translator of the sermon, explains: "The entire writing echoes his experience as a pastor and confessor constantly in contact with men and women who were terrified by the maze of popular customs and practices observed by the church in connection with death. To Schart and others like him Luther speaks with intimate and comforting understanding."[1]

The sermon is a classic example of Luther's application of the gospel to all of life—including suffering. From his own spiritual experience, Luther understood that the absence of faith in God during the presence of suffering led to a terrified conscience that perceived God to be angry and evil instead of loving and good. As Luther pondered how the gospel applied to people experiencing such excruciating inner suffering, he painted five pastoral soul care portraits: (1) the trial of faith, (2) *coram Deo* faith, (3) the perspective of faith, (4) the scriptural context of faith, and (5) the gospel content of faith.

Luther's Portrait of the Depth of Suffering: The Trial of Faith

Luther perceived two levels of suffering based upon two kinds of evil in our fallen world. Level one suffering happened *to* a person—external suffering such as illness, persecution, rejection, or death. Level two suffering happened *in* a person—the internal suffering of the trial of faith as sufferers reflected on their external suffering. Level one suffering was the result of living in a fallen world, while level two suffering resulted from temptations to doubt God arising from the world, the flesh, and the devil.

While not minimizing the pain of external suffering, Luther emphasized the internal suffering of the trial of faith (*anfechtungen*). This deep suffering involves a person's internal reaction of depression, fear, anxiety, panic, and loss of faith in response to external evils. Thus, for Luther, the greatest evil was the suffering of the conscience when it moved away from God due to lack of faith in his goodness. The worst thing that happened was not the evil suffered, as bad as that was. The tragedy was the potential hemorrhage in the relationship with God when the individual responded to evil by doubting God's goodness.

Luther utilized this twin portrait of suffering in his letter of spiritual counsel to the Saxon Elector, Frederick the Wise. In 1519, the Elector was stricken with a serious illness and his court feared for his life. Frederick's chaplain, George Spalatin, suggested that Luther prepare some writings of spiritual comfort for Frederick. Indebted to the Elector for unyielding protection against his enemies, Luther felt a special sense of obligation to fulfill Spalatin's request and thus penned "The Fourteen Consolations: For Those Who Labor and Are Heavy-Laden."[2]

In his letter, Luther empathized with Frederick's external suffering while also emphasizing his internal suffering: "And if there are that many diseases, how great do you think will be the number of misfortunes that assail our possessions, our friends, and even our very mind, which, after all, is the main target of all evils and the one trysting place of sorrow and every ill?"[3] Diseases and misfortunes constituted level one external suffering, and distresses and doubts of the mind comprised level two internal suffering.

Luther labeled these level two internal sufferings spiritual trials, trials of the faith, or *anfechtungen*. In relationship to suffering, Luther defined these spiritual trials of faith as satanic temptations to doubt God.[4]

From his personal and pastoral experience, Luther understood that the worst *anfechtungen* were trials of faith—doubts about God's goodness produced by the mind's reflection on and reaction to external suffering. Satan was always complicit in nurturing these doubts:

> When God sends us tribulation, it is not as reason and Satan argue: "See there God flings you into prison, endangers your life. Surely He hates you. He is angry with you; for if He did not hate you, He would not allow this thing to happen." In this way Satan turns the rod of a Father into the rope of a hangman and the most salutary remedy into the deadliest poison. He is an incredible master at devising thoughts of this nature. Therefore, it is very difficult to differentiate in tribulations between him who kills and Him who chastises in a friendly way.[5]

For Luther, suffering is God's medicine of choice to awake us from our slumbering self-sufficiency and turn us to heightened Christ-sufficiency. Satan seeks to turn God's medicine into poison by causing us to doubt God's goodness and thus create a breach in our relationship with God.

Genesis 50:20 explains that what people intend for evil, God weaves together for good. Satan twists this truth and tempts us to believe that what God intends for good is really evil—God is getting back at us instead of getting us back to himself. In the trial of faith, Satan tempts us to put God's heart on trial. That temptation is the deepest suffering a child of God can ever endure.

Luther's Portrait of the Focus on Christ: *Coram Deo* Faith

Since Luther defined the deepest level of suffering as a trial of faith, his spiritual counsel was primarily concerned with sustaining, healing, reconciling, and guiding faith. In sustaining, Luther aimed to maintain faith in the goodness of God during times of suffering. Put in our vernacular, we would say, *God is good even when life is bad*. Luther was convinced that in the midst of suffering, people needed to perceive God as a good Father who has good intentions for his children. Thus, Luther sought to sustain faith in the wisdom, plan, and purposes of God as revealed in Christ.

In comforting the Elector Frederick, Luther repeatedly returns to images of God's goodness. He speaks of the psalmist in Psalm 139, "marveling among other things at the goodness of God." Luther applauds Augustine in his *Confessions* reciting, "so beautifully the benefits of God toward him from his mother's womb." Luther urges Frederick to reflect on his past so he could "understand God's ever-present care and providence over us." Luther encourages Frederick to recall to mind Psalm 40:17, "I am poor and needy, may the Lord think of me." He directs Frederick to Psalm 139:15–16 and asks, "What does the psalmist intend with such words except to show us by this marvelous illustration how God has always cared for us without any help from us! Thus we see how without all our doing divine compassion and comfort sustain us."[6]

Luther taught that true faith perceived the presence of God in the presence of suffering. He used the Latin phrase, *coram Deo*—before the face of God, in the presence of God, in the sight of God—to picture people living face-to-face with God every moment in every situation.[7] For Luther, all existence found its final meaning and object in God and all affections, cognitions, motivations, actions, and emotions had God as their circumference. All of life was a story of personal encounter with God and the deepest questions in life were questions about God. So in suffering, people vocalize the questions, *Where is God in my suffering? Is he for me or against me? Has he abandoned me?*

Luther's ultimate answer to these questions was a one-word response: *Christ!* Luther presented Christ to Elector Frederick as a Savior who experienced human suffering and continues to suffer with humanity—and with Frederick:

When, therefore, I learned, most illustrious prince, that Your Lordship has been afflicted with a grave illness and that Christ has at the same time become ill in you, I counted it my duty to visit Your Lordship with a little writing of mine. I cannot pretend that I do not hear the voice of Christ crying out to me from Your Lordship's body and flesh saying, "Behold, I am sick." This is so because such evils as illness and the like are not borne by us who are Christians but by Christ himself, our Lord and Savior, in whom we live even as Christ plainly testifies in the Gospel when he says, "Inasmuch as ye have done it unto one of the least of these my brethren, ye have done it unto me."[8]

Here Luther is discussing *coram Deo* from God's perspective. Not only do God's children ever live in his fatherly presence, but God ever lives in our presence, in us, and in our suffering. Luther saw Christ dwelling in and with his children, and therefore, Christ suffers when his children suffer.

When someone was suffering from spiritual doubt as a result of their internal response to an external event, Luther prescribed *coram Deo* faith as his remedy for doubts about the goodness of God. Luther sought to move people face-to-face with God so they could encounter the love of God through faith in the crucified, suffering Christ.

Luther's Portrait of Spiritual Comfort: The Perspective of Faith

In his spiritual counsel, Luther emphasized the development of a faith perspective. Luther saw faith as the divine perspective on life from which people could erect a platform to respond to their suffering.

Luther believed that how a person viewed life made all the difference in life. As he writes to the Elector Frederick, "The Holy Spirit knows that a thing only has such value and meaning to a man as he assigns to it in his thoughts."[9] Therefore, Luther sought to help suffering people reshape their perspective or interpretation of their life situation.

The words Luther writes to Frederick demonstrate the value he attached to changing people's perspective and interpretation of events. He urged the Elector to "be mindful," "remember, meditate, ponder," "comfort yourself by the remembering of God's works," "perceive the blessings of Christ," and "try to attain to the knowledge and love of this blessing." Luther selected similar words when he explains how to change perspective:

- "if we consider this (the broader rule and plan of God) rightly, we shall see how greatly we are favored by God"
- "we thus see that all our suffering is nothing when we consider and ponder the afflictions of men"
- "oh, if we could only see the heart of Christ as he was suspended from the cross, anguishing to make death contemptible and dead for us"
- "this (delighting in suffering) will come to pass if this image (of Christ's resurrection) finds its way into our heart and abides in the innermost affections of our mind."[10]

Luther focused on renewing people's faith perspective regarding God's gracious character because he believed:

> If only a man could see his God in such a light of love . . . how happy, how calm, how safe he would be! He would then truly have a God from whom he would know with certainty that all his fortunes—whatever they might be—had come to him and were still coming to him under the guidance of God's most gracious will.[11]

Summarizing his letter of consolation, Luther wrote, "by means of such splendid symbols the mercy of God shows us in our infirmity that even though death should not be taken away, its power has been reduced by him to a mere shadow."[12] Luther wanted Frederick's non-faith or earth-bound, human story of suffering to give way to God's narrative of the cross and resurrection: "He who does not believe this [Christ is risen] is like a deaf man hearing a story. . . . If we considered it properly and with an attentive heart, this one image [of the resurrected Christ]—even if there were no other—would suffice to fill us with such comfort that we should not only not grieve over our evils, but should also glory in our tribulations, scarcely feeling them for the joy that we have in Christ."[13]

Luther encourages Frederick to consider a new way of looking at life—the way of Christ's grand victory narrative: "All that remains is for us now to pray that our eyes, that is the eyes of our faith, may be opened that we may see. Then there will be nothing for us to fear."[14]

Luther taught the Elector that it was not what happened to him that mattered most, but how he scripturally framed and biblically interpreted what happened to him: "And it is equally true that we measure, feel, or do not feel our evils not on the basis of the facts, but on the basis of our thoughts and feelings about them."[15] For Luther, we must look at everything in life, including our suffering, through the lens of Christ's gospel victory narrative.

Luther's Portrait of the Source of Consolation: The Scriptural Context of Faith

Luther believed that the Scriptures were the irreplaceable context for realigning our faith perspective. In his letter to Frederick, Luther contrasted scriptural consolation with the consolation popular in his day:

> I have put together these fourteen chapters after the fashion of an altar screen and have given them the name *Fourteen Consolations*. They are to replace the fourteen saints whom our superstition has invented and called "The Fourteen Defenders Against All Evils." Now this is a spiritual [scriptural] screen and not made of silver. The book is not meant to adorn the walls of churches, but to uplift and strengthen the pious heart.[16]

Luther expresses his high view of Scripture to Frederick: "In speaking of the consolations which Christians have, the Apostle Paul in Romans 15:4 writes, 'Brethren, whatever was written, was written for our instruction, so that through the patience and comfort of the Scriptures we might have hope.' In this passage he plainly teaches us that our consolations are to be drawn from the Holy Scriptures."[17]

Luther taught that the Bible provided God's grand narrative of and explanation for the human condition. The Bible was his source book for developing a faith perspective concerning suffering: "It is thus very true that we shall find consolation only through the Scriptures, which in the days of evil call us to the contemplation of our blessings, either present or to come."[18] So strong is Luther's conviction that he quotes or refers to Scripture 169 times in his 45-page letter to Frederick.

The beauty and power of Luther's scriptural focus was his ability to encourage suffering people to grieve deeply and honestly and to encourage them to cling to scriptural hope. Ambrose Brendt had studied in Wittenberg and received his master's degree, and thus was well-known to Luther. Brendt's wife died in childbirth and her newborn son died with her. Luther writes to his friend, giving him permission to grieve and encouragement to hope:

> I am not so inhumane that I cannot appreciate how deeply the death of Margaret distresses you. For the great and godly affection which binds a husband to his wife is so strong that it cannot easily be shaken off, and this feeling of sorrow is not displeasing to God . . . since it is an expression of what God has assuredly implanted in you. Nor would I account you a man, to say nothing of a good husband, if you could at once throw off your grief.[19]

Then, toward the end of his letter of spiritual consolation to Brendt, Luther adds this crucial reminder: "Comfort yourself with the Word of God, *the pre-eminent consolation.*"[20]

Luther's Portrait of the Christ of the Cross: The Gospel Content of Faith

If the Scriptures were Luther's main text, then the crucified Christ was the gospel content for renewing the faith perspective. Repeatedly, Luther directed believers to the narrative of Christ suffering on the cross. Theologians have named this Luther's *theologia crucis*—his theology of the cross—the Christ of the cross.

The events of life made no sense to Luther apart from Christ's death on the cross on behalf of sinners. The Christian must suffer, because Christ also suffered: "Did Christ not offer himself? It is true that he offered himself on the cross for every one of us who believes in him. But by this very act he at the same time also offers us, so that it is necessary for all those who believe in him to suffer too and to be put to death according to the flesh, as happened in this case."[21]

Luther wanted to help Frederick to understand that the death of Christ for him and the suffering of Christ with him could change Frederick's perspective:

> How does this come to pass? Surely, it comes to pass when you hear that Jesus Christ, God's Son, has by his most holy touch consecrated and hallowed all sufferings, even death itself, has blessed the curse, and has glorified shame and enriched poverty so that death is now a door to life, the curse a fount of blessing, and shame the mother of glory. Suffering has been touched and bathed by Christ's pure and holy flesh and blood and thus have become holy, harmless, and wholesome, blessed, and full of joy for you. There is nothing, not even death, that his passion cannot sweeten.[22]

Luther urged Frederick to not "fail to perceive"[23] the implications of Christ's passion. He counseled the Elector that in his suffering he should turn to the image of the compassionate Christ, "firmly believing and certain that it is not we alone, but Christ and the church who are in pain and are suffering and dying with us."[24]

The Christ of the cross pointed not only to a suffering Savior, but also and ultimately to a victorious Savior. Luther's fourteenth and final image focused Frederick's vision on "Jesus Christ, the King of glory, rising from the dead. . . . This then is the most sublime image. . . . It is on this that our faith relies, firmly trusting that he is such a Christ as we have described."[25]

Luther concluded his letter by asking, "What is it that he has wrought by his resurrection?"[26] It is vital to note that his answer focused Frederick's mind on his good standing with his good God because of the eternal goodness of the resurrected Christ:

> I am a sinner, but I am borne by his righteousness which is given to me. I am unclean, but his holiness is my sanctification, in which I ride gently. . . . Thus the Christian (if he but believes it) may glory in the merits of Christ and in all his blessings as though he himself had won them. . . . Such a great thing is faith, such blessings does it bring us, such glorious sons of God does it make us. . . . Therefore, just as it is impossible for Christ with his righteousness not to please God, so it is impossible for us, with our faith clinging to his righteousness, not to please him. It is in this way that a Christian becomes almighty lord of all, having all things and doing all things, wholly without sin. Even if he is in sins, these cannot do him harm; they are forgiven for the sake of the inexhaustible righteousness of Christ that removes all sins.[27]

In our suffering, Satan is like Job's wife, demanding, "Curse God and die!" That is, *Give up on God and give up on yourself! God must be bad since he allows such bad circumstances into your life. Or, you must be bad and God is punishing and rejecting you.* Satan is like Job's miserable counselors who saw God as a tit-for-tat God—doing good to the good and doing evil to the evil.

Luther repels miserable counsel with counseling under the cross. Luther was convinced that we can only make sense of seemingly senseless suffering by looking to our suffering Savior. It is as if Luther says to us, *Look to the cross and the empty tomb and learn the truth: God is good even when life is bad.* The cross and the resurrection forever squelch the lies and quiet the whispers of Satan. The cross and the resurrection once and forever shout the truth that even our suffering comes to us from the hands and the heart of our good God—our gracious Father who relates to us as his beloved children.

Timeless Truth for Life and Ministry Today

God calls all believers to comfort one another with the comfort we receive from the Father of compassion and the God of all comfort (2 Corinthians 1:3–11). What central truth does Luther teach us about our calling? We can encapsulate Luther's theology of sustaining in tweet-size fashion:

> When life is bad, we defeat satanic doubts about God's goodness by facing our suffering face-to-face with God in the face of Christ.

Yes, understanding and empathizing with people's external suffering is important. Luther shows us just how important in our next chapter. However, as soul physicians, what is most important is understanding the internal suffering—the potential internal bleeding as the heart struggles for faith to believe in God's good heart.

We not only compassionately ask, "How are you doing as you face this?" We also wisely ask, "How are you doing with God as you face this?"

Luther does not brush off people's grief or rush them toward shallow trust. Rather, Luther journeys with people in their grief, giving them biblical permission to grieve. Chapter 5 illustrates the how-to of Luther's spiritual consolation: what does it look like, feel like, and sound like to help people to confront their suffering face-to-face with Christ?

CHAPTER FIVE
GOSPEL-CENTERED COMFORT FOR SUFFERING:
LUTHER'S METHODOLOGY OF SUSTAINING

ON JANUARY 3, 1530, Luther wrote to Conrad Cordatus, pastor in Zwickau, to congratulate him on the birth of his son. Less than three months later, on April 2, 1530, Luther wrote again to Cordatus, this time to grieve with him over the death of his son:

> My dear Cordatus: May Christ comfort you in this sorrow and affliction of yours. Who else can soothe such a grief? I can easily believe what you write, for I too have had experience of such a calamity, which comes to a father's heart sharper than a two-edged sword, piercing even to the marrow. But you ought to remember that it is not to be marveled at if he, who is more truly and properly a father than you were, preferred for his own glory that your son—nay, rather his son—should be with him rather than with you, for he is safer there than here. But all of this is vain, a story that falls on deaf ears, when your grief is so new. I therefore yield to your sorrows. Greater and better men than we are have given way to grief and are not blamed for it.[1]

Luther compassionately journeyed with Cordatus, entering his earthly story of suffering. He empathized with Cordatus's honest struggle by sharing how he felt when his daughter, Elizabeth, died at seven months. In doing so, Luther gave Cordatus permission to grieve without guilt. Cordatus did not have to feel "un-Christian" in grief because

Luther and other people greater than they have grieved deeply. And Luther pointed Cordatus to Christ—the Ultimate Comforter.

Outlining essential principles can cloud that fact that Luther, the master pastor, understood that soul care was a complex, messy, relational process—not a rote, linear progression. For example, when Luther said that he "yields to his grief," he recognizes that truth (that this precious boy is now in the hands of his heavenly Father) cannot always be immediately heard and internalized. The Christian calling to grieve with hope does not obliterate the need for grief; it expects and respects the grief process. The companion phrase, "that fall on deaf ears," likewise demonstrated the multifaceted journey of grief and the importance of timing in the offer of comfort.

Compassionately Journeying with Sufferers: Entering the Earthly Story

We live life between two worlds—the earthly and the heavenly. The pastoral counselor, therefore, must constantly pivot between two stories—the temporal and the eternal. With Cordatus, Luther did not focus exclusively on the eternal story of Christ's comfort and hope. Instead, he also sought to understand and enter the earthly story of human hurt and despair. Luther entered the sufferer's situation, story, and soul by seeking to know the person's unique personality, disposition toward God, and core issues.

Sensing the Person's Unique Personality

Luther believed that various remedies could be effective for different types of people. During a November 30, 1531 table talk, "Treatment of Melancholy," Luther explained, "But this you ought to know, that other remedies are suitable for other persons."[2] Luther continued this dialogue by insisting that caregivers must understand the person before prescribing the treatment.

Luther gained insight about people in a number of ways. In many of his letters, it is evident that he knew a great deal about the individual through personal contact or through detailed information provided by a mutual friend. We discern more about his approach to learning the character of a person through this description of what Luther would do when he visited someone who was sick:

> When Dr. Martin Luther approached any sick person, whom he visited in time of bodily weakness, he conversed with him in a very friendly way, bent down over him and inquired in the first place about his sickness, what his ailment was, how long he had been weak, what physicians he had employed, and what kind of medicine had been given him. Afterwards, he began to inquire whether in his bodily weakness he had been patient before God.[3]

Sensing the Person's Disposition toward God

The last part of the previous quotation serves to introduce a second aspect of Luther's commitment to journeying with people. Luther inquired about how people were responding to their bodily weakness. The rest of that interview describes the distinctive ways Luther responded, depending on the level of faith evidenced by the individual "when he had now learned, how the sick man had borne himself in his weakness, and what was his disposition toward God."[4] If the person evidenced strong faith, then Luther would respond with praise and encouragement. If the person did not display a clinging trust in Christ, then he might confront the person for lack of faith, or he might attempt to strengthen the person's faith.

As we saw in chapter 4, Luther viewed people as *coram Deo* beings living continuously in the presence of God. Luther used this perception as a primary pastoral care tool. He wanted to know where people stood in terms of their relationship with God.

Luther's ministry to Dr. Jerome Weller provides a pertinent example. Dr. Weller was a professor of theology in Freiberg who was struggling with depression. In ministering to Weller, Luther began by asking whether he was angry with God, with Luther, or with himself. Weller replies, "I confess that I am murmuring against God."[5] Luther then provides comfort by sharing that he, too, had experienced many bouts of anger with God. A lengthy conversation ensues in which Luther helps Weller to see that God was not angry at him, even though Weller was angry at God. Luther knew Weller and used his knowledge as the context for his counsel.

If Luther sensed that a person's faith was weak, especially due to severe trial and spiritual depression, he recommended fellowship with other Christians who could strengthen and help the person: "Thereupon, he entreated Weller to cultivate the company of men when he is afflicted with such melancholy and not live alone."[6] If, on the other hand, he sensed great faith, even in the midst of severe trial, Luther affirmed people and encouraged them to continue what they were already doing so well. This is the case with his letter to Lambert Thorn who was arrested and tried for heresy:

> Christ has given me abundant testimony of you, dear brother Lambert, that you do not need my words, for He Himself suffers in you and is glorified in you. He is taken captive in you and reigns in you, He is oppressed in you and triumphs in you, for He has given you that holy knowledge of Himself which is hidden from the world. . . . There is little need, then, to burden you with my consolations.[7]

Sensing the Person's Core Issues: Applying the Plasters of Scripture

Though Luther held a strong spiritual focus, he did not see every issue as a spiritual issue in terms of cause and cure. Luther worked hand-in-hand with physicians because he saw ministers as physicians of the soul and doctors as physicians of the body. For Luther, the wise physician of soul or body distinguishes causes then prescribes the appropriate cure.

In one table talk, Luther states that though Satan was the first cause of sickness and death, this did not negate the need for physical remedies: "Generally speaking, therefore, I think that all dangerous diseases are blows of the devil. For this, however, he employs the instruments of nature."[8] Since this is the case, when one battles sickness, the battle is on two levels, both the spiritual and the physical: "God also employs means for the preservation of health, such as sleep for the body, food, and drink, for he does nothing except through instruments."[9] Therefore, it is appropriate and necessary to treat the whole person:

> Accordingly a physician is our Lord God's mender of the body, as we theologians are his healers of the spirit; we are to restore what the devil has damaged. So a physician administers theriaca (an antidote for poison) when Satan gives poison. Healing comes from the application of nature to the creature. . . . It's our Lord God who created all things, and they are good. Wherefore it's permissible to use medicine, for it is a creature of God. Thus I replied to Hohndorf, who inquired of me when he heard from Karlstadt that it's not permissible to make use of medicine. I said to him, "Do you eat when you're hungry?"[10]

On the other hand, when convinced that an issue was spiritual in nature, Luther did not hesitate to call for spiritual, rather than medicinal cures. He writes to his friend John Agricola concerning John's wife: "Her illness is, as you see, rather of the mind than of the body. I am comforting her as much as I can, with my knowledge."[11]

Two concepts stand out in Luther's response. First, it was important for Luther that causes be sensed. Second, even when he sensed that causes were spiritual, Luther did not believe he was the expert with the last word on everything. This passage and others reflect a pastor who was willing to refer to physicians when the issue was physical and to other Christians when the issue was spiritual, but beyond his realm of expertise. Luther continued by telling Agricola: "In a word, her disease is not for the apothecaries (as they call them), nor is it to be treated with the salves of Hippocrates, but by constantly applying plasters of Scripture and the Word of God. For what has conscience to do with Hippocrates? Therefore, I would dissuade you from the use of medicine and advise the power of God's Word."[12] Scripture is God's prescription, God's choice medicine, for soul sickness.

Luther speaks to those today who maintain a materialistic worldview that assumes that every issue is biologically-based and, therefore, treatable only by psychotropic medication. He also speaks to those today who maintain a spiritualistic worldview that assumes that every issue is soul-based and, therefore, treatable only by speaking the truth in love.

Empathizing with Sufferers: Joining the Earthly Story

Luther prepared for soul care by understanding the life context of those to whom he ministered. He entered their earthly story by sensing their personalities, backgrounds, situations, faith, relationship to God, and their specific areas of suffering. All of these relational activities prepared him to sustain sufferers by empathizing with their suffering. Throughout church history, this has been known as compassionate commiseration—feeling the pathos, the pain, of another. We care so deeply that we experience another person's misery as our own.

Personal Suffering: I Have Wrestled with Suffering

Luther was convinced through his study of Scripture, his work with people, and his personal experience that only the person who had honestly wrestled with suffering could be of help to others struggling through suffering. Therefore, he taught that the spiritual director had to be willing to wrestle with both level one and level two suffering.

John Schlaginhaufen, an auditor, recorded this table talk in which Luther addressed Schlaginhaufen's spiritual need and shared his own spiritual suffering.

> Then, after Master Philip had departed, he (Martin Luther) said to me, "Be of good cheer. Things will surely be better with you, for I know that your trials contribute to the glory of God and to your profit and that of many others. I, too, suffered from such trials, and at the time I had nobody to console me. When I complained about such spiritual assaults to my good Staupitz, he replied, 'I don't understand this; I know nothing about it.' You now have the advantage that you can come to me, to Philip (Melanchthon), or to Cordatus to seek comfort."[13]

Though Staupitz was Luther's beloved mentor, in Luther's deepest spiritual suffering, Staupitz could neither understand nor assist Luther. Luther and Schlaginhaufen needed someone who had also wrestled honestly with their own conscience. Begalke, speaking of how Luther learned his theology and his pastoral care from his own struggles with suffering, notes, "Luther gained a tremendous awareness and acceptance of the human condition. Troubled persons could sense in him, a humble fellow-sojourner who experienced many of the same depressive anxieties as they did."[14]

Luther's open sharing of his *anfechtungen* is a primary example of his honesty in dealing with inner, or level two, suffering. Luther also freely shared his honest response to level one, or external suffering. When his fourteen-year-old daughter, Magdalene, took sick (after a brief illness, she died on September 20, 1542), Luther openly expresses his struggle: "I love her so very much, but if it is thy will, dear God, to take her, I shall be glad to know that she is with thee." He speaks words of comfort to Magdalene about heaven, but also admits, "The spirit is willing, but the flesh is weak. I love her very much. If this flesh is so strong, what must the spirit be?"[15] When his daughter was in the agony of death, he fell upon his knees before her bed and, weeping bitterly, prayed that God might save her if it be his will.

Likewise, after his father's death, Luther writes of his own raw grief:

> This death has cast me into deep mourning, not only because of the ties of nature but also because it was through his sweet love to me that my Creator endowed me with all that I am and have. Although it is consoling to me that, as he writes, my father fell asleep softly and strong in his faith in Christ, yet his kindness and the memory of his pleasant conversation have caused so deep a wound in my heart that I have scarcely ever held death in such low esteem.[16]

Luther faced his suffering with integrity by bringing his loss directly to God. Since the person's relationship to God in suffering was so important to Luther, he felt that facing suffering *coram Deo* was a prerequisite for anyone seeking to offer sustaining care.

Participation in Suffering: I Suffer with You

Luther suffered with others with great intensity. Frederick Myconius, pastor in Gotha and known as the Reformer of Thuringia, had for some time been suffering from a pulmonary infection. By the summer of 1540, he had the symptoms of tuberculosis; soon afterward he lay down on what he thought was his deathbed. Luther wrote to him, "So I pray that the Lord will make me sick in your place."[17] This is the essence of Luther's sustaining comfort—joint-sharing of suffering to the point of experiencing others' pain with them. Luther entered another's world by looking at life through the person's eyes. He was willing to be a joint-participant in another's suffering because he believed that this was the Christian's duty of love. "We must support one another and be supported," he writes to an ill Urban Rhegius.[18]

Three months before his father died, Luther wrote a lengthy letter of comfort to him in his illness. Luther speaks of his desire to participate with his father in his suffering: "I wish to write this to you because I am anxious about your illness (for we know not the hour), that I might become a participant of your faith, temptation, consolation, and thanks to God for his holy Word."[19]

Luther believed that a sufferer often could not embrace loss unless and until another Christian shared in that loss. For Luther, support through sympathy, or compassionate commiseration, could prevent the person from retreating from life. He wrote about the power of shared suffering in his preface to "The Fourteen Consolations," when he wrote of Christ crying out, "Behold, I am sick," and the Christian crying out, "I suffer with you."[20] Luther lived out the conviction that shared sorrow was endurable sorrow.

Permission to Grieve in Suffering: I Respect Your Struggle in Suffering

Luther taught that candid grieving could be encouraged if others first provided sincere expressions of grief. It is as if he wanted the pastoral counselor to say, *I will grieve for you first, so that you can then allow yourself to grieve. I will feel your pain and express your suffering and thus become a window or mirror of your soul so that you can honestly struggle with your own suffering.*

John Zink was a young graduate student at Wittenberg and a frequent guest in Luther's home. On April 20, 1532, he died, and Luther wrote his parents to express the great personal loss John's death was to him and to empathize with their grief: "Accordingly we all are deeply grieved by his death. . . . As is natural, your son's death, and the report of it, will distress and grieve your heart and that of your wife, since you are his parents. I do not blame you for this, for all of us—I in particular—are stricken with sorrow."[21]

Luther frequently offered permission to grieve by communicating that it was abnormal and unhealthy not to grieve. For instance, Mr. and Mrs. Matthias Knudsen were the parents of John Knudsen, a graduate of the university in Wittenberg. Luther wrote to them after their son's death. After expressing consolation in the experience of the death of their son, Luther writes, "It is quite inconceivable that you should not be mourning. In fact, it would not be encouraging to learn that a father and mother are not grieved over the death of their son."[22]

Pointing Sufferers to Christ and the Body of Christ

Recall the essence of historical biblical sustaining. Our fallen world falls on us and then Satan tempts us with his false reasoning, *Life is bad; God is sovereign; God must be bad, too.* Everything around us and in us tempts us to retreat from trust. Sustaining draws a line in the sand of spiritual retreat so that faith survives. It may not yet thrive—that is the work of historical biblical healing. Sustaining provides comfort—co-fortitude—because shared sorrow is endurable sorrow. And sorrow shared with the ultimate Comforter—the Father, Son, and Holy Spirit—is surely endurable sorrow.

Pointing People to Christ: The Supreme Comforter

Picture how Luther draws this line in the sand of spiritual retreat with the Knudsens after the death of their son, John. Having given them permission to grieve, Luther now encourages them to find comfort in Christ:

> So you too, when you have mourned and wept, should be comforted again. The Lord and supreme Comforter Jesus Christ, who loved your son even more than you did and who, having first called him through his Word, afterward summoned him to himself and took him from you, comfort and strengthen you, with his grace until the day when you will see your son again in eternal joy.[23]

Luther wanted the Knudsens to embrace loss (grieve) and to embrace life (find comfort). For Luther, life meant this earthly life and the larger story of life beyond what is seen with the eyes and known by the mind. He wanted Mr. and Mrs. Knudsen to embrace this full-ness of life in the midst of pain so that their pain did not shut them off from the giver of life.

Luther pointed persecuted Christians to Christ. The local priests suppressed the evangelical movement in Miltenberg, and some evan-gelicals were beheaded. Luther wrote an open letter of consolation to these persecuted Christians. His letter included an exposition of Psalm 120,[24] which begins with the words, "In my distress I cried unto the LORD, and he heard me." Luther's exposition and application of this verse illustrate his belief that God is our supreme comforter and the one to whom we must turn in our suffering:

> The first verse teaches us where we should turn when misfor-tune comes upon us—not to the emperor, not to the sword, not to our own devices and wisdom, but to the LORD, who is our only real help in time of need. "I cried unto the LORD in my distress," he says. That we should do this confidently, cheerfully, and without fail he makes clear when he says, "And he heard me." It is as if he would say, "The LORD is pleased to have us turn to him in our distress and is glad to hear and help us."[25]

For Luther, it is not only pain (level one suffering) that we are to bring honestly to God, but also lament (level two suffering). Luther was convinced that God knew all that the sufferer felt and thought; therefore, all feelings and thoughts could be expressed openly to God. For example, Veit Dietrich writes of a conversation he and Luther had concerning what a Christian was free to share with Christ:

> When I asked him about the passage in which Jeremiah cursed the day in which he had been born and suggested that such impatience was a sin, he (Martin Luther) replied, "Sometimes one has to wake up our Lord God with such words. Otherwise he doesn't hear. It is a case of real murmuring on the part of

Jeremiah. Christ spoke in this way. 'How long am I to be with you?' (Mark 9:19). Moses went so far as to throw his keys at our Lord God's feet when he asked, 'Did I conceive all this people?' (Num. 11:12)."[26]

The ongoing dialogue is quite intriguing. Luther continues by saying that everyone feels and thinks such things, and those who say that Christians should not express them to God are unrealistic: "Accordingly it is only speculative theologians who condemn such impatience and recommend patience. If they get down to the realm of practice, they will be aware of this."[27] An open, candid relationship with God was important to Luther's soul care because it halted retreat in the midst of suffering. He taught that speaking directly and candidly to God helped hurting people to maintain their faith in God.

Pointing People to the Larger Story of Who God Is: Loving Father

But what if a person does not see God as trustworthy? In 1 Peter 5:7, Peter encourages us to cast all our cares on God, because he cares for us. Luther understood that if we do not see God as caring, then exhortations to turn to God for comfort will fall on deaf ears. Whenever Luther pointed people to Christ for comfort, he also nurtured a biblical image of God the Father and Christ the Son. Hart notes that "Luther's approach to pastoral care begins with his understanding of who God is."[28] There were no atheists in Luther's mental universe. A god is anything to which people look for all good and in which they find refuge in every time of need. To have a god is nothing else than to trust in that god with the whole heart. Kolb explains that by Luther's definition, "every person has a god; there is no such thing as an atheist. For everyone must put trust in something or someone, or some combination of persons and things, or life will disappear."[29] Suffering forces us to declare our god; it surfaces our true image of God.

Luther found that this image was often distorted. In a table talk from 1533, Luther affirmed that, according to reason alone, "our God is always in the wrong, no matter what he does."[30] When we think about God and see what happens in this world, without faith, we conclude that either God is very weak and cannot stop suffering, or he is very wicked and delights in suffering.

In suffering, doubt about God's goodness and grace is the core problem preventing consolation. Luther's personal and pastoral solution to this problem was to rest in God as a loving heavenly Father. He believed Father was the central image of God that was necessary in all of the Christian life, especially in suffering.

When prescribing his treatment for depression, Luther explained that the words of the creed are of utmost importance, "I believe in God the Father." He furthered expounded that by reason it never occurs to people that, "God is Father."[31] To the human mind, unaided by faith, it never occurs that the God who is Father is a loving Father. Instead, people see God, especially in suffering, as an angry Father who uses suffering as a punishment. Luther rejected the notion that all personal suffering be viewed as punishment for personal sin. His God was not an angry, but a loving, Father. His God was not against us, but for us.

In his commentary on Genesis, Luther developed this line of biblical reasoning: "True faith draws forth the following conclusion: God is God for me because He speaks to me. He forgives my sins. He is not angry with me, just as He promises: 'I am the Lord your God.' Now search your heart, and ask whether you believe that God is your God, Father, Savior, and Deliverer, who wants to rescue you."[32]

Luther constantly reminded people of God's fatherly love and friendship. This was his counsel and consolation to his father when he lay ill and near death: "Herewith I commend you to Him who loves you more than you love yourself."[33] In a letter of pastoral counsel to the Elector John, Luther wrote, "God's friendship is a bigger comfort than that of the whole world."[34]

When someone is suffering, the temptation is to look at life through the eyes of reason unaided by faith. Luther consoled people by helping them to look at life holistically—through the eyes of reason redeemed by faith. He pointed hurting people to a faith which saw God as good and fatherly and to a faith that saw suffering as coming from the kindly hands of the Father of compassion and the God of all comfort, not from the punishing hands of an angry despot.

This is the larger story that was so important to Luther. The physical world was real and suffering was real and tragic, but there was more to life's story than the physical world. The spiritual reality of relationship to God was Luther's ultimate story. Luther strove to blend these two stories, these two realities. When the only son of Benedict Pauli died in June of 1533, Luther wrote him a letter of consolation. As usual, Luther begins with words of sympathy and comfort. He then expresses the normalcy of grieving, "The Scriptures do not prohibit mourning and grieving over deceased children. On the contrary, we have many examples of godly patriarchs and kings who mournfully bewailed the death of their sons."[35] Luther continued, "We concede, of course, that the evil that has befallen you is a very grave one."[36]

Yet, he also told Pauli, "at the same time you ought to leave room for consolation."[37] The Christian can grieve, but not as one who has no hope. Luther then gave Pauli the hope or consolation that God is sovereign and therefore in control. God is good and therefore has the best interest of his son and himself at heart. He reminded Pauli that he has "the favor of Christ" and "a Heavenly Father who is gracious to you through him," and "a God who consoles us by saying, 'Because I live, ye shall live also.'"[38] Luther enlightened Pauli's eyes of faith to see that God was a loving Father and therefore had brought his son to eternal life.

Pointing People to the Larger Story of Who Christ Is: Caring Savior

The largest story of all, for Luther, was the story of the cross. When all else seemed to point to the conclusion that God did not care, Luther counseled people to look to the cross. Luther saw Christ's sufferings on our behalf as God's clear declaration, his once-for-all pronouncement, that he is for his children, not against them.

Luther encouraged people to observe life through the lens or eyeglasses of Christ-centered faith: "Faith, is, as it were, the center of a circle. If anybody strays from the center, it is impossible for him to have the circle around him, and he must blunder. The center is Christ."[39]

Luther directly connected Christ as a suffering Savior to God as a loving Father: "The flesh cries out against the belief that God is good, but the suffering Savior brings consolation that this is indeed true."[40] Through Christ people can grasp with assurance that God is Father and cry out, "Abba, dear Father."[41]

Luther understood that in this life such a belief was hard to maintain. To Matthias Weller, he writes that he should not depend on his own thoughts and reasoning in his attempts to work his way out of depression. Rather, he should turn to the Scriptures, which make plain the truth "that you should be cheerful in Christ, who is your gracious Lord and Deliverer, and let him care for you, as he most assuredly does."[42]

We can find comfort from Christ in our suffering because Christ is our suffering Savior. Luther used this picture in writing to the wife of a man in prison for his evangelical faith: "Our sufferings have not yet become so deep and bitter as were those of his own dear Son and of the mother of our Lord. By the thought of these we should be comforted and strengthened in our sufferings, as St. Peter teaches us (first epistle, iii.18): 'Christ has once suffered for us, the just for the unjust.'"[43]

Pointing People to the Body of Christ

Historically, sustaining included the mobilization of faith resources so that Christians could candidly face and courageously embrace life in Christ. Luther believed we could best accomplish this sustaining task by meeting together as the body of Christ—a priesthood of all believers—to encourage one another individually and in small groups.

Luther taught that all those who placed their faith in Christ as Savior were baptized into the universal church, the body of Christ. Every believer was thus connected as the parts of the body are connected and as members in a human family are connected. Out of this doctrine, Luther developed his teaching on the priesthood of all believers. He used the phrase to emphasize the spiritual equality, duties, and qualifications of every member of God's family:

> All Christians truly are of the spiritual estate, and there is no difference among them except to office. Paul says in I Corinthians 12 that we are all one body, yet every member has its own work by which it serves the others. This is because we all have one baptism, one gospel, and faith, and are all Christians alike; for baptism, gospel, and faith alone make us spiritual and a Christian people.[44]

Luther's thinking continued to develop over the years. In *The Babylonian Captivity of the Church*, he maintained and elaborated upon this doctrine, "Let everyone, therefore, who knows himself to be a Christian, be assured of this, that we are all equally priests."[45]

The corporate body of Christ, through the sympathetic sharing of sorrow and of strength, consolidated the individual's faith resources and empowered each other to embrace life. The body of Christ provided its members with the shared strength to find the courage to grieve with hope.

The priesthood of believers made a profound difference in Luther's pastoral care because it democratized soul care. Every believer was now viewed as capable and responsible to be a sustainer because every believer could provide shared strength to someone experiencing suffering. Individuals and small groups of Christians could meet together to consolidate faith resources by strengthening one another's faith perspective concerning God's plans and purposes.

It was dogma for Luther that life could not be embraced alone: "Luther knew full well that persons in sorrow have not always power to exorcise the spirit of sadness, and to draw for themselves the proper comfort from the Word and works of God."[46] In a table talk dated February 18, 1538, Luther spoke of a period of melancholy that his dear friend and colleague Philip Melanchthon was experiencing. He complained that Philip was seeking solitude in his affliction and affirmed that instead he should seek companionship:

"He's gnawing at his own heart," said Luther. "I, too, often suffer from severe trials and sorrows. At such times I seek the fellowship of men, for the humblest maid has often comforted me. A man doesn't have control of himself when he is downcast and alone, even if he is well equipped with a knowledge of the Scriptures. It is not for nothing that Christ gathers his church around the Word and the sacraments and around prayer and hymns and is unwilling to let these be hidden in a corner. Away with monks and hermits! These are inventions of Satan because they exist apart from all the godly ordinances and arrangements of God. According to the plan of creation every man is either a domestic or a political or an ecclesiastical person. Outside of these ordinances he is not a man, unless he is miraculously exempted. Accordingly a solitary life should be avoided as much as possible."[47]

Luther based his thoughts both on experience and Scripture. He knew that the humblest person had comforted him. He experienced as a spiritual director that people could not shake themselves of melancholy without help. He believed that Christ had called the body of Christ to unite in Word, sacrament, prayer, and hymns. From a sociological and spiritual perspective, Luther believed that men and women ceased to be fully human when in isolation.

Mutual sustaining was also a theological issue for Luther. In another table talk, this one from 1532, Luther accused both the papists and Anabaptists of breaking the Ten Commandments through their teaching that spiritual maturity came through solitude: "The papists and Anabaptists teach: 'If you wish to know Christ, try to be alone, don't associate with men, become a separatist.' This is plainly diabolical advice which is in conflict with the first and second table."[48]

When Jerome Weller was depressed, Luther urged him to give his heart to the Lord and "seek fellowship with men."[49] A table talk records the continuation of this exhortation, "Thereupon he entreated Weller to cultivate the company of men when he is afflicted with such melancholy and not live alone. 'Woe to him who is alone,' the preacher says (Eccles. 4:10). When I'm morose I flee above all from solitude."[50]

Much as a counselor would say today, Luther insisted that the wife of a suicidal man not leave her husband alone: "Be very careful not to leave your husband alone for a single moment, and leave nothing lying about with which he might harm himself. Solitude is poison to him. For this reason the devil drives him to it."[51] To another friend he wrote, "This is my only and best advice: Don't remain alone when you are assailed! Flee solitude!"[52]

Luther's thinking was practical—solitude produces melancholy because, when people are alone, the worst and saddest thoughts come to mind. When alone, people magnify those thoughts, leaping to conclusions and interpreting everything in the worst light: "We imagine that other people are very happy, and it distresses us that things go well with them and evil with us."[53]

Mutual ministry was also a theological issue because Luther believed that Christians were commanded to comfort one another. Luther quoted 2 Corinthians 1:3–5 concerning the duty of Christians to take the comfort they receive from God and then to pass on that comfort to others in distress.[54] In a table talk recorded in 1534, Luther stated several theological truths that lay behind his insistence upon the avoidance of solitude and the need for fellowship. He noted that God created people for society and not for solitude and that more and graver sins were committed in solitude than in mutual fellowship. Luther repeated Christ's promise that where two or three are gathered in his name, there Christ would be. He supported this thinking by the arguments that God created two sexes, that God founded the Christian church as the communion of the saints, and that the church is to be a place of consolation.[55]

Luther's thinking on individual encouragement is clear. Alone, the individual is vulnerable to satanically inspired distorted thinking about self, God, and the world. When enduring suffering, it is very difficult to consolidate one's own resources as the spiral seemed to proceed endlessly downward. To embrace life again, people need one another. Consolidation of personal resources requires consolidation through corporate resources.

Those corporate resources included both individual and small group encouragement. In his work *Concerning the Order of Public Worship*, Luther exhorted his followers to return to the New Testament model of meeting for worship weekly in a larger celebration group and of meeting daily for fellowship (support and sustaining, encouragement and healing) in smaller groups or cells. He suggested that during these times, every person should share, pray, praise, sing, and interpret Scripture so that they could have "free reign to uplift and quicken souls so that they do not become weary."[56]

David Zersen goes so far as to claim a Lutheran root for modern-day small group ministry:

> Thomas Oden has shown that the small group movement has its roots in the Lutheran Pietism of the 17th century. Whether secular proponents of small groups will acknowledge it or not, the historical precedent for the movement is to be found in

the small groups founded by Lutheran pastor Philip Jakob Spener. He claimed that he was merely drawing implications from and providing functional realization for Luther's doctrine of the priesthood of all believers.[57]

Luther intended for Christians to be priests to one another and his writings make it clear that this involved the spiritual care of one Christian for another. Zersen lists five examples from the life of Luther which promoted the idea of ministry through small groups: Luther's small group devotional times in his home, his table talk groups, his Bible study time in groups at his home, his proposal for the use of the catechism in small group settings, and his proposal for the order of worship and fellowship in homes.[58]

In his *Preface to the German Mass and Order of Service*, Luther urged Christians to meet in small groups in homes to pray, to read Scripture, and to promote ministries of love. These groups were also to make it possible for members to know each other well enough so that they could console, challenge, confront, and strengthen one another.[59]

Luther believed that the consolidation of faith resources came about as a result of the joint resources of the faith community. Through the one-another ministry of the body of Christ, people were strengthened individually so that they could endure suffering, embrace their loss, and be prepared to embrace life again through the ministry of healing.

Timeless Truth for Life and Ministry Today

If we made a movie of Luther's letters of sustaining counsel, there are several scenes we would not see. We would not see Luther wagging his finger as he shamed people saying, *If you really trusted Christ you wouldn't be experiencing grief!* We would not see Luther shoving people from behind as he rushed and pushed them toward the cross.

There are several scenes we would see. We would view Luther weeping with those who weep as he cried out, *It's normal to hurt. Of all people, Christians can grieve the most candidly as they face their loss with integrity.* We would view Luther walking side-by-side with people as he patiently journeyed with them toward their suffering Savior. We would hear Luther sharing: *I get it. I've been there. There have been times I've begun to turn my back to God in doubt. In those moments, I needed a Christian to be "Jesus with skin on" by entering my pain and slowly helping me to turn my face back to the face of God.*

We can encapsulate Luther's practice or methodology of sustaining in tweet-size fashion:

> The human comforter is a sorrow sharer who points people
> to the supreme Comforter by incarnationally entering the
> sufferer's earthly story.

Through sustaining soul care, we help one another grasp the reality that there is comfort in Christ alone. Sustaining begins to turn the suffering Christian back to Christ. Living face-to-face with Christ, we now begin the healing process where we learn that it's possible to hope—in Christ alone.

This is where real growth, real hope, and real healing occur. This is where faith not only survives; it can begin to thrive. And faith is needed because turning back to Christ does not mean that he snaps his fingers and makes everything in our situation better. No. Many times, most times, when we face Christ in the midst of our suffering, he says, *Wait. Wait for the better day—hope in my future promise.* As you wait, worship. So . . . on to chapter 6 where we learn Luther's theology of waiting on God as we find healing hope.

CHAPTER SIX

THE SPIRITUAL SIGNIFICANCE OF SUFFERING: LUTHER'S THEOLOGY OF HEALING

LUTHER COMPOSED numerous letters to men whose wives had passed away. Such was the case in 1539 to his friendly sponsor, Hans of Taubenheim, after the death of Hans's wife:

> Most worthy, steadfast, dear Lord and kind Sponsor. I have learned how our dear Lord God has again suffered his counsel to be wrought out upon you, in taking to himself also your dear wife. This, your sorrow and pain, causes me sincere and heartfelt grief. . . . Bear, then, the stroke of the dear Father's gentle rod in such a way that you may find in his gracious and paternal will towards you a comfort deeper than the pain; and, in the conflict of your grief, let the peace of God, which soars above all our reason and senses, be triumphant, however the flesh may sob and whimper. . . . I am confident that you yourself, taught by the word of God, know without my admonitions that the peace of God must dwell, not in the five senses nor in the reason, but far above in the region of faith.[1]

Woven into this one interaction, we hear Luther's creative mingling of sustaining and healing. Luther sustained Hans by climbing in the casket with him, comforting or co-fortifying Hans to face God again courageously.

Having turned to face God, does Hans perceive the face of God in the face of Christ, or does he misperceive the face of God through the lies of Satan? In his candor, Hans might still be lamenting, *Why?*

How long, O, Lord? Who is this God who would allow such suffering?
These are the questions that move us into the terrain of historic biblical healing.

Knowing this, Luther journeyed toward healing hope by helping
Hans gain a biblical, faith-inspired glimpse of the face of God. Luther
wrote, "the peace of God must dwell, not in the five senses nor in the
reason, but far above in the region of faith." Hans needed to know,
Who is this God of peace? Luther answered: the "dear Father" with the
"gentle rod" who is "gracious and paternal."

Knowing the true God is the central pivot, the core movement
between sustaining and healing. Healing journeys with the sufferer
back to the God of holy love, of affectionate sovereignty. As Isaiah
40:10–11 explains, God's almighty arms rule for sufferers and his all-
loving arms carry his children close to his heart.

Luther's Healing Counsel: Glimpsing the God of Resurrection Hope

To say that historical, pastoral healing focuses on hope requires that
we have a theology of hope. What is biblical hope in suffering? What
is it that the Bible urges us to hope for? Is it hope that the suffering,
loss, grief, and pain would go away? While certainly desirable, pain
alleviation is not our ultimate hope.

Biblical hope directs people like Hans of Taubenheim to weave into
their heart, soul, mind, will, and spirit the biblical image of God. This
in turn inspires us to worship God which results in growth in grace and
becoming more like Christ. If sustaining focuses on fortifying faith to
resist retreat, then healing stresses deepening faith to promote spiritual
maturity—loving God and loving others (Matthew 22:35–40). We find
God even if we do not find relief. Our souls are restored even if our situation is not. We find our hope not in changing circumstances, but in
our changeless Savior. We place our hope not in a new level of improved
external circumstances, but in a new level of biblical wisdom, worship,
and wholeness—growth in Christlikeness.

Recall that Luther shifted the focus of healing from the medieval emphasis on physical recovery through ritual to a biblical emphasis on spiritual growth through dependence upon God. In ministering to the Elector Frederick, Luther resolved in healing "to strengthen the pious heart."[2] The medieval person looked for something that was efficacious to relieve dire difficulties; Luther pointed to someone who was efficacious to promote spiritual maturity. He pointed people away from relief and to rich relationship to Christ. Instead of emphasizing earthly well-being and the end of suffering, Luther emphasized the well-being of the soul.

It was Luther's theology of biblical healing that led to such a significant departure in viewpoint and practice. Luther based his theory and practice of healing upon his interpretation of:

- The biblical promise concerning healing.
- The biblical diagnosis of our worst sickness.
- The biblical significance of suffering.
- The biblical definition of health.

The Biblical Promise Concerning Healing

Throughout his ministry, Luther addressed three primary areas of healing: external suffering through persecution, physical sickness, and spiritual depression. Luther believed that God could end persecution, bring physical healing, and relieve spiritual depression. However, he knew that God did not guarantee such healing.

Still, in each of these areas, Luther fervently prayed for healing. On June 27, 1535, Luther wrote to the believers in the town of Mittweida who were being persecuted for their refusal to receive communion according to the Catholic belief and practice: "I deplore the suffering and persecution of innocent people. May my dear Lord Jesus Christ, for whose sake you are suffering, comfort and strengthen you for his glory and your deliverance. Meanwhile it is incumbent on us to be prayerful in hope that God will make haste and put an end to the matter."[3]

Luther experienced answered prayer for physical healing in the life of his dear friend Philip Melanchthon. In June 1540, Melanchthon lay dying at Weimar. Traveling day and night from Wittenberg, when Luther arrived he found Melanchthon's "eyes had already become dim, reason had entirely vanished, the power of speech was lost, hearing was gone, and his countenance and temples were sunken. It was indeed, as Luther said, the Hypocratic face. He recognized no one, ate and drank nothing."[4] When Luther first looked upon his friend, he was shocked beyond measure, and said to his companions, "God forbid! How has the devil marred this instrument!"[5] Turning immediately to the window, Luther prayed earnestly to God.

"Then and there," Luther said afterwards, "was our Lord God obliged to listen to me, for I cast my burden before his door, and besieged his ear with all the promises to answer prayer that I could repeat from the Holy Scriptures."[6] He then took Philip by the hand, and said, "Be of good courage, Philip, you will not die. . . . Therefore, do not give way to despondency, and thus become your own murderer, but trust in the Lord, who is able to kill and make alive again."[7] Philip became more and more animated, and Luther, ordering some food to be quickly prepared, took it to him. Gradually, Philip regained his strength and returned to health and ministry.

Luther also prayed ardently for his soul and the souls of others who were experiencing spiritual depression or *anfechtungen*. Writing to a good friend experiencing depression, Luther shared, "I am truly sorry that you are called to bear this burden and sorrow. I pray that Christ, the very best Comforter of all the distressed, may comfort you, as he certainly can and will. Amen."[8]

While Luther undoubtedly believed that God could heal, he was not persuaded that the goodness of God required him to always heal. Luther believed the Scriptures taught that God never guaranteed that

Christians would be shielded from persecution, physical illness, or spiritual depression; nor promised that tribulation, physical suffering, or *anfechtungen* would be relieved. Rather than focusing on cure, Luther highlighted spiritual care by encouraging believers to mature spiritually through their suffering.

Regarding persecution, Luther wrote to exiled believers in Leipzig, "Peace is not to be found anywhere until the Lord comes and overthrows the enemy of peace."[9] He continued, telling the believers, who experienced Duke George's persecution, "If you get nowhere with that willful man, and if you cannot secure a certificate of your upright walk from him, still you have achieved more than enough, seeing that both God, and the world, and even Duke George's own adherents, testify that you do and suffer all this in a Christian spirit and solely for Christ's sake."[10]

Luther wrote to John Ruehel, "I am sorry to learn of your infirmity from your Justus' letter and am even more sorry to learn that you take your infirmity so hard."[11] Luther was disappointed that Ruehel was bearing his sickness so poorly by failing to understand the work of God even in sickness. He continued, "Are you not together with us, a friend, member, and confessor of that Man who speaks to all of us in Saint Paul, 'My strength is made perfect in weakness.'"[12]

Luther's response reveals his view of sickness and healing: suffering is bad, but since God does not guarantee the end of suffering, the failure to grow from suffering is worse because it wastes a spiritual opportunity. Believing that God did not promise healing, Luther significantly altered the medieval approach to healing by focusing on internal spiritual growth rather than on external physical cure.

In sustaining, Luther was saying, *What can't be cured can be endured*. In healing, Luther was saying, *What can't be cured, can help you mature*.

The Biblical Diagnosis of Our Worst Sickness

We have consistently witnessed Luther's commitment to comprehensive pastoral care that deals thoroughly both with the evils we have suffered and with the sins we have committed. Luther persistently exhorted that the worst suffering is spiritual sickness—sin that causes estrangement from God. Spiritual sickness was so prominent in Luther's theology of healing that even as the Elector Frederick lay on his deathbed, Luther explains the evil greater than death—the evil within, the evil of sin: "Whether man believes it or not, it is most certain and true that no torture can compare with the worst of all evils, namely, the evil within man himself. The evils of sin within him are more numerous and far greater than any which he feels. If a man were to feel his evil, he would feel hell, for he has hell within himself."[13]

For Luther, highlighting recovery from persecution, illness, or spiritual depression while minimizing recovery from spiritual estrangement would be like a physician today refusing chemotherapy for cancer patients because they are taking aspirin for their headache. Because of his spiritual interpretation of sickness, Luther essentially was saying, *Do not focus on ending persecution, healing physical illness, or relieving spiritual depression because there is a much greater sickness that must take priority.*

Luther's view of sickness informs the significance he saw in suffering, his definition of health, and his practice of soul care by healing. In Luther's view of spiritual sickness we are spiritually dead and therefore separated from God, and we are spiritually deceived and therefore unaware that any problem exists.

Spiritually Dead and Therefore Separated from God

For Luther, we are so sick that we are the walking dead. In *The Bondage of the Will*, Luther teaches that we live under the complete mastery of sin and "have a nature that is corrupt and turned from God." Every "thought and imagination of man's heart is inclined to evil from his youth. Every imagination of man's heart is intent on evil continually."[14]

It's horrible to exist as the walking dead. What is worse is that our sin results in alienation from God and judgment by God unless a cure is found from the Great Physician who alone has the remedy: "The wrath of God is revealed from heaven against all the ungodliness and unrighteousness of men, who hold down the truth in unrighteousness. Do you hear this general judgment against all men, that they are under the wrath of God?"[15]

Our critical condition is made even more serious because we are spiritually impotent—totally unable to heal ourselves by fighting off the disease of sin. A central premise of Luther's ministry and of his healing soul care was to use God's Word to "admonish and awaken a man to see his own impotence."[16]

Spiritually Deceived and Therefore Unaware That Any Problem Exists

The plot thickens and our dilemma deepens because we are unaware that we are dead. In *The Bondage of the Will*, Luther summarizes the apostle Paul's teaching that all people are ignorant of sin, death, righteousness, and eternal life; sitting ignorantly in darkness and knowing not that "they are certainly under wrath and condemnation, and by reason of their ignorance they cannot thence extricate themselves, nor endeavor to do so. How can you endeavor, if you do not know what, or how, or why, or to what extent, you must endeavor?"[17]

Luther constantly keeps in the foreground this understanding of our ultimate sickness: we are unaware that we are spiritually dead. As a pastoral counselor, he was concerned that focusing primarily on stopping persecution, curing illness, and relieving spiritual depression might hinder the deeper work of God in which he uses trials to reveal our deepest need for God. Using biblical language, Luther warned his followers, "let him who stands take heed that he does not fall," explaining that as long as a person is healthy and life is going well, "he is always likely to fall into more sins, thus constantly thwarting the loving will of his loving Father."[18]

Luther radically shifted the focus of healing away from a sense of external cure and toward an internal cure that leads to spiritual wholeness. Ironically, Luther viewed suffering as the medicine of choice to heal spiritual sickness.

The Biblical Significance of Suffering

A generation ago, C. S. Lewis taught about the purpose of pain, saying, "God whispers to us in our pleasure, but shouts to us in our pain. Pain is God's megaphone to rouse a sleeping world."[19]

We hear a similar message about the significance of suffering when we accompany Luther to a house of mourning, that of painter Lucas Cranach, to whom we owe one of the finest portraits of Luther. A message had come to Luther that Cranach's son, John, had died on October 9, 1536: "The poor parents, in addition to the natural grief of their loving hearts, were enduring also great torment of conscience, as though they themselves were the cause of his death, insomuch as they had sent him to Italy."[20]

Luther, the faithful friend, visited the brokenhearted father. After sharing his grief and assuaging his conscience, Luther moved forcefully into a discussion of God's purposes in our losses. God sends pain and suffering because he "wishes to break your will. He is apt to lay his hand upon us just where it will give us the most pain, in order to slay our old Adam."[21] Suffering is not only God's megaphone; it is God's anvil upon which he fashions in us the image of Christ.

Urban Rhegius was a Catholic priest who became an evangelical pastor and rose to a position of great influence. On December 30, 1534, Luther wrote to Rhegius to comfort him in an illness. After communicating words of consolation, Luther shared with Rhegius God's primary purpose for affliction: "By these vicissitudes he teaches us not to be arrogant, as we might be if we were always strong. We are best off when we ourselves acknowledge that we are framed of dust and are mere dust."[22]

Luther reminded Rhegius of what he already knows and has preached to others. God allows suffering so that we can become "conformed to the image of God's Son." And this "trial comes to you, as it does to other brethren who occupy high stations, in order that we may be humbled." Rhegius is to wait on the Lord, who said to Paul in his suffering, "My strength is made perfect in weakness."[23]

The Spiritual Significance of Level One External Suffering

Luther believed that God uses both external and internal suffering (level one and two suffering) to reveal to us our desperate need for him. The Reformer taught that persecution and physical suffering opened channels for dependence upon God. Clebsch and Jaekle, speaking of Luther's healing ministry, write:

> Sickness, therefore, was to be seen by the sufferer in two ways: on the one hand, for what it was, a painful and debilitating event which the believer wished to be ended; but on the other hand, sickness had a meaning for faith, an inside meaning, as it were, for which the believer was to raise his voice in thanksgiving. By sickness he was being driven to participate in the grace of God which in this world was still "via passionis" of Christ.[24]

Writing to the Elector John of Saxony, who was deathly ill, Luther clearly conveyed how God uses tribulations, suffering, and pain to draw us nearer to him and make us more like him: "This is the school in which God chastens us and teaches us to trust in him so that our faith may not always stay in our ears and hover on our lips but may have its true dwelling place in the depths of our hearts. Your grace is now in this school."[25] When evil intrudes into the usual rhythms of life, God brings us to a full stop and moves us to the verge of defenselessness—fertile ground for the growth of faith.

Strohl pictures Luther meeting people at the border of despair to promote profound trust in Christ. Concerning Luther's healing ministry and view of suffering, Strohl writes, "Suffering can render the believer more susceptible to the divine activity, which as sheer grace can transform the emptiness of deprivation into the fullness of God."[26]

The Spiritual Significance of Level Two Internal Suffering

God also makes therapeutic use of internal suffering. Recall how Luther pictured *anfechtungen* as inner conflicts, trials, temptations, and profoundly disturbing experiences of the soul. *Anfechtungen* contain a sense of being estranged, abandoned, or rejected by God. Luther experienced it as spiritual depression involving a complex inner struggle and anguish of heart in which his relationship to God was called into question and marked not by friendship but by isolation and alienation.

Luther described many forms of *anfechtungen*. Foremost in intensity was the *anfechtung* of faith which involved the temptation to lose faith in God's pardoning grace. In this *anfechtung*, Luther felt as if God were angry and ready to reject him, rather than sensing God as good, loving, and accepting. Luther called such spiritual depression "the strongest, greatest, most severe temptation."[27]

As we have seen, Luther believed that the greatest suffering was the conscience at enmity with God. The conscience would stay alienated from God unless suffering entered life to produce weakness and dependence. Without such weakness, the conscience remained autonomous, trusting in itself, rather than in God. In this way, Luther argues for the necessity of *anfechtungen*: "The most dangerous trial of all is when there is no trial, when everything is all right and running smoothly. That is when a man tends to forget God, to become too independent and put his time of prosperity to a wrong use. In fact, at this time he has more need to call upon God's name than in adversity."[28]

While calling *anfechtungen* "the greatest grief,"[29] Luther also considered them to be necessary trials. God reveals our need for total dependence upon him. These repeated experiences of *anfechtungen* are opportunities for God to divulge more of himself. Luther concluded, "Therefore, we should willingly endure the hand of God in this and in all suffering. Do not be worried; indeed such a trial is the very best sign revealing God's grace and love for man."[30]

Luther wrote twice to the Magdeburg chancellor, Laurentius Zoch, after Zoch's wife had died. Luther focused his first letter more on the pain of level one suffering, and then concentrated his second letter more on the faith struggle of level two suffering. In his second letter, Luther explained why Zoch might not be enjoying the felt experience of God's comfort: "Therefore, he often withdraws from us the comfort of visible things, in order that the comfort of the scriptures may find room and opportunity within us, and not remain standing uselessly in the bare letter without exercise."[31]

Luther recognized how difficult and painful it was to wait patiently on God when our flesh is crying out for fixed feelings and changed circumstances. Yet, this painful process teaches us dependent trust, "All of this, both such patience and such comfort, is the work of God and beyond our power. This is the school of Christians. They take lessons daily in this art and cannot comprehend it, much less learn it thoroughly, but they always remain children, spelling the A B C of this art."[32]

Clearly, Luther saw a positive role for deep internal suffering, even describing it as a "delicious despair."[33] Spiritual depression brought the sufferer to the border of despair in order to produce profound faith in Christ. In clarifying Luther's view of faith and suffering, Mildenberger notes that Luther saw human beings as typically untroubled persons, people at ease, who imagine faith to be within their control:

> The Reformers taught that we receive God's salvation in Christ only when we are past the point of being able to do anything. At this point, the point at which we are unable to do anything for ourselves, the Holy Spirit works faith. This

kind of faith, therefore, comes only at a specific time and place. The time and place at which we experience spiritual temptations is the time and place at which God wills to create the faith which is God's own work in us.[34]

Luther taught that we need to face suffering with stark realism because undiminished suffering is God's catalyst for faith.

The Biblical Definition of Health

For Luther, the healthiest people are those who know how spiritually unhealthy they are. Since strength is found in weakness, our greatest need is neediness and our greatest enemy is needlessness. Since spiritual sickness is essentially our refusal to depend upon God, Luther defined spiritual health as the awareness and acceptance of our consummate need for Christ. To become whole, we first have to experience the fragmentation of sin and suffering; to become integrated, we first have to experience the paradoxical stage of disintegration or desperation.

Into this need for neediness, God sends *anfechtungen* for the express purpose of producing humble faith, desperate dependence, clinging trust. Luther viewed *anfechtungen* as assaults through which God recalls the attention of the soul back to himself. The love of this world lulls the soul away from a passionate relationship with God, "But, as if by a thunderstroke, the ache of the soul sent by God startles us and awakens us to life lived *coram Deo*. The trials of faith are a prerequisite to knowing God deeply and loving him passionately."[35]

McGrath further outlines Luther's understanding of God's health-giving purposes in sending *anfechtungen*: "God Himself must be recognized as the ultimate source of *anfechtungen*: it is His 'opus alienum,' which is intended to destroy man's self-confidence and complacency, and reduce him to a state of utter despair and humiliation, in order that he may finally turn to God, devoid of all the obstacles to justification which formerly existed."[36]

Anfechtungen make room for faith. According to Luther, faith and *anfechtungen* are God's healing medicine against the disease of self-trust:

> Inasmuch as tribulation serves the same purpose as rhubarb, myrrh, aloes, or an antidote against all the worms, poison, decay, and dung of this body of death, it ought not to be despised. We must not willingly seek or select afflictions, but we must accept those which God sees fit to visit upon us, for he knows which are suitable and salutary for us and how many and how heavy they should be.[37]

We do not ask for *anfechtungen*, nor are we expected to enjoy the experience. However, we can grow if we face the dark night of the soul *coram Deo*.

Luther saw the healing task as restoring the suffering Christian to wholeness—the renewal of a faith perspective in which doubts about the goodness of God are transformed into dependence upon God's good heart and gracious purposes. When people raised the question, *What good are my trials?* Luther encouraged them to face the paradox of a good God who uses bad things to produce good results. He pointed people to the benefits of faith to perceive the benefits of trials.

Timeless Truth for Life and Ministry Today

If we are to provide Luther-like pastoral counseling, then we need to see sustaining and healing as God-given medicine for treating suffering. In sustaining, we seek to promote the spiritual survival of faith; in healing, we desire to promote the spiritual maturity or growth of faith. Through sustaining, we help men and women to face life honestly and to begin to seek God for comfort. In healing, we journey with people a giant step further by encouraging them to enjoy God's good heart and to explore God's grace purposes for life's bad events. When suffering enters the normal flow of life, the natural response is to retreat from life, to deny either the reality of evil or the goodness of God. Through sustaining and healing, like Luther, we encourage people to face both truths: life is bad and God is good.

If we are to maintain a Luther-like theology of the spiritual significance of suffering, then we need to understand that God sends suffering to cure our deepest sickness of estrangement from God caused by our independence from him. We need to help one another perceive by faith the deeper work of God. He uses trials as his medicine of choice to convince us of our desperate need for Christ. We need to journey with our spiritual friends so that their suffering can lead them to a greater susceptibility to the divine activity, develop profound trust, and serve as a catalyst for humble faith.

We can capture Luther's theology of healing in two tweet-size summaries.

> God's good heart always produces good purposes in our suffering: he sometimes chooses to cure us; he always chooses to mature us.

> God uses suffering to form and transform us.

And, God chooses to use us in his creative process of forming the face of Christ in one another. As Lake pictures it, "there is no human experience which cannot be put on the anvil of a lively relationship with God and man, and battered into a meaningful shape."[38] In this chapter we have witnessed Luther's understanding of God's role. In chapter 7, we'll observe Luther modeling our role.

CHAPTER SEVEN
CHRIST'S GOSPEL MEDICINE FOR SUFFERING:
LUTHER'S METHODOLOGY OF HEALING

IN 1523, an Augustinian friar, Lambert Thorn, was arrested for adhering to his evangelical faith. Thorn spent five years in prison where he eventually died in 1528—without recanting. On January 19, 1524, early in Thorn's imprisonment, Luther sent Thorn a letter of spiritual encouragement.

Luther led with reminders of Thorn's union with Christ and the strength this union provides: "Christ, who is in you, has given abundant testimony that you do not need my words, for he himself suffers in you and is glorified in you. He is taken captive in you and reigns in you. He is oppressed in you and triumphs in you."[1] Christ in us is not only the hope of glory; our union with him is also our sure hope this side of glory.

Luther continued by underscoring the relational nature of Thorn's union with Christ and again linked that union to courage during life's storms. Lambert was to be "mindful that you are not suffering alone but that He is with you who says, 'I will be with him in trouble; because he hath set his love upon me, therefore will I deliver him. I will set him on high because he hath known my name'. . . . Be of good courage and he will strengthen your heart."[2]

Luther's counsel is the counsel of the Word: "He has said: 'In the world ye shall have tribulation: but be of good cheer; I have overcome the world.'" Luther's reasoning is faith-based. "Do not argue with Satan but fix your eyes on the Lord, relying in simple faith on Jesus Christ, and know that by his blood we are saved."[3]

Luther draws out the courage already resident within Thorn by applauding the impact Lambert's testimony was having on Luther and the whole world. "He strengthens you inwardly by his Spirit in these outward tribulations and consoles you with the double example of John and Henry. Thus both they and you are to me a great consolation and strength, to the whole world a sweet savor, and to the gospel of Christ a special glory." It is not going too far to say that Luther bragged on Thorn. "I rejoice with you and congratulate you with my whole heart, giving thanks to the faithful Saviour who has given me to see in you the rich and splendid increase of his grace."[4]

Luther concludes with words of challenge and comfort: "You have become a member of him by the holy calling of our Father. May he perfect his calling in you to the glory of his name and of his Word. Amen. Farewell in Christ, my brother."[5]

Luther's Healing Counsel: Speaking Gospel Healing

In a letter of approximately 600 words—less than a brief blog post by today's standards—Luther illustrates three dynamic aspects of healing pastoral counsel. Luther speaks gospel healing: (1) to the soul, (2) to the mind, and (3) to the will.

Luther heals the soul through constant conversations about the Christian's union with Christ. Satan seeks to misuse suffering to suggest a breach in our relationship with God. This sucker punch can stagger even the strongest Christian. Luther becomes the Spirit's advocate by reintegrating God's children with their heavenly Father through emphasis on their union with Christ.

Luther heals the mind through gospel conversations that urge Christians to fix their "eyes on the Lord, relying in simple faith on Jesus Christ, and know that by his blood we are saved." Satan seeks to misinterpret suffering to insinuate that God is angry with us. This kidney punch can double-over even the most mature believer. Luther becomes the Spirit's advocate by teaching Christians how to reinterpret their suffering through a gospel lens. The gospel is the divine smelling salt that jolts our minds back to the eternal reality that in suffering God is not getting back at us; he is getting us back to himself.

Luther heals the will through encouragement counseling. Encourage—to implant courage into our wills by enlightening our minds to the reality that Christ is implanted in and united with us. Satan seeks to dis-courage us—to suck the courage out of us—by causing us to doubt God and ourselves. This one-two combination can knock even the greatest spiritual athlete to the canvas. Luther becomes the Spirit's advocate by challenging Christians to reinvigorate their faith: "Be of good courage and he will strengthen your heart."

Relational Healing of the Soul: Reintegrating Christians to God and Themselves

To grasp the essence of reintegrating, we need to time travel back before suffering and sin invaded planet earth. God created humanity for shalom—peace, wholeness, holiness, integrity. United as one, Adam and Eve experienced their identity and wholeness in their relationship to God. The man and his wife were both naked and they felt no shame as they walked with God in the cool of the day. Their identity was integrated. Then, sin shattered shalom. Shame entered the soul—hiding, covering, self-sufficiency, fear, doubt, despair, brokenness, dis-integration, blaming, self-centeredness.

For Luther, *anfechtungen* was the fallout of the fall. Created for peace with God, with one another, and within our own souls, we now experience alienation from God, separation from one another, and dis-integration within our souls. Luther poignantly describes this *anfechtungen* of his soul as being afflicted with "sadness, despair or other heart-sorrow" and as "a worm gnawing in his conscience."[6] Satan is always all too happy to feed the worm: "The more you give way to the thoughts with which the devil attacks and wearies you, the more vigorously and quickly does he set himself against you, until at length he drives you to despair."[7] Luther counteracted the worm's gnawing with biblical truth about reconciliation with God and redemptive relationships.

Relational Healing through Reconciliation with God

Satan's fundamental strategy is to paint pictures of God shaking a wrathful, angry finger at Christians: "This one line of attack the devil pursues to the utmost against us, undertaking to break down our faith and confidence by the thought that God is angry with us."[8] Luther's spiritual warfare counter-strategy promotes healing by painting gospel-centered images of God's relationship to his children. Luther heals in light of Christ-centered *coram Deo* because wholeness and holiness, integration and shalom, were impossible to him apart from the spiritual dynamic of relationship to God through Christ.

Gospel-Centered Images of God's Relationship to His Children

Losing faith in the grace and goodness of God was the gravest temptation Luther could imagine:

> By the temptation of faith is meant that the evil conscience drives out of a person his confidence in the pardoning grace of God, and leads him to imagine that God is angry and wishes the death of the sinner, or that, in other words, the conscience places Moses upon the judgment-seat, and casts down the Savior of sinners from the throne of grace. This is the strongest, greatest and severest temptation of the devil, that he says: "God is the enemy of sinners, you are a sinner, therefore, God is your enemy." This is the noose which Satan throws over the head of the poor child of man in order to strangle him.[9]

What is the believer to do when confronted with the devil's lie? The heart of Luther's healing counsel involved turning people back to the heart of God—revealed in Christ: "I know nothing of any other Christ than he whom the Father gave and who died for me and for my

sins, and I know that he is not angry with me, but is kind and gracious
to me; for he would not otherwise have had the heart to die for me
and for my benefit."[10]

Luther is very specific in teaching how to counter Satan's deception about God's relationship to the Christian:

> For the spirit and heart of man is not able to endure the
> thought of the wrath of God, as the devil represents and urges
> it. Therefore, whatever thoughts the devil awakens within us
> in temptation we should put away from us and cast out of
> our minds, so that we can see and hear nothing else than the
> kind, comforting word of the promise of Christ, and of the
> gracious will of the heavenly Father, who has given his own
> Son for us, as Christ, our dear Lord, declares in John iii. 16:
> "God so loved the world that he gave his only begotten Son,
> that whosoever believeth on him should not perish, but have
> everlasting life." Everything else, now, which the devil may
> suggest to us beyond this, that God the Father is reconciled
> to us, and graciously inclined to us, and merciful and pow-
> erful for the sake of his dear Son, we should cast out of our
> minds as wandering and unprofitable thoughts.[11]

These words reveal a pivotal concept in Luther's healing ministry:
God the Father is reconciled to and graciously inclined toward his
children.

When Johann Schlaginhaufen of Kothen battled melancholy, Luther counseled him not to view his spiritual temptations as signs of
God's wrath, but as signs of the paternal love of God: "Let it be granted
that God appears to be angry when we are vexed and tempted; yet, if
we repent and believe, we shall come to see that beneath the wrath of
God lie hidden grace and goodness, just as his strength and power lie
concealed beneath our weakness."[12]

On another occasion, Luther counseled a person "assailed by temptations to doubt" to "bury himself in the Holy Scriptures."[13] And what is the center of the Scripture? It is the comfort of the gospel: "It is a falsehood, that God is an enemy of sinners, for Christ roundly and plainly declares, by commandment of the Father: 'I am come to save sinners.'"[14]

When tempted by the devil to doubt the grace of God, Luther encouraged his followers to mock the devil rather than debate him:

> When the devil casts up to us our sin, and declares us unworthy of death and hell, we must say: "I confess that I am worthy of death and hell. What more have you to say?" "Then you will be lost forever!" "Not in the least: for I know One who suffered for me and made satisfaction for my sins, and his name is Jesus Christ, the Son of God. So long as he shall live, I shall live also." Therefore treat the devil thus: Spit on him, and say: "Have I sinned? Well, then I have sinned, and I am sorry; but I will not on that account despair, for Christ has borne and taken away all my sin, yes, and the sin of the whole world, if it will only confess its sin, reform and believe on Christ. What should I do if I had committed murder or adultery, or even crucified Christ? Why, even then, I should be forgiven, as he prayed on the cross: "Father, forgive them" (Luke xxiii. 34). This I am in duty bound to believe. I have been acquitted. Then away with you, devil![15]

In these words of counsel, Luther highlights the perspective that both sins and sinners are forgiven. Therefore, the believer is no longer separated from God. Luther urged his followers to "depend boldly upon this"[16] in order to experience peace with God. Luther counseled Christians to draw near to Christ with full confidence and assurance of his love. The Reformer promised that such an understanding can bring hope, joy, peace, confidence, and love. To Schlaginhaufen, he wrote, "believe that he esteems and loves you more than does Dr. Luther or any other Christian."[17] Awareness of God's friendship has the power to entice prodigals to return home to the Father: "The conscience, spurred by the devil, the flesh, and the fallen world; says, 'God is your enemy. Give up in despair.' God, in His own Fatherly love and through His Son's grace and through His Word and through the witness of His people; says, 'I have no wrath. You are accepted in the beloved. I am not angry with you. We are reconciled!'"[18]

Grace-Centered Images of God's Character

For Luther, integration with God was based upon a rich, relational, integrated biblical understanding of God. Luther taught that holy love was the essence of God's character. He saw God's holiness as his absolute power, righteousness, and separateness from humanity. He viewed God's love as his absolute kindness, mercy, and nearness to humanity. Luther's God is eternally transcendent (always above) and immanent (always near). Luther's God is the eternal God of affectionate sovereign grace.

Luther was convinced that attacks on God's holy love were a staple of the devil: "This, then, is the most furious and sudden of all attacks, in which the devil exerts to the full extent all his powers and arts, and transforms himself into the likeness of the angry and ungracious God."[19]

The theology of God as a God of holy love served as the foundation for Luther's letters to people suffering in the throes of spiritual depression. Luther desired that Christians grasp the depths of God's perfect love at a personal level: "One should therefore banish from his mind and heart the grievous thoughts of sin and of the wrath of God, and cherish the very opposite thoughts."[20]

We witness how Luther counseled people struggling with doubts about God's holy love in his interactions with Benedict Pauli. In June of 1533, Pauli's only son fell off the roof of their home and died. Luther visited Pauli at his home and Veit Dietrich recorded his words of comfort and encouragement "as they fell from Luther's lips in the home of Dr. Benedict."[21]

We learned about Luther's sustaining ministry to Pauli in chapter 5. Luther's subsequent words of healing consolation communicated that God's grace comes to us in the form of his affectionate sovereignty. Luther directed Pauli to Job with the reminder that God sovereignly gives and takes away. Experiencing guilt that his son died an accidental death, Luther forcefully asked Pauli, "Why do you torment yourself so much about this? God is omnipotent."[22] But is this omnipotent God in control but uncaring? Luther addressed this question directly: "Are you afraid, then, that the Lord took your son in wrath?"[23] That is the essence of Satan's lying, condemning narrative: he seeks to disintegrate our relationship with God by seeking to denigrate the character of God. So Luther continues: "Certainly it is the good will of God that your son should die, although human nature cries out against this and imagines that God is angry. It is characteristic of our human nature to think that what we wish is best and what God does is unsatisfactory to us. . . . *It is enough for us that we have a gracious God.*"[24]

This last line summarizes Luther's healing ministry: *it is enough for us that we have a gracious God.* Our Father is enough to console his children and to give them hope. His will, which at times may seem unkind, does in fact always flow out of his eternal kindness—out of his holy love.

Relational Healing through Redemptive Relationships

Luther taught that the soul could experience re-integration through personal encounters with others who carried the voice of the gospel. Bernard von Dolen had been an evangelical clergyman in St. Peter's Church in Freiberg, Saxony. In addressing von Dolen's deep dissatisfaction with life and ministry, Luther wrote, "Perhaps your temptation is too severe to be relieved by a brief letter; it can better be cured, God willing, *by a personal encounter with me and my living voice.*"[25]

Schleiner examined Luther's view of integration through personal encounter in its historical context—researching 500 years of treatment for schizophrenia, psychosis, and melancholy from the Renaissance through the Reformation.[26] He concluded, "medical writers of the period rarely show any sympathy for such delusive conditions." Renaissance doctors delighted in mocking psychotics (persons thinking themselves other than they were—a clay jar, a cock with flapping wings): "The sense of ridicule overcomes pity. Of course the pain and inhumanity resulting from unsympathetic attitudes towards psychotics have mostly gone unrecorded."[27]

Schleiner set as his task finding some source whose treatment and healing methodology might be more compassionate. According to Schleiner, "one must look to theologians . . . to find sympathetic treatments of the condition" (of schizophrenia).[28] Only in Luther did he find someone manifesting "an encompassing sympathy for the psychotic."[29]

Schleiner's work bears examination because it highlights what was so important to Luther—personal encounter or cure by redemptive relationships. He called Luther's cure, the cure by charity and company—"societas." Compassionate care was a major part of the cure in Luther: "Indeed it can be said that this sense of caring becomes a vehicle of therapy. . . . Clearly human company is the essential ingredient in the cure of the melancholic."[30]

What sort of strugglers does Luther minister to? One was a "melancholic who refused to eat and drink and hides in a cellar. He rebuffs any charitable helpers with the words 'Don't you see that I am a corpse and have died? How can I eat?'"[31] Here is a person who is both depressed and psychotic—thinking he is dead. In a second case, Luther treated an individual who thought he was a rooster "with a red comb on his head, a long beak, and a crowing voice."[32]

What was Luther's care and cure for these two individuals? Schleiner says the two elements common in every one of Luther's cases were "the consideration of the psychotic's past and the role of societas (company, relationship) in re-integrating such a person into the community."[33] Reintegrating the soul through compassionate relationships was an essential element in Luther's soul care. He used his personal relationship as a way of encountering another person on behalf of God so that the other person's image of God and relationship to God could be altered in ways that brought integration to their personality. In fact, Schleiner even labeled Luther's approach "compassionate reintegration."[34] Schleiner's summary of Luther's pastoral counseling is instructive: "Luther shows none of the dehumanizing amusement that often animates even learned physicians when they report certain kinds of cases. The 'cure' is brought about not by trickery but by friendly persuasion, by appeal to common humanity, by company. The entire story is informed by a strong sense of sympathy for a patient who becomes stigmatized by society."[35]

Luther believed that spiritual wholeness or integration was achieved through personal encounter. This was true in his ministry to others and also in his openness to being ministered to by others. After reading thousands of pages of firsthand accounts of Luther's interactions, Nebe writes of Luther, "He never regarded himself as all-sufficient, nor as highly lifted up above all others; humbly and urgently he besought help in hours of trial."[36]

Rational Healing of the Mind: Reinterpreting Suffering

Schleiner discussed a third difficult case that Luther counseled. This person was labeled a "voluntary retentive"—someone who refused to urinate. In most Renaissance cases like this, no history was taken or given. Not so with Luther. He traced the beginning of this disorder to a sermon this person heard about works-righteousness. The person came to believe that if he could perfectly control his body and soul, that he would be accepted by God.[37]

Having gleaned this history, Luther then diagnosed a cause, calling this person a "'*iustitiarius*'—someone attempting to justify himself by works rather than by faith."[38] His cure was redemptive/gospel-centered—pointing the person away from works of righteousness to the righteousness of Christ. Luther's interactions with the voluntary retentive person helped him to see that his behavior was rooted in the pride of self-sufficiency. Luther also helped this man see that he must put on renewed images of God in Christ as a God of grace.

This vignette is one of many examples of how Luther encouraged his followers to reinterpret life by exegeting it from a gospel perspective. He cared for souls by promoting the curative attitude of spiritual insight into the redemptive meaning behind events and experiences.

Reason Redeemed by Grace

When healing the mind, Luther was asking and answering the question: *How is faith to win over despair?* Luther taught people what to do with despair in order to move from doubt to trust: maintain confident reliance on God developed through the perspective of reason redeemed by grace in contrast to reason apart from faith.

McGrath explains Luther's view of life as a constant battleground between trust and doubt:

> The Christian life is characterized by the unending tension between faith and experience. For Luther, experience can only stand in contradiction to faith, in that revealed truth must be revealed under its opposite form. This dialectic between experienced perception and hidden revelation inevitably leads to radical questioning and doubt on the part of the believer, as he finds himself unable to reconcile what he believes with what he experiences.[39]

Luther realized that there were definite, apparent contradictions when people reflect on experience and on the Scriptures. Circumstances shout, *God does not care about me!* The Scriptures proclaim, *God loves you!* Which narrative does the Christian believe?

Luther discerned two primary approaches to resolving such apparent contradictions. One approach was to examine the situation based on reason unaided by faith or grace; the other was to scrutinize the situation based upon reason aided by faith and grace.

Luther chose the holistic approach of reason redeemed by grace. Grislis explored Luther's thinking through a study of Luther's commentary on the life of Joseph. Luther first recorded the plight of Joseph—rejected by his brothers, falsely accused by Potiphar's wife, and cast into prison. Luther then pondered the questions that arose for Joseph: "Where is God now? Where are those very great and precious promises that He loves, guards, and preserves His saints?" Grislis describes this as the paradox of faith—by human reason no one could interpret such events as good or as sent from the hands of a good and loving God. In Joseph's life, God did not seem merciful and kind, yet he was—according to the insight of faith combating the insight of reason.[40]

Luther rejected the vantage point of unaided reason. The divine promises are meaningless and empty words to the counsel of reason. By reason, the flesh is compelled to shout, "God is a liar!"[41] For Luther, this battle was necessary. Within the darkness of despair, the light of faith emerged, for only in the struggle with unbelief could faith be won and nurtured. Luther insisted that doubt be faced, that the resources of reason be used and shown faulty, and that the resources of faith be retained.

Hart explains that "Luther saw that the reality of faith was often expressed by a courageous reliance on God."[42] This courageous faith was not unreasonable—it was reason redeemed by grace. It was reason which, with the benefit of faith, saw the benefits of trials: "With the assistance of reason-redeemed-by-grace, Luther taught that the believer should be able to recognize several distinctive benefits which arise on account of the *anfechtungen*."[43] Luther believed that God's good purposes were discerned through a perspective which was not unreasonable, but which was beyond mere reason.

Luther thus counseled people to cling to the source of reason aided by grace—the Scriptures. He explained, "I have learned by experience how one should act under temptation, namely, when any one is afflicted with sadness. . . . Let him first lay hold of the comfort of the divine Word."[44]

In his commentary on Isaiah, Luther used the circumstances surrounding Hezekiah's trials to illustrate his point. Hezekiah's advisers suggested a course based upon reason unaided by grace. Luther explained that this course only served to "whet the devil's tongue."[45] And that "human reason cannot be content until it has looked about for human help."[46] In his ongoing commentary, Luther taught a method of mental healing based upon biblical reinterpretation:

> Therefore, whenever any one is assailed by temptation of any sort whatever, the very best that he can do in the case is either to read something in the Holy Scriptures, or think about the Word of God, and apply it to his heart. . . . Just here is especially seen the power and might of the Word of God, namely, that in the most admirable way, it heals and restores again to health the mind and heart of man when wounded by the arrows of the devil.[47]

In dispensing the medicine of reason redeemed by grace, Luther consistently urges sufferers to turn to the Scriptures as their interpretive narrative:

> Christ heals people by means of his precious Word, as he also declares in the 50th chapter of Isaiah (verse 4): "The Lord hath given me a learned tongue, that I should know how to speak a word in season to the weary." St. Paul also teaches likewise, in Romans xv 14, that we should obtain and

strengthen hope from the comfort of the Holy Scriptures, which the devil endeavors to tear out of people's hearts in times of temptations. Accordingly, as there is no better nor more powerful remedy in temptations than to diligently read and heed the Word of God.[48]

Luther directed Christians to a higher truth and a deeper reality than their earthly suffering by guiding them to the reality of God's healing power contained in the Scriptures. In healing, Luther taught his parishioners how to use the Word to cause their faith to thrive. Without the Word, he said that a Christian was like a soldier, "entering upon conflict naked and unprotected."[49] With the Word, the Christian could defeat even the "most practiced and experienced warrior."[50]

The Medicine for Healing the Mind: A Faith Perspective on Suffering

In Luther's healing ministry, he encouraged men and women to grasp the good purposes of a good God when he allowed evil to enter the natural rhythms of life. While suffering is always painful; it also is purposeful. Luther deepened faith in God's good purposes in pain by teaching that hardship united the believer with Christ in his suffering and made them more like Christ as they clung to him in their suffering.

Luther maintained a balance of pain and purpose in his letter to his father, Hans Luther. As Hans' health deteriorated, Luther proposed that his parents move to Wittenberg where Luther resided. But the weakness of his father made this impossible, and Hans died on May 29, 1530. Three months earlier, Luther's brother, James, informed him that Hans was seriously ill. In response, Luther pens a letter of consolation to his father, in which he wrote candidly about the pain of our fallen world: "If it is his divine will that you should postpone that better life and continue to suffer with us in this troubled and unhappy vale of tears, to see and hear sorrow and help other Christians to suffer and conquer, he will give you the grace to accept all this willingly."[51]

Then Luther moved seamlessly into God's good heart and grace purposes: "In the meantime I pray from the bottom of my heart that our Father, who has made you my father, will strengthen you according to his immeasurable kindness." Hans could see this kindness even in his pain if he understood that his suffering resulted in current growth ("the true marks of our likeness to the Lord Christ") and future glory ("as Paul says, that we may be like him also in future glory"). Knowing this, Hans could "Let your heart be strong and at ease in your trouble, for we have yonder a true mediator with God, Jesus Christ, who has overcome death and sin for us. . . . I commend you to Him who loves you more than you love yourself."[52]

The suffering Christian is united with God because Luther's God suffers. His God is not apathetic (without feeling, lacking empathy), but full of pathos. Christ's crucifixion is the ultimate demonstration of God's care, and Luther forms his theology of the cross upon it. Jensen contrasts the theology of the cross to a theology of glory that teaches God and his children will not suffer:

> It is in reaction to such a view (the theology of glory) that Luther makes his statement that suffering is the Christian's greatest treasure. He is not suggesting that suffering is something to be glorified. What he is saying, however, is that faith is not an eternal fire insurance policy. Rather, it is a daily risking of one's self to God's care. A theology of the cross stresses that *God is to be found in the struggles and uncertainties of this earthly life.* This is the way God has chosen to be revealed. Consequently, true faith also involves living in the midst of uncertainties. It is a "theology of *anfechtungen*" where the outcome always depends totally on God. Only in the midst of trials can a true hope emerge, a hope which does not avoid the struggles of life. By facing one's challenges head on, as Christ did, rather than running from them, an undeniable hope is the result. One is not abandoned in personal and communal struggles, for God

is present. God suffers and dwells with us in order to lead us to an unquenchable hope.[53]

Our great hope in suffering is that pain has a divine purpose; it increases our awareness of our union with Christ; it heightens our dependence upon Christ; it promotes our growth in Christlikeness. This was Luther's counsel to Laurentius Zoch upon the loss of his wife: "But it is a much greater comfort, that Christ has formed you in his likeness, to suffer as he suffered, i.e., to be punished and distressed, not alone by the devil, but as though by God, who is and must be your comfort."[54]

Luther's perspective on suffering is the perspective of faith in a God who is larger than, but not immune to, human suffering. His purposes in suffering are good purposes. This truth could never be learned through reason. Rather, this larger story can be read and understood only with the eyes of faith in the goodness of God. Luther merged these two stories in his final words to Zoch: "Heavy is thy (God's) rod, but I know assuredly that thou art Father still."[55] The smaller story is real and it is heavy (hurtful). The larger story is real, and it is light, for Christ's burden is light and his yoke is easy because it flows from his fatherly love for his children.

The reality of God's comfort was a faith-sensed reality for Luther: "We are told that faith consists in that which cannot be seen, and which does not appear."[56] Because "We must turn our faces to the unseen things of grace and to the hidden things of comfort, hoping and waiting upon these; and our backs to things that are seen, that we may accustom ourselves to leave these and depart from them, as St. Paul says: 'Who look not at the things which are seen, but at the things which are unseen' (2 Cor. iv. 18)."[57] The healing which God offers is his intimate presence in union with Christ. It is the knowledge that when Christians suffer, Christ suffers in them.

Healing calls for a higher medicine—the medicine of faith—reason redeemed by grace. When Elizabeth Agricola became anxious about her life circumstances, Luther counsels her to "remember that

Christ is near and bears your ills, for he has not forsaken you, as your flesh and blood make you imagine."[58] Rather than interpreting life through the flesh, she—and we—are to interpret life through the lens of our suffering Savior: "Remember that he has suffered far more for you than you can ever suffer for his sake or your own."[59]

Volitional Healing of the Will: Reengaging the World for Christ

Picture the process theologically: First, we are relationally reintegrated with Christ as we come to understand who we are in Christ and who Christ is. Then, we rationally reinterpret life through the lens of the cross of Christ. Now, we are prepared for volitional healing—reengaging the world for Christ.

Picture the process personally: Suffering invades life. Doubts ensue. Faces turn away from God. We retreat. Sustaining draws the line in the sand of retreat. Now faith arises. Faces turn back to face God in Christ. Healing moves from retreat to advance—advance in our union with Christ, dependence upon Christ, and likeness to Christ. Do we stop here, content in our renewed relationship with Christ? Not for Luther. It was unthinkable for Luther to imagine that Christians rejoicing in God's grace would isolate themselves from the larger community.

Luther exhorted redeemed sufferers to reengage the world, believing that the human heart must have something to do, and that isolation, idleness, and purposelessness would lead back to despair. Engagement with the world was both the result of healing and part of the process of healing. Luther encouraged volitional healing through courageously affirming existing faith resources, bluntly confronting lack of faith, and boldly challenging the further use of existing faith resources.

Courageously Affirming Existing Faith Resources

When Frederick of Myconius lay dying of consumption, Luther wrote him a letter that Nebe described as a "heroic epistle."[60] Luther fills his epistle with affirmations of Myconius's strength in weakness: "I have, dear Frederick, received your letter, in which you inform me that you are lying sick unto death, or, as you rightly and in a true Christian spirit explain, 'sick unto life.'"[61]

Luther affirmed the faith that allowed Myconius to reinterpret life from God's eternal perspective. Luther also shared how Myconius is impacting Luther's life. Twice he mentions, "it gives me a peculiar joy, that you are so unterrified in view of death."[62] Throughout his brief letter, Luther identified specific details in Myconius's faith-response that so impressed him.

In affirming faith resources, Luther drew out specific instances of courage and faith. He recounted in detail how the Elector John of Saxony had endured an extremely negative situation. He then described the fruit of John's faithfulness and explained how God was using John's faith to impact others for good. Seeing his words as insufficient, Luther spoke words of affirmation of John on behalf of God: "It is as if he [God] would say, 'To you dear Duke John, I entrust my most precious treasure, my pleasant paradise, and ask you to preside over it as father. I place it under your protection and government and do you the honor of making you my gardener and caretaker.'"[63]

As part of his heroic narratives, Luther would identify strengths in one area and then encourage his followers to apply them in other pressing matters. For instance, when his friend Philip Melanchthon became anxious and discouraged, Luther wrote, "You who are so pugnacious in everything else, fight against yourself."[64] As always, Luther reminded Philip that he does not fight in his own strength: "Great though our cause is, it's Author and Champion is also great, for the cause is not ours."[65]

Luther, hearing reports of Melanchthon's revived courage, wrote again to affirm and applaud Philip's victorious living: "I believe that you have wrestled manfully with the demons this past week."[66] Luther pointed Philip to the ultimate champion wrestler: "Only see to it, dear

Philip, that you do not worry about a cause that is not in your hands but in the hands of Him who is greater than the prince of this world and from whose hands no one can pluck us."[67]

Gregory Bruck, chancellor of the elector of Saxony, was assailed by doubts and uncertainty about the Reformation. In response, Luther told Bruck, "I have recently seen two miracles." They were miracles of God's power in nature. Immediately after sharing these two miracle stories, Luther continued, "I take the liberty of engaging in such pleasantries with Your Honor, and yet I write with more than pleasantries in mind, for I found special pleasure in learning that Your Honor, above all others, has been of good courage and stout heart in this trial of ours."[68] From the nature of the two stories and from what follows in his letter, Luther connected God's faithfulness and power to Bruck's faith in God's power. Luther stirred up and fanned into flame the embers of Bruck's faith with reminders of God's faithfulness. God, who is providentially and all-powerfully at work every second, will continue to sovereignly shepherd their Reformation cause: "By his Spirit, God will bless and further this work which he has graciously given us to do, and he will find the fitting time, place, and method to help us."[69]

Bluntly Confronting the Refusal to Use Existing Faith Resources

We would be mistaken to assume that Luther only affirmed positives, such as instances of courage. Luther also confronted and exposed instances of cowardice. After affirming Philip, Luther sharply confronted him: "I pray for you very earnestly, and I am deeply pained that you keep sucking up cares like a leech."[70]

The Elector John the Steadfast of Saxony died of apoplexy on August 16, 1532. His chamberlain and confidant, John Riedesel, fell under the displeasure of the new elector, John Frederick, and was deeply distressed by his sudden change of fortune. Luther frankly challenged John: "I beg you for God's sake to be a man now. God is trying you a little. Be steadfast and you will learn what kind of God God is and how he reigns."[71]

Boldly Challenging the Further Use of Faith Resources

When Luther saw a failure to exercise faith, after confronting it, he then challenged the person to grow up in Christ. When he saw successes in exercising faith, he affirmed them and then challenged the person to continue growing. Part of his challenge included courageous imagery. To those being persecuted, he wrote, you are as "guests in an inn whose keeper is a villain. Be strong through this evil."[72] Luther validated their trials, affirmed their faith, and motivated them to ongoing courage.

Luther exhorted a weary Jonas of Stockhausen to "pluck up courage and confidence" and to fight strongly against the devil's temptations. Jonas was to lay hold of himself and to fight the good fight in God's strength. Luther concluded by linking Jonas to Christ. He called Christ the "true Conqueror" and exhorted Jonas to celebrate their (Jonas and Christ) shared triumph over the devil.[73]

To individuals suffering externally or internally, Luther would encourage grief plus growth. To Catherine Metzler, whose husband and son had died within an eight-month span, he wrote:

> I could not refrain from writing to you and, in so far as God enables me, sending you these lines of comfort since I can well imagine the cross which God has now laid upon you through the death of your beloved son sorely oppresses and hurts you. It is natural and right that you should grieve, especially for one who is of your own flesh and blood. For God has not created us without feeling or to be like stones or sticks, but it is his will that we should mourn and bewail our dead. Otherwise it would appear that we had no love, particularly in the case of members of our own family. However, our grief should be mingled with hope, for our dear Father is testing us here to see whether we can fear and love him in sorrow as well as in joy and whether we can give back to him what he has given us . . . . I pray you, therefore, that you acknowledge

the gracious and good will of God and that you patiently bear this cross for his sake.[74]

Luther challenged Catherine to use her knowledge of and relationship to God in Christ as the means by which she could embrace life again.

Timeless Truth for Life and Ministry Today

If we are to provide Luther-like pastoral counseling for suffering, then we must see suffering for what it is—a spiritual battleground between faith and doubt, between God and the devil. If suffering involved only or primarily external events that happened to us, then the medicine for healing would not have to be spiritual. It could be circumstantial—changed situations, settings, and surroundings. But for Luther, suffering is primarily internal—how we spiritually and theologically interpret what happens to us. That's why healing for suffering requires Christ's gospel medicine.

Relationally, Satan deviously strives to misuse suffering to rip us apart—from God, others, and within our own souls. Christ's gospel medicine heals the relational gash by reminding us that we are once and forever reconciled to the Father through the Son—reintegrating.

Rationally, Satan deceptively works to misuse suffering to infiltrate our minds with doubts about the goodness of God. Christ's gospel medicine heals the rational virus by reminding us of God's good purposes flowing from God's good heart—reinterpreting.

Volitionally, Satan desperately desires to misuse suffering to weaken our wills, causing us to cave in on ourselves, curl up, and quit. Christ's gospel medicine heals the volitional faintness by reviving with en-couragement—the courage of Christ stirred up within us—reengaging.

We can condense Luther's practice of healing pastoral care with this tweet-size summary:

When suffering tempts us to despair, we prescribe Christ's
gospel medicine of healing hope—reconciled relationships,
renewed minds, and revived courage.

We know that pastoral care is defective unless it can deal thoroughly both with the evils we have suffered and with the sins we have committed. Thus far, we have observed Luther the master pastor applying gospel medicine to the wound of suffering. Now, we will watch and learn as Luther performs spiritual heart surgery as he applies gospel medicine to the disease of sin.

CHAPTER EIGHT

THE SPIRITUAL ANATOMY OF THE SOUL: LUTHER'S THEOLOGY OF RECONCILING

BARBARA LISCHNER, sister to Jerome and Peter Weller, was disturbed by doubts about her eternal security, allowing questions about whether she was a true child of God to torment her. In counseling Barbara in a letter Luther wrote on April 30, 1531, he referred to his own experience with this struggle: "Dear and virtuous lady: Your dear brother, Jerome Weller, has informed me that you are deeply distressed about eternal election. I am truly sorry to hear this. . . . I know all about this sickness. I was myself brought to the brink of eternal death by it. . . . I will tell you how God helped me out of this trouble, and by what means I even yet daily guard myself against it."[1]

What was Luther's daily guard? He preached the gospel to himself every day: "The highest of all God's commands is this, that we ever hold up before our eyes the image of his dear Son, our Lord Jesus Christ. He must daily be to our hearts the perfect mirror, in which we behold how much God loves us and how well, in his infinite goodness, as a faithful God, he has grandly cared for us in that he gave his dear Son for us."[2] Luther's exhortation to Barbara is a powerful reminder to us today: "Do not let this mirror and throne of grace be torn away from before your eyes."[3]

Luther quickly exposed the ultimate source of such doubts about God's grace: "First, you must firmly fix in your mind the conviction that such thoughts as yours are assuredly the suggestions and fiery darts of the wretched devil."[4] Luther was equally swift to urge Barbara to fix her mind on truth about God from God's Word:

Learn to say: "Begone, wretched devil! You are trying to make me worry about myself. But God declares everywhere that I should let him care for me. He says, 'I am thy God.' This means, 'I take care of you.'" This is what Saint Peter taught, "Cast all thy care upon him, for he careth for you." And David taught, "Cast thy burden upon the Lord, and he shall sustain thee."[5]

Ever the spiritual diagnostician, Luther exposed Satan's strategy and how his scheme aligned with our fleshly compulsion to save ourselves:

The wretched devil, who is the enemy of God and Christ, tries by such thoughts to tear us away from Christ and God and to make us think about ourselves and our own cares. If we do this, we take upon ourselves the function of God, which is to care for us and be our God. In paradise the devil desired to make Adam equal with God so that Adam might be his own god and care for himself, thus robbing God of his divine work of caring for him. The result was the terrible Fall of Adam.[6]

Luther's Creation, Fall, Redemption Narrative of Reconciling

In these words, we discover many of the theological insights and methodological practices embedded throughout Luther's reconciling ministry. It was, first of all, a theologically-grounded ministry. Whether encouraging people who doubt their salvation, exhorting unsaved people to cling to Christ for salvation, or confronting hypocritical Christians, Luther unswervingly highlighted Christ's grace, Satan's condemning lies, the flesh's infatuation with self-salvation, and the Christian's battle to live by the Spirit.

Luther's reconciling was secondly a gospel-centered ministry. Luther preached the gospel to non-Christians who were alienated from

God. He also preached the gospel to Christians who falsely believed they were alienated from God. To the believer with a tender conscience and to the believer with a seared conscience, Luther held up the mirror of the throne of grace.

Chapter 3 summarized historic reconciling as "a ministry which seeks to re-establish broken relationships between man and fellow man and between man and God."[7] Luther might have worded it like this, *How do we help alienated people to establish or renew peaceful relationships with God and with each other?*

Throughout church history, pastors and theologians answered this question by developing a culturally relevant spiritual diagnostic system. Through a biblical study of the nature of the soul, sin, and salvation, they identified, classified, and helped people to experience victory over besetting sins. Franz Delitzsch labeled this a "biblical psychology."[8] We can categorize it even further. Throughout church history and in Luther, historic reconciling is a theological understanding of people, problems, and solutions:

- Biblical Psychology/Understanding People/Creation: The nature of the soul; understanding whose we are.
- Biblical Psychopathology/Diagnosing Problems/Fall: The nature of sin (the pathology, sickness, and sin of the soul); diagnosing what went wrong.
- Biblical Psychotherapy/Prescribing Solutions/Redemption: The nature of salvation; prescribing the gospel cure; how Christ changes us and brings us peace with God.

It is particularly important that we understand Luther's theology of reconciling since our means of justification and peaceful relationship with God was the polarizing soul care issue of the Reformation era. Luther greatly altered the approach to granting certainty of right relationship with God, reconciling sinners to God, and reestablishing relationships between people. Luther based his reconciling ministry upon his views of: (1) the struggle of the conscience, (2) the design of the soul (people, biblical anthropology, biblical psychology), (3) the essence of sin (problems, biblical hamartiology, biblical psychopathology), and (4) the nature of salvation (solutions, biblical soteriology, biblical psychotherapy).

The Struggle of the Conscience

In his reconciling ministry, Luther made the struggle of the conscience his pastoral care theme. Sin shattered shalom—obliterating our peace with God, with others, and even within our own soul. Luther was convinced that finding peace with God was the soul's ultimate struggle, and he counseled people concerning how they could obtain a good conscience before God.[9]

Luther maintained a robust understanding of the struggle of the conscience. Like the Puritans after him, Luther sought to load the conscience with guilt for those who were truly alienated from God. He also sought to lighten the conscience with grace for those who were at peace with God but were tormented by doubts.[10] A table talk entitled, "Forgiveness of Sin Is Hard to Believe," exemplifies Luther's dual ministry to the conscience: "So it comes about that those who are truly sinners don't want to be considered sinners, and those who are saints don't want to be called saints either."[11] Luther's diagnosis of the conscience was precise: "The latter don't believe the gospel which comforts them and the former don't believe the law which accuses them."[12]

Startling One Another with the Gospel

Luther sought to apply the doctrines of justification and reconciliation. Since by justification and reconciliation, our eternal relationship to God is secure, Luther wanted people to understand by faith that their present, day-by-day relationship to God was equally secure. How do we speak to our cleansed but doubting conscience?

But the Christian says: I believe and cling to him who is in heaven as a Savior. . . . Thus the Christian faith differs from other religions in this, that the Christian hopes even in the midst of evils and sins. Without the Holy Spirit natural man can't do this. He can only seek refuge in works. To say, "I am a child of God," is accordingly not to doubt even when good works are lacking, as they always are in all of us. This is so great a thing that one is startled by it.[13]

In reconciling soul care, we seek to startle one another with the gospel. Daily, we hold up the mirror of grace to the tender conscience and speak on behalf of God: *Sins do not separate Christ from sinners who believe.*

In his commentary on Galatians, Luther further developed the relationship between eternal acceptance in Christ, the believer's daily battles with sin, and the conscience's doubts about acceptance. Luther experienced a practical problem in his own Christian life and in the lives of Christians to whom he ministered—people with a righteous conscience fail to live consistently righteous lives.

In commenting on Galatians 5 and the reality that, in the Christian, the flesh lusts against the Spirit, Luther acknowledged about himself, "I myself have good experience. I have suffered many and various passions, and the same also very vehement and great."[14] Speaking of all Christians, Luther admitted, "Hereby we may see who are very saints indeed. They are not sticks and stones so that they are never moved with anything, never feel any lust or desires of the flesh."[15]

Luther explained that when Christians sin, the temptation is to become overwhelmed with guilt and believe Satan's vicious lie that God is now angry, full of wrath, condemning, and rejecting. In his reconciling ministry, Luther endeavored to empower a righteous conscience to flourish even in the midst of such unrighteousness.

In the religious culture of his day, the remedy involved constant attempts to subdue the flesh perfectly. Soul physicians taught people to defeat the flesh by works of the flesh: calm your conscience by never sinning. In reading Galatians, Luther became convinced that this was impossible because the flesh always wrestles against the Spirit (Galatians 5:17). In fact, the biblical truth that every Christian struggles with sin was to be a comfort!

> Let no man marvel therefore or be dismayed when he feels in his body this battle of the flesh against the Spirit; but let him pluck up his heart and comfort himself with these words of Paul: "The flesh lusteth against the Spirit," and "These are contrary one to another, so that ye do not those things that ye would." For by these verses he comforts those who are tempted. As if he should say: "It is impossible for you to follow the guiding of the Spirit in all things without any feeling or hindrance of the flesh."[16]

Luther knew well the typical response to such teaching: "But here may some man say that it is dangerous to teach that a man is not condemned, if eventually he overcome not the emotions and passions of the flesh which he feels. For when this doctrine is taught among the common people, it makes them careless, negligent, and slothful."[17] Luther's retort? "But it does not therefore follow that you should make a light matter of sin, because God does not impute it. . . . They make not their sin less than it is, but amplify it and set it out as it is indeed; for they know that it cannot be put away by satisfactions, works, or righteousness, but only by the death of Christ."[18]

We take sin seriously, and we take our serious sin to Christ. Yet, we still will struggle with serious sin and searing guilt:

> And with these words: "If ye be led by the Spirit, ye are not under the law," you may greatly comfort yourself and others that are grievously tempted. For it often comes to pass that a man is so vehemently assailed with wrath, hatred, impatience, carnal desire, heaviness of spirit, or some other lust of

the flesh, that he cannot shake it off. What should he do in this case? Should he despair? No.[19]

Prescribing the Gospel Remedy

The battle worsens when Satan adds his condemning lies to our condemning conscience: "And let not him that suffers this temptation be dismayed, in that the devil can so aggravate sin, that during the conflict he thinks himself to be utterly overthrown, and feels nothing else but the wrath of God and desperation." Now what? What is Luther's gospel remedy? First, "let him not follow his own feelings." Second, "comfort yourselves through faith in Christ" and remind yourself that "ye be not under the law."[20] Third, apply Christ's gospel of grace to your tender conscience: "And yet the greatness and enormity of their sin does not cause them to despair, but they assure themselves that it shall not be imputed to them, for Christ's sake." Fourth, hold up the mirror of grace to your tender conscience:

> So shall he have a strong buckler wherewith he may beat back all the fiery darts with which the wicked fiend assails him. Therefore, when the emotions of the flesh rage, the only remedy is to take the sword of the Spirit, that is, the Word of salvation, and to fight against them. If we do this, we shall obtain the victory. But if we do not use the Word, there is no counsel or help remaining.[21]

This is counseling under the cross. This is the counsel of the Word.

With suffering, Luther saw two levels: what happened to us and what happened in us. The worst suffering was the internal suffering of doubts about the goodness of God. Likewise, with sin, Luther saw two levels: the sins we committed and our condemning conscience. The worst sin-related battle was the inner struggle in our conscience about doubts about the grace of God. For Luther, the gospel is the double cure: it forgives our sin and it assures our conscience of our peace with God through Christ.

Luther's Biblical Psychology: Understanding People

Writing in 1899, Delitzsch noted, "Biblical psychology is no science of yesterday. It is one of the oldest sciences of the church."[22] It is in this historical tradition that Luther develops his biblical psychology—his understanding of people based upon a system of diagnosis built on his theological understanding of our creation in the image of God.

In Luther's eyes, the Bible does not present a study of the nature of humanity as an end or even a focus in itself. Rather, the Bible describes the human constitution (personhood, personality, inner nature) in light of humanity's relationship to God. Luther's theological psychology rests upon the fulcrum of biblical truth regarding the God-human relationship—it is a *coram Deo* psychology.

Knowing the Creature through the Creator

Luther seeks to know the creature through the Creator instead of knowing the creature through the creature. The source of reality for Luther is not the human mind; therefore, Luther's assumptions about humanity do not emerge from what we could understand and say about ourselves. Secular psychology proceeds from *anthropos* (humanity) and excludes *theos* (God). Luther develops a *coram Deo* psychology through which he studies *anthropos* in light of *theos*.

Luther understood people in terms of our orientation to God—we are oriented either with our faces or our backs toward God. Within this *coram Deo* framework, Luther develops views on the original nature of the human personality (biblical anthropology/psychology), on the fallen nature of the human personality (biblical hamartiology/psychopathology), and on the redeemed nature of the human personality (biblical soteriology/psychotherapy).

Luther saw all people as in-relationship-to-deity beings. In the innermost chamber of the soul, we are worshiping beings. God designed us with a fundamental nature that must worship—we are designed to trust, place faith in, and display loyalty to someone or something that transcends us. Commenting on Romans 1:19–20, Luther showed that even God-deniers are worshippers:

> All men therefore, in particular all idolators, had a clear knowledge of God, especially of His Godhead and His omnipotence. They proved this by calling the idols which they made "gods," and even "God," and they revered them as eternal and almighty, at least as strong enough to help them. This demonstrates that there was in their hearts a knowledge of a divine sovereign Being. . . . "From the creation of the world" (1:20). This phrase emphasizes the fact that God was known ever since the world came into existence.[23]

We must worship: "The human mind is so inclined by nature that as it turns from the one, it of necessity becomes addicted to the other. He who rejects the Creator needs must worship the creature."[24] The human personality is inclined to worship, and this inclination could be filled in God or it could be filled outside of God. We all live every moment either with a worship disorder or with a worship order.

Luther taught that the ability to worship from the heart was, in fact, what made people truly human. Kolb explains that Luther describes the essence of humanity as "our relationship of love and trust with our Creator Father."[25] Kolb further depicts Luther's view of what constitutes our original nature as worshipping beings—the longing for peace and harmony with a gracious heavenly Father. God created us as worshipping beings designed to long for the God who is the Father of grace.[26]

Understanding Who God Is and Whose We Are

Luther constantly related his biblical understanding of people to daily life issues. For instance, on November 30, 1531, Luther engaged in a table talk focused on the "Treatment of Melancholy and Despair." He began by diagnosing the heart problem behind depression: "In short, it does not occur to man that God is Father."[27] He continued by sharing his prescription: "If we only had the first three words of the Creed, 'I believe in God the Father' (three words in Latin: *Credo in Deum*), they would still be far beyond our understanding and reason"[28] Where do we learn of the gracious fatherhood of God? From our forgiving Savior, "Since Christ accepted the thief on the cross just as he was and received Paul after all his blasphemies and persecutions, we have no reason to despair."[29]

Luther passionately counsels us to apply gospel comfort when we are battling spiritual depression: "Good God, what do you think it means that he has given his only Son? It means that he also offers whatever else he possesses. We have no reason, therefore, to fear his wrath."[30] Luther's biblical theology (who God is) and his biblical psychology (whose we are) undergird his biblical counseling. As Kolb affirms, "Luther's approach to pastoral care begins with his understanding of who God is. We usually think of Luther's theology centering on the Second person of the Holy Trinity. Luther's theology, though, arises out of the First Article, out of his understanding of who God is and who we are in relationship to God."[31]

Luther did not simply ask, *Who are we?* He asks, *Whose are we and who do we long for?* The human personality is comprised of the longing to worship, trust in, and relate to God the gracious Father. This biblical theology/psychology plays a crucial role in Luther's ongoing development of what it means to minister to the soul by lightening the conscience with grace.

Luther's Biblical Psychopathology: Diagnosing the Problem

Biblical psychology asks, *Whose are we?* It responds, *We are worshippers created for relationship with the Father of grace.* Biblical psychopathology (or hamartiology—the theology of sin) asks, *What went wrong? What is our core problem? What is the sinful pathogen sickening our heart?* Luther answers, *false worship.*

Drinking from Broken Cisterns

Through the fall into sin, people are now oriented with their backs to God. Fallen life is one titanic worship disorder: the longing for God remains, but people turn in any and every other direction to satisfy their hunger for the gracious Father. People forsake God the spring of living water and seek to quench their thirst in broken cisterns that can hold no water (Jeremiah 2:13). Every fallen person is now a moving-away-from-God being.

Sin mars God's original design. Consequently, "He who rejects the Creator needs must worship the creature."[32] The capacity to worship was disrupted and distorted by rebellious self-centeredness. Accordingly, as worshiping beings created to know the Father, but divided by the pull of a sinful nature, people resort to worshiping the creature instead of the Creator. For Luther, the foundation of sin was putting one's ultimate faith, trust, and loving commitment in anything but God. Luther saw false worship and idolatry at the heart of all sin. Kolb summarizes the essence of Luther's view:

> In the explanation of the First Commandment he wrote, "A god is that to which we look for all and in which we find refuge in every time of need. To have a god is nothing else than to trust and believe him with our whole heart. If your faith and trust are right, then your God is the true God." By this definition, of course, every person has a god: there is no such thing as an atheist. For everyone must put trust in something, or some combination of other persons and things, or life will disappear.[33]

Originally designed as faith-in-God beings, now people are faith-in-anything-but-God beings.

Moving from Faith to Fear

Had Luther's biblical understanding of our core problem stopped here, it might have been accepted for presentation at the theological society of his day, but it might not have had much relevance for pastoral care. Luther did not stop here. In his psychology of sin, Luther develops the further implication that fear is now the controlling passion in the fallen soul: "The poets fancied that souls were terrified by the bark of Cerberus; but real terror arises when the voice of the wrathful God is heard, that is, when it is felt by the conscience. Then God, who previously was nowhere, is everywhere. Then He who earlier appeared to be asleep hears and sees everything; and His wrath burns, rages, and kills like fire."[34]

The human personality descended from a center of faith to a nucleus of fear, and not just some angst or generalized fear. Rather, at the heart of humanity resides a spiritual fear: all human beings experience spiritual separation anxiety. Luther taught that the soul's original essence consists of faith in the Father, while the essence of the fallen soul consists of fear of the Father.

The Reformer held that people were in flight from the Father, but still in need of the Father. Consequently, people stubbornly search for substitutes. In Luther's commentary on Romans, he traced the steps in the process of flight from God and the commensurate emptiness. The first stage is idolatry (false worship/false love). The next stage is vanity in which the mind, for a time, actually believes that the substitute deities will work. The next step is futility. In this stage, Luther described the many efforts, plans, and endeavors that humanity makes to fulfill their desire for God. But this search is hopeless: "In and through them they seek whatever they desire; nevertheless, all their efforts remain vain since they seek only themselves."[35] The final stage emphasizes addictive passions where lusts of the flesh control people who by now are in a desperate attempt to fill the void in their soul.

Kolb summarizes Luther's view of the process. In the absence of God, fallen humanity has to impose for themselves some substitute source of identity, security, and meaning:

> Our substitutes can never adequately serve as proper sources for life, but following the Deceiver who led Adam and Eve to doubt, we lie to ourselves and learn to live with our idols. At some level of semi or sub-consciousness, though, we recognize our lie, and therefore we live in dread, dread that the gods we have fashioned for ourselves will fall apart. That makes us defensive: Luther's term was that we are "turned in upon ourselves," and protecting ourselves from the evils that assault us.[36]

Luther, the pastor, centered his message, his life, and his pastoral care in God's coming to retrieve the broken sinner. Humanity is fleeing; God is pursing. Humanity is in fearful flight from God; God is in passionate flight to humanity. Luther worked to restore people to Eden—to their original shape—turned upward to God and turned outward to others instead of turned inward on self. Luther cared for tender consciences, terrified by the breakdown of their false gods and in search of the true source that would quench their thirst for the Father's gracious acceptance.

In his role as spiritual director, Luther counseled that when we discover there is nothing to fear from God the Father, then we can face the lesser fears of life. Luther pointed us to the ultimate resolution of all fears by first facing the greatest fear—the fear that God is not a loving, forgiving, accepting, gracious Father.

Luther sees fear clutching at the heart of every person, and he develops an understanding of fear's psychological and theological meaning. Commenting on Isaiah 43:5, Luther wrote:

> "Fear not for I am with you." Why does He say: "Fear not?" Because there are fears within and terrors without, the church

is a tumult and a frightened people, beset by fear, despair, and sins. For that reason it has the Word, which is the breath of its life, so that it may be consoled by the Word. "Why are you afraid? Do not be afraid. I am with you." Since the conscience feels that God is very far away from us, it is necessary for Him to say, "I am with you." These are hidden words. It seems that God is against us.[37]

Luther diagnosed our core problem as a worship disorder that lies beneath every other disorder. Trust in the Father is our creational design. Our core evil is our refusal to entrust ourselves to the Father. And the core result is our fearful flight from the Father—who we imagine as a vindictive, vengeful, merciless judge. No wonder we despair. No wonder we need hope found in Christ alone.

Luther's Biblical Psychotherapy: Prescribing the Gospel Solution

When people entrust themselves to anything or anyone other than the God of the Bible—who is revealed as a gracious Father—they become false worshippers and foolish idolaters. However, none of these false lovers or foolish idols is ultimately able to satisfy. The God-shaped, gracious Father-shaped, vacuum inside the soul leaves the soul restless until it rests in the Father of grace. Therefore, a fearfulness, restlessness, and emptiness resides in the soul that drives and motivates the fallen human personality. This worship disorder leads to fear—a specific kind of core fear—spiritual separation anxiety.

Believing that God is not a gracious and caring Father, people do not cast their care and spiritual anxiety on him. This leads to movement away from God and away from others as the soul increasingly turns in upon itself.

Coming to Our Senses and Coming Home to Our Father

Some seek to quell their fear and quench their thirst with sins of the flesh—like the prodigal son. Others seek to quell their fear and quench their thirst with works of the flesh—like the older brother of the prodigal. Luther and Luke 15 prescribe God's solution: we must come to our senses and come back home to our forgiving Father.

For Luther, coming to our senses involves applying salvation by grace to our daily lives. It involves coming to our senses about who God is in Christ and about who we are in Christ. Luther taught that those who placed their faith in Christ are forgiven (justification), forever accepted by God in Christ (reconciliation), made new as saints in Christ (regeneration), and empowered as victors in Christ (redemption).

As new creations in Christ, Christians are turned back to Christ in worship. Believers entrust themselves in desperate, submissive, dependent worship to Christ for forgiveness (justification), acceptance (reconciliation), holiness (regeneration), and victory (redemption). All people are faith-in-something beings. Christians are faith-in-Christ beings and under-the-grace-of-God beings. As Christians, we become reoriented toward God as we see God through Christ and see ourselves in Christ.

Luther's biblical psychotherapy (his understanding of the soul's healing in Christ) played itself out constantly in his letters of spiritual counsel. Luther applied this theology to the life of a "Mrs. M," in a letter dated January 11, 1543. Though we do not know the identity of Mrs. M, we do know that she was an over-scrupulous woman who was troubled by words she uttered in a fit of anger. Luther pointed Mrs. M to Christ to show her God's identity—God is forgiving, and to show Mrs. M her identity—she is forgiven:

> Certainly it was not Christ who put into your mind the notion that you belong to the devil, for Christ died in order that those who belong to the devil may be released from his power. Therefore, do this: Spit on the devil and say: "Have I sinned? Well I have sinned, and I am sorry. But I shall not despair, for Christ has taken away the sins of the whole world, of all who confess

their sins. So it is certain that this sin of mine has also been taken away. Begone, devil, for I am absolved. This I am bound to believe. And if I had committed murder or adultery, or had even crucified Christ himself, this too would be forgiven if I repented and acknowledged the sin, as Christ said on the cross, 'Father, forgive them.'"[38]

Looking into the Gospel Mirror of Justification, Reconciliation, Regeneration, and Redemption

Luther's letter to Mrs. M highlights gospel memory aids that held up to her the mirror of justification so she could see her forgiveness in Christ. Luther's letter to Barbara Lischner (from the opening of this chapter) held up the mirror of reconciliation so she could see the Father's welcoming love: "He must daily be to our hearts the perfect mirror, in which we behold how much God loves us and how well, in his infinite goodness, as a faithful God, he has grandly cared for us in that he gave his dear Son for us."[39]

To Christians struggling with gospel amnesia, Luther also offers gospel memory aids that hold up the mirror of regeneration so Christians can see they are new creations in Christ: "The Holy Scriptures call Christians saints and the people of God. It's a pity that it's forgotten that we are saints, for to forget this is to forget Christ."[40]

To Christians struggling with despair and spiritual depression, Luther held up the mirror of sainthood so they could see who God is who and they are in Christ: "Praise be to God, who gave us the Word and also allowed his only Son to die for us! He did not do this in vain. Accordingly we should entertain the hope that we are saints, that we are saved, and that this will be manifest when it is revealed."[41]

Luther returned again to the salvation imagery of sainthood in his commentary on Galatians: "When I was a monk I often wished that I might once see the life of some saint or holy man."[42] Luther then shared that he imagined such a saint living in the wilderness, abstaining from meat and drink, and living only with roots of herbs and cold water. Luther counters this works-based imagery with gospel imagery:

> But now in the light of the gospel we plainly see who they are whom Christ and His Apostles call saints: not they who live a single life, or observe days, meats, apparel, and such other things, or in outward appearance do other great works, but they which believe that they are sanctified and cleansed by the death and blood of Christ. So Paul everywhere calls them holy, the children and heirs of God. Whoever then believes in Christ, whether he or she is man or woman, bond or free, is a saint; not by his own works, but by the works of God.[43]

To Christians struggling with gospel amnesia, Luther also offered gospel memory aids that hold up the mirror of redemption—our victory in Christ. Luther shared this gospel mirror with his mother:

> We are unable to accomplish anything against sin, death, and the devil by our own works. Therefore, another appears for us and in our stead who definitely can do better; he gives us his victory, and commands us to accept it and not doubt it. He says: "Be of good cheer; I have overcome the world;" and again: "I live, and you will live also, and no one will take your jour from you."[44]

For Luther, salvation is by faith alone, while daily Christian living (sanctification) is by faith active in love. When tempted to sin, by faith Luther's mother must reckon on the victory she already has in Christ—counting herself dead to sin but alive to God in Christ Jesus (Romans 6:11). On the basis of this victory already won by Christ and in Christ (Colossians 2:13–15), the Spirit empowered Mrs. Luther to not let sin reign, not to obey sin's evil desires, not to offer herself to sin, but instead to offer herself to God as one who has been raised from death to life (Romans 6:12–13). Luther exhorted his mother to see herself with eyes of faith through the lens of the cross: through the mirror of the grace of redemption—her victory in Christ.

Timeless Truth for Life and Ministry Today

If we are to provide Luther-like pastoral reconciling, then we must have a robust, gospel-centered theology of people, problems, and solutions. Having moved from faith in our gracious Father to fear of an imagined, unforgiving father, it is no wonder that we are now in flight from the Father. We perceive God through the mirror of the world, the flesh, and the devil. We need a new mirror: a mirror of Christ's grace. This gospel mirror calls our soul back to its first home—the Father's home—away from false gods and controlling passions of the soul.

Luther offered us gospel reminders that cure our gospel amnesia about who God is through Christ and whose we are in Christ. Christ's grace—justification/forgiveness, reconciliation/acceptance, regeneration/sainthood, and redemption/victory—is the only power able to woo our heart back to the Father's good heart.

We can digest Luther's theology of reconciling with this tweet-size summary:

> Daily behold in Christ's gospel mirror your gracious Father saying to you: "Forgiven! Welcome home! Saint! Victor!"

What does it look like to help one another behold Christ's gospel mirror? Luther shows us in chapter 9. Let's take a look into that mirror together.

CHAPTER NINE
CHRIST'S GRACE PRESCRIPTION FOR THE SOUL:
LUTHER'S METHODOLOGY OF RECONCILING

FOR MANY years, individual families oversaw mines in Thuringia, but then, in order to increase his income, Count Albert of Mansfeld confiscated their mines. Luther challenged Count Albert's actions in a letter dated May 24, 1540. When the Count refused to change his ways, on December 28, 1541, Luther penned a sharper letter of spiritual restoration.

Rather than launch into a harsh confrontation, Luther opened with a narrative of grace relationship: "Gracious Sir: I desire from the bottom of my heart that you may receive in a Christian and gracious way what I write here." Luther continued with words of spiritual affirmation: "God did many laudable things through Your Grace at the beginning of the gospel: churches, pulpits, and schools were well ordered to the praise and honor of God." Next, Luther expressed his pastoral care: "For these and other reasons I cannot readily forget Your Grace or cease to pray for you and be concerned about you."[1]

Only then did Luther introduce his loving confrontation. First, Luther exposed how Albert is living in contradiction to his identity as a new creation in Christ: "But it appears to me, especially from rumors and complaints that have reached me, that Your Grace has fallen away from such good beginnings and has become a very different person." Luther continued, "Your Grace too must be aware that you have become cold, have given your heart to Mammon, and have the ambition to become very rich." Luther's compassion spilled over as he shared, "As Your Grace may well believe, this causes me great heartache on your account."[2]

Second, Luther revealed how the Count is living in contraction to the law of love: "According to complaints Your Grace is also sharply and severely oppressive to subjects and proposes to confiscate their forges and goods and to make what amounts to vassals out of them."[3] Third, Luther laid bare how Albert is living in contradiction to the holiness of God: "God will not suffer this."[4]

Throughout his letter, Luther wove in a narrative of scriptural consequences, showing how God removes his blessing on leaders when they sin against who they are in Christ, against others, and against God. Turning to Haggai 1:6, Luther wrote, "He will allow your land to become impoverished and go to ruin, for he can take away what is his own gift without giving an accounting for it; as Haggai says: 'Ye have sown much, and bring in little; and he that earneth wages, earneth wages to put into a bag with holes.'"[5] In frankness, Luther summarized, "This is what happens when God and his Word are despised."[6]

Since Luther wrote a letter of spiritual restoration, he continued with a narrative of sanctification. Luther spoke first about heart change: "I pray again that Your Grace may be more gentle and gracious with your subjects." Then he wrote of actions fit for repentance: "Let them [the mine owners] remain as before."[7]

Luther then shared a narrative of loving motivation. Why was Luther even penning his letter? "In short, I am concerned about Your Grace's soul. I cannot permit myself to cease praying for you and being concerned about you, for then I am convinced that I would cease being in the Church."[8] Just as it is the Christian's calling to comfort one another in suffering, so also it is the calling of the body of Christ to speak gospel truth to one another when sin rears its ugly head. To refuse to do so is to refuse to be a part of Christ's body. Having spoken as a spiritual shepherd to a political shepherd, Luther concluded by directing Count Albert to the Great Shepherd: "Herewith I commit you to God in all his grace and mercy."[9]

Luther the Shepherd of Wandering Sheep

In Luther's letter to Count Albert, we encounter many of the shepherding practices embedded throughout Luther's reconciling ministry. In ministering to Albert, Luther sandwiched his restoration ministry between a narrative of grace relationships and a narrative of loving motivation. At the start, at the end, and everywhere in between, Luther embraced Galatians 6:1: "Brothers, if someone is caught in a sin, you who are spiritual should restore him gently. But watch yourself, or you also may be tempted." Gentle restoration was vital to Luther because of his theological understanding of the struggle of the conscience.

Luther's reconciling ministry is also reminiscent of Paul's ministry in 1 Thessalonians 2:8 where he, too, sandwiches gospel ministry between affirmations of loving relationships: "We loved you so much that we were delighted to share with you not only the gospel of God but our lives as well, because you had become so dear to us." Likewise, Luther, in between expressions of love for Count Albert, shared gospel truth in the form of his narrative of confrontation of sin, of scriptural consequences of sin, and of sanctification and victory over sin. Out of concern for Albert's soul or conscience, Luther sought to restore Albert's conscience to a state of peace with God.

In his reconciling ministry to Albert and countless others, Luther followed a number of practices as he journeys with the struggling conscience from a place of alienation from God to a place of reconciliation through Christ. Luther empowered Christians to apply Christ's gospel prescription for their souls through discerning the conscience, calming the conscience, enlightening the conscience, liberating the conscience, renewing the conscience, strengthening the conscience, forgiving the conscience, and battling the fleshly conscience.

Applying the Gospel to the Conscience

Luther's letters were his personal efforts to underscore the daily significance of the gospel. Kolb describes Luther's ministry as "the 'how to'
of taking care of our people's relationship with their God" by "applying the living voice of the Gospel to people's lives."[10]

Luther saw salvation as a joyous exchange. A transaction has
taken place in which our sinfulness has been transferred to Christ and
where Christ's righteousness has been transferred to us. So, the essence
of Luther's reconciliation ministry involves teaching those already reconciled to God that God loves them, and they can live out that love.
Experiencing the gospel is central to victory over temptation and victory over a sense of condemnation when we succumb to temptation.
As Kolb summarizes, "The combating of evil with the Gospel stood at
the heart of his pastoral care."[11]

It is the daily duty of fellow believers, through mutual conversation and consolation, to enable each other to hear the gospel's personal
meaning. Through Christian sisters and brothers, God says to the
tempted soul, *Out of gratitude to your gracious Father, and through the
resurrection power of Christ, say, "No!" to ungodliness and worldly passions
and say, "Yes!" to Christlike living that pleases your Father.* This is gospel
motivation and power for victory over temptation. The gospel is preventative medicine and vitamin supplements that strengthen us to fight
off the virus of temptation.

Of course, as Christians we do not always avail ourselves of this
gospel motivation and medicine. The flesh lusts against the spirit. We
say, "No!" to righteousness and we say, "Yes!" to unrighteousness. Then,
Satan, who first tempted us to sin, tempts us to despair over our having sinned. As chapter 8 explained, this is the ultimate struggle of the
Christian conscience—to place our faith in the grace of Christ to us
and for us in the midst of our current sin. Rather than despair, Luther
pointed us to gospel hope. When the Christian does yield to sin, there
is gospel victory over the guilt of sin and the condemnation of Satan.

Discerning the Conscience

Guided by Paul's exhortation to restore the sinner gently (Galatians 6:1), Luther believed that it was crucial to discern the different ways that sin worked in different people. Then, Luther could idiosyncratically apply the gospel to the individual conscience. Luther saw this as vital in the pulpit ministry of the Word: "To distinguish between two kinds of sinners, the penitent and the secure, is especially necessary for the preacher, otherwise all Scripture remains closed."[12] To the proud, Luther preached the gospel of repentance to disturb their conscience. To the poor and afflicted, Luther preached the gospel of grace to comfort their conscience.

Discernment of the conscience is equally crucial in the personal ministry of the Word. To the tender, repentant, remorseful conscience—speak gospel love. To the hard, impenitent, shameless conscience—speak gospel holiness. Luther notes how Paul spoke gospel grace to the penitent:

> So Paul did bear the infirmity and fall of the Galatians and others when they heartily repented. So he received into grace that unchaste Corinthian (2 Corinthians 2:7); also he reconciled Onesimus the runaway slave. . . . Therefore, that which he teaches here concerning the duty of supporting the weak and restoring the fallen, that he did also himself perform, but towards such only as could be healed: that is to say, such as heartily confessed their sin, their fall, their error, and returned to the right way.[13]

Luther also described how Paul spoke gospel holiness to the hardhearted: "Contrariwise, towards the false apostles, which were obstinate and defended their doctrine, saying that it was not error, but the very truth, he showed himself very hard and severe."[14]

Luther used Paul's ministry to the repentant believer in 2 Corinthians to further illustrate two ways of ministry to two types of consciences:

> Those who are in the ministry of the Word should not forget the fatherly and motherly affection which Paul here requires of them. And of this precept he has set forth an example (2 Corinthians 2:6), where he said that it was sufficient that he who was excommunicated was rebuked by many, and that they ought now to forgive him and comfort him, lest he should be swallowed up with overmuch sorrow. . . . Therefore, pastors and ministers must indeed sharply rebuke those which are fallen, but when they see that they are sorrowful for their offenses, then let them begin to raise them up again, to comfort them, and to diminish and qualify their faults as much as they can, lest they that be fallen be swallowed up with overmuch heaviness.[15]

Paul's message in 2 Corinthians 2:5–11, and Luther's method are the same. Pastoral caregivers lovingly, humbly, and gently confront sin; and then they lovingly forgive, comfort, and reaffirm their love for repentant believers so their conscience is not overwhelmed by excessive sorrow. We do this "in order that Satan might not outwit us. For we are not unaware of his schemes" (2 Corinthians 2:11).

Calming the Conscience

Luther taught that despairing of grace was the greatest conflict, for sin can be forgiven, but believing that sin cannot be forgiven leaves the soul in hopeless despair: "The temptation of faith is the very greatest and most severe, for it is the province of faith to overcome all other temptations. . . . By the temptation of faith is meant that the evil conscience drives out of a person his confidence in the pardoning grace of God."[16] Thus the most dangerous battle of all occurs when we allow sin to overwhelm the conscience. When we exaggerate sin beyond Christ's grace, we minimize the work of Christ and magnify our sin as greater than Christ's forgiving grace. "Consequently one ought to be disposed to say, 'It is true. I have sinned. But I will not despair on this account.'"[17]

Luther noticed that little counsel could be received when the conscience was in intense turmoil. Therefore, he sought to calm the conscience by separating sin from temptation and by comforting the conscience with grace.

Separating Sin from Temptation

Luther's intention was to alleviate the sting of false guilt. When temptations toward sinful thoughts came into the minds of his followers, Luther would communicate, "Now such thoughts are nothing but a web spun by the devil; which we do not make or do, but suffer; they are not the works of men, but their sufferings. For those who will not learn this, all is lost."[18] Luther also was fond of quoting an unnamed ancient father who said: "As it is not in your power to forbid the birds to fly in the air over your head, although you can prevent them from making their nests in your hair; so, too, you cannot protect yourself from the thoughts of the devil, but give all diligence that the thoughts of the devil do not take and hold the entire possession of your heart."[19] Luther calmed the tender conscience by helping Christians to discern between external temptation toward sin and internal choices to sin.

Comforting the Conscience with Grace

In addition to rejecting false guilt, Luther also dismissed the thought that true guilt should lead to despair. Luther calmed the disquieted conscience by encouraging the faithful to refuse to let sin overwhelm them. When his close friend, George Spalatin, bitterly reproached himself for a decision he made, Luther wrote, "It is enough to have sinned; let the sin now vanish, and let sadness, which is a much greater sin, depart."[20]

But how is this done in the midst of Satan's condemnation? Satan preaches law to the believer: *You are condemned for not doing this good work and for doing this bad work.* Christ preaches gospel to the believer, as Luther communicated in one of his table talks, "Once I debate about what I have done and left undone, I am finished. But if I reply on the basis of the gospel, 'The forgiveness of sins covers it all,' I have won." Luther continued, "On the other hand, if the devil gets me involved in what I have done and left undone, he has won, unless God helps and says, 'Indeed! Even if you had not done anything, you would still be saved by forgiveness.'"[21] The gospel reminds us that Christianity is not about what I have done, but what Christ did once for all.

In the same table talk, Luther passionately described how we must preach the gospel to ourselves—and to the devil: "It's the supreme art of the devil that he can make the law out of the gospel. If I can hold on to the distinction between law and gospel, I can say to him any and every time that he should kiss my backside. Even if I sinned, I would say, 'Should I deny the gospel on this account?'"[22] We calm and comfort the conscience by distinguishing between law (works, doing) and gospel (faith in what Christ has already done).

We are not only responsible for preaching the gospel to ourselves; we also must preach the gospel to one another in the midst of temptations toward condemnation. Speaking of Galatians 6:1 and restoring a Christian who has sinned, Luther first exhorted us what not to do: "Do not trouble him or make him more sorrowful; be not bitter toward him; do not reject or condemn him." Instead:

> Therefore, if you see a brother cast down and afflicted by occasion of sin which he has committed, run to him and, reaching out your hand, raise him up again, comfort him with sweet words, and embrace him with motherly arms. A brother ought to comfort his fallen brother with a loving and

meek spirit. For God would not have those that are bruised to be cast away.[23]

Enlightening the Conscience

Of course, human comfort must always point to the Divine Comforter and the eternal comfort we have as a result of our union with Christ. As in sustaining and healing, so also in reconciling, Luther's counseling emphasized the need to enlighten Christians to their identity in Christ based upon their union with Christ.

Luther highlighted how as Christians we need the eyes of our heart opened to see that, in our central identity, we are loved by God. Luther reflected on his spiritual struggle during which for a long time, "I went astray and didn't know what I was about" because he saw himself through the eyes of his self-sufficient attempts at righteousness. It was only when Luther saw himself as a recipient of Christ's righteousness that he found freedom from the law.[24] What freed him was the realization that he was indeed someone who was loved by God—his core identity was a beloved child of God: "I began to experience a change when I read about the love of God and what it signifies passively, namely, that by which we are loved by God. Before I had always taken love actively (namely, that by which we love God)."[25] In other words, the greatest thing about us is not that we love God, but that God loves us!

Luther found that the love of the Father was central to his joyous walk with Christ. With fond recollection, he recalled the words that helped him to experience reconciliation with God: "Sometimes my confessor said to me when I repeatedly discussed silly sins with him. 'You are a fool. God is not incensed against you, but you are incensed against God. God is not angry with you, but you are angry with God.' This was magnificently said."[26]

Enlightened to the Unfailing Parental Love of the Father

Luther found that illustrations and images from human relationships often provided powerful illumination and enlightenment about God's unfailing love. In a table talk on how hard it is to believe in the forgiveness of sin, Luther shares this powerful imagery:

> You say that the sins which we commit every day offend God, and therefore we are not saints. To this I reply: Mother love is stronger than the filth and scabbiness on a child, and so the love of God toward us is stronger than the dirt that clings to us. Accordingly, although we are sinners, we do not lose our filial relation on account of our filthiness, nor do we fall from grace on account of our sin.[27]

Luther made this potent image of a mother's love even more staggering by personalizing it further as he related the love of his wife Katy for their son Martin to the love of God for his children:

> God must be much friendlier to me and speak to me in friendlier fashion than my Katy to little Martin. Neither Katy nor I could intentionally gouge out the eye or tear off the head of our child. Nor could God. God must have patience with us. He has given evidence of it, and therefore he sent his Son into our flesh in order that we may look to him for the best. . . . When I reflect on the magnitude of God's mercy and majesty, I am myself horrified at how far God has humbled himself.[28]

When Satan holds before our eyes images of our sinfulness, the gospel provides laser surgery that enlightens our vision to see the unfailing parental love of God.

To this powerful image of God's unfailing parental love, Luther added the imagery of adoption. In his commentary on Romans, Luther contrasted the spirit of bondage with the spirit of sonship and adoption. The spirit of bondage is the fleshly conscience which feels like it is still under the law's weight and sees itself under the condemnation of God, a harsh judge. The spirit of sonship and adoption is the spiritual conscience that knows that it is under the freedom of grace and sees itself under the love of God, a forgiving heavenly Father. This biblical image of God impacts our image of ourselves and in turn impacts how we live life—out of faith active in bold love instead of out of self-protective fear:

> You have become free from fear and have received the Spirit
> of adoption by which you trust God. This trust he shows very
> clearly by the words: "Whereby we cry, Abba, Father." This is
> the cry of a heart which is full of childlike trusts and knows
> no fear. That the cry is not one of the mouth but of the heart,
> is clear from Galatians 4:6,7: "Because ye are sons, God hath
> sent forth the Spirit of his Son into your hearts, crying, Abba,
> Father. Wherefore thou art no more a servant, but a son; and
> if a son, then an heir of God through Christ."[29]

Enlightened to the Unfailing Friendship of the Son

Luther encouraged those struggling with sin to cling to the friendly heart and finished work of Christ. If one does not do so, condemnation will engulf the conscience: "Satan speaks according to the law and says to you in your heart, 'God doesn't want to forgive you.'" Luther asked in this situation, "How will you as a sinner cheer yourself, especially if signs of wrath, like illness, etc., are added?"[30] Satan and suffering grow cataracts over our spiritual eyesight. What spiritual laser surgery will heal our faith vision?

Luther's answer clears our vision: "Then the Christian must come and say, 'I have been incorporated in Christ.'"[31] Incorporation or identification and union with Christ is essential in defeating the blinding lies of Satan: "A Christian remains firmly attached to Christ, and says, 'If I'm not good, Peter wasn't either, but Christ is good. . . . Christ is the bishop of souls. To him will I cling, even if I sin.' It is thus that one has assurance."[32]

Luther enlightens us to the truth that God does not reject us in anger when we sin. Rather, in Christ, God is always the Friend of sinners. Luther contrasts finite human friendship and the infinite friendship of Christ: "Christ is friendlier than we are. If I can be good to a friend, how much more will Christ be good to us!"[33]

Luther insisted that this knowledge is not simply cognitive or academic, but affective and relational: "The principal lesson of theology is that Christ can be known. . . . This isn't a knowledge of the law, or dialectical skill, or of some other art, but it's the knowledge that Christ is the most just and the most merciful One, in whom alone we dwell."[34]

Gospel counsel helps people to grasp together with all the saints a personal knowledge of Christ as merciful Friend. This is the most basic knowledge that the soul needs—the knowledge that the soul can trust Christ as best Friend.

Liberating the Conscience

The Christian life is a constant battle between faith and fear, freedom and bondage. One moment we experience the joy of spiritual life. The next moment we give into temptation and give up under the duress of Satan's condemnation—and move again from freedom to bondage.

In his commentary on Galatians, Luther applied Paul's doctrine of freedom in Christ. Luther tried every human means of finding liberation from his troubled conscience. He attempted all manner of physical and ritualistic devotions and deprivations. He did all of this to harness his sinfulness, his desires, and his flesh. He tried to find peace with God through human effort. Galatians directed Luther away from self-sufficiency and into Christ-sufficiency as the only pathway for a liberated conscience.

Luther based his understanding of the liberated conscience on Galatians 5:1, "Stand fast therefore in the liberty wherewith Christ hath made us free."

> This is that liberty whereby Christ has made us free, not from an earthly bondage, from the Babylonian captivity, or from the tyranny of the Turks, but from God's everlasting wrath. And where is this done? In the conscience. There rests our liberty, and goes no farther. For Christ has made us free, not civilly, nor carnally, but divinely; that is to say, we are made free in that our conscience is now free and quiet, not fearing the wrath to come.[35]

Feel the sigh of relief, the release of burden, the removal of weight. Sense the freedom: free from wrath, free in Christ, free from condemnation, free to return home to the Father. This is true liberation theology—personal, eternal, and universal liberation in Christ.

Luther counseled us to preach this gospel of liberation to ourselves as a preventative measure against the taunts of Satan:

> Therefore, our conscience must be instructed and prepared beforehand so when we feel the accusation of the law, the terrors of sin, the horror of death, and the wrath of God, we may remove these heavy sights and fearful fantasies out of our minds, and set in their place the freedom purchased by Christ, the forgiveness of sins, righteousness, life, and the everlasting mercy of God.[36]

Luther also counseled pastoral counselors to magnify this liberty as he did:

> For who is able to express what a thing it is, when a man is assured in his heart that God neither is nor will be angry with him, but will be forever a merciful and loving Father to him for Christ's sake? This is indeed a marvelous and incomprehensible

liberty, to have the most high and sovereign Majesty so favor-able to us. Wherefore, this is an inestimable liberty, that we are made free from the wrath of God forever; and is greater than heaven and earth and all other creatures.[37]

Luther used Christ's grace as a magnet to attract the cowering soul back to the Father's forgiving heart.

Renewing the Conscience

Though made new in Christ, Christians live with internal conflict. The forces of the flesh and of the spirit wage an ongoing battle. Be-cause the believer is a saint who battles against sin, the Christian is always becoming, always moving, always growing. This growth occurs in the depths of the heart—in mind renewal and the renewal of the conscience.

Luther's mind renewal does not equate with modern rational-emotive therapy or modern cognitive-behavioral therapy; rather, it is the renewal of faith. Faith renewal involves a renewed trust in the love of God who motivates and empowers Christians to grow in faith active in love. Commenting on Romans 12:2 ("That you may prove what is the good, and acceptable, and perfect will of God"), Luther wrote:

> However, when the Apostle says that the proving of the three-fold divine will comes from the transformation or the renewing of the mind, he may think of something that goes much deeper than what the words can express, something which we can learn only from experience. Only faith transforms the mind and leads us to where we may prove the will of God.[38]

Luther is saying that mind renewal is gospel renewal applied to the depths of the heart, the recesses of the conscience. He developed this further: "The Apostle Paul speaks of this in Ephesians 3:17ff: 'That ye may be able to comprehend with all saints what is the breadth, and length, and depth, and height; and to know the love of Christ, which passeth knowledge, that ye might be filled with all the fullness of God.'"[39] Together with all the saints, we grasp in our soul the love of God in a way that is not simply informational but transformational.

This transformation happens in the midst of life's messes, as Luther explained: "These words are overflowingly rich in consolation; for just then when afflictions come over us, we should be of good courage, because that is the good will of God. Therefore we should be greatly pleased when things happen to us which displease us. The 'good' will of God creates good out of evil."[40] Our fallen world falls on us. We are tempted to doubt God's goodness and to doubt our relationship with God. Conscience renewal helps us to grasp in our inner being the infinite, inexhaustible, bottomless loveliness of God and love of God.

Strengthening the Conscience

But how is the conscience renewed? How do we grasp the loveliness and love of God in the depths of our soul? Luther answered that we strengthen the conscience through the people of God and the Word of God.

Strengthening the Conscience through the People of God

Luther believed in the power of community, the power of words, and the power of God's Word. He united all three of these active powers in his doctrine of the communion of the saints. When entangled in temptations and struggling with sin, the Christian should remember, "the word of a fellow-Christian has wonderful power."[41] Luther shared this conviction in the context of satanic attacks "undertaking to break down our faith and confidence by the thought that God is angry with us."[42]

During these times of spiritual temptation and spiritual depression, Luther counseled toward spiritual conversations. The voice and words of "brethren and fellow Christians are to be heard and believed as the word and voice of God himself, as though God were speaking to them."[43] God encounters the conscience through his Word mediated through his people. Luther was convinced that there is only one Mediator between God and humanity—Christ Jesus. He was also convinced that God calls on the body of Christ to speak on behalf of Christ about Christ's gospel of grace.

The tormented conscience will lose the battle between the flesh and the spirit if it is left alone. To one individual experiencing great upheaval of conscience, Luther wrote, "I beseech you by the Lord Christ, as earnestly as I can, not to depend upon yourself and your own thoughts, but to hear the brother in Christ who now speaks to you."[44]

Strengthening the Conscience through the Word of God

Speaking again of the devil's attempts to convince us that God is through with us, Luther wrote, "If you now attempt, in this spiritual conflict, to protect yourself by the help of man without the Word of God, you simply enter upon the conflict with that mighty spirit, the devil, naked and unprotected." Such an endeavor would be worse than David against Goliath—without God's supernatural power helping David: "You may, therefore, if you so please, oppose your power to the might of the devil. It will then be very easily seen what an utterly unequal conflict it is, if one does not have at hand in the beginning the Word of God."[45] In strengthening the conscience, Luther directed troubled people to the sufficiency of the Spirit of God, the people of God, and the Word of God.

For Luther, sufficiency of Scripture was not an academic term for theological discussion but an experiential reality for daily application. God's Word is authoritative, sufficient, relevant, potent, robust, profound—useful for all faith and practice; beneficial for teaching, training, instruction, encouragement, confrontation, exhortation, and consolation—for pastoral counseling: "He who was assailed by temptation should bury himself in the Holy Scriptures. He should diligently read them, should meditate deeply upon them and lay them to heart."[46] Luther was not speaking of burying problems or of hiding from reality. He was insisting that reality must be taken to Scripture—to gain eternal perspective for daily struggles.

Luther encouraged prayerful meditation on the Word during times of turmoil. The Psalms are especially helpful, directing the conscience toward the right path for handling tribulation. When Valentine Hausmann struggled with terror regarding his acceptance before God, Luther counseled him to read aloud and listen attentively to the Psalms and the New Testament. Why? "For at such time you must accustom yourself not to wrap yourself up in your misfortune and sink into your own thoughts, without the Word of God."[47] Luther was not counseling Hausmann to deny his feelings or thoughts, but instead to wrap his feelings and thoughts in the wisdom and deeper reality of the Word.

Forgiving the Conscience

Luther was a realist who knew firsthand that all the discerning, calming, enlightening, liberating, renewing, and strengthening of the conscience would not eliminate all sin. Saints will continue to sin. It was that simple for Luther. Therefore, the conscience needs to receive forgiveness.

Luther saw confession and absolution as the means by which the guilty conscience could experience forgiveness. The word "experience" is the key. All sins—past, present, and future—were already forgiven in Christ. But the sinning penitent's conscience experienced a condemning alienation from God. The truth of ongoing forgiveness needed to be mediated to the conscience through confession and absolution.

In his pastoral counseling, Luther emphasized the depth of forgiveness rather than the depth of confession. Recall that in his early life, Luther would confess sins for hours and still feel as though he had forgotten some sin. Later, he rejected this sort of confession, calling it the "papal kind of confession."[48] Instead, he taught that it was enough that the person be contrite. The attitude of heart mattered, not the remembrance of every sin.

Luther focused on confession and absolution centering in the proclamation of the Word in the congregation (blending the Word of God and the people of God). Luther "spoke about the efficacy of the Word of God and the joy in the church when brethren comfort one another with the Word of God. There's something great about the employment of the keys and of private absolution when the conscience can be put to rest."[49] The Catholic Church saw the "keys" (Matthew 18) as gifts given only to ordained priests. Luther encouraged the radical idea that every believer has the keys, can hear the confession of fellow believers, and can privately absolve them, thus giving rest to their conscience. A well-known passage from *The Babylonian Captivity of the Church* captures this memorably: "When we have laid bare our conscience to our brother and privately make known to him the evil that lurked within, we receive from our brother's lips the word of comfort spoken by God himself. And if we accept this in faith, we find peace in the mercy of God speaking to us through our brother."[50] Let that sink in. We receive from our brother's lips the word of comfort spoken by God himself. We are Christ's gospel messengers of peace and mercy.

Historically, lay confession became known as *consolatio fratrum*.[51] The mutual consolation of the brethren through private confession was a primary means of absolving the conscience of guilt. Luther based this teaching on his view "that all Christians are priests in equal degrees"[52] (the doctrine of the priesthood of all believers). Since all are priests, all can bind and loose sin; that is, all can announce the absolution or forgiveness of sins. Forgiveness was vital to Luther because he was convinced that the forgiven conscience could bear anything. The unforgiven conscience would be so tormented that inner suffering, outer suffering, and temptations to sin would easily overwhelm the soul.

For Luther, the priesthood of believers did not eliminate the calling and role of the pastor. So, to Mrs. M (from chapter 8) who struggled to accept her forgiveness in Christ, Luther speaks words of pastoral absolution: "Be contented, therefore, and of good cheer; your sins are forgiven you. Depend boldly upon this; turn not to your own thoughts, but listen only to that which your pastors and preachers repeat to you out of God's Word. Do not despise their word and comfort; for it is Christ himself who speaks to you through them."[53]

To absolve the conscience, Luther encouraged the personal ministry of the Word (believers speaking grace to one another), the pulpit ministry of the Word (pastors preaching grace to the congregation), and the private ministry of the Word (believers preaching the gospel to themselves). He suggested the private ministry of the Word to Mrs. M as she struggled to believe Christ's forgiveness: "But if you are still weak in faith, say to yourself: 'I wish that I could believe more firmly, for I know very well that this is true and that it ought to be believed. But even though I cannot believe it as I should, yet I know that it is the pure truth.'"[54]

Battling the Fleshly Conscience

In his commentary on Galatians, Luther imagined the meeting of two Christians. Absolution has just been granted. A lengthy discussion follows in which the conscience is discerned, calmed, enlightened, liberated, renewed, strengthened, and forgiven. But Christians who have received absolution may express the fear that they might sin in the same way. Though delighted by the prospects of endless forgiveness, Christians should still desire victory over this sin.

Luther then explained how to help a penitent Christian in this situation to find victory over sin by battling the fleshly conscience. Luther models three primary methods for overcoming sin: expose the sinning conscience, warn the erring conscience, and despise and cast out the evil conscience.

Nebe expresses the priority that Luther gave to the ministry of exposing the sinning conscience: "Throughout his entire life, the Reformer was, to a most extraordinary extent, brought into contact with people who cherished erroneous opinions, or whose consciences were perverted, especially with people who, unable to find the right way, wandered about in uncertainty or had actually started upon some course that was utterly wrong."[55] When someone cherished wrong beliefs, Luther looked to the Scriptures as his source of authority for correct beliefs. He used the teaching of the Scriptures to explain truth and to expose waywardness from that truth.

Luther followed a common process when using the Word to expose sin. First, he quoted the Word. Second, he related the Word to the situation at hand. Third, he prayed for conviction of error in the heart of his reader. Fourth, he rebuked the reader for sinning. Fifth, he expressed his outrage and anger over the failure to return to God's Word. Sixth, he exhorted repentance and a return to godly living. Luther followed this process when he wrote to Hans Kohlhase who had taken malicious revenge on a neighbor for stealing his horse:

> It would have been better in the first place not to have undertaken revenge, since it cannot be undertaken without burdening of the conscience; for a private vengeance is forbidden by God, Deut. xxxii. 35, Rom xii. 19: "Vengeance is mine, saith the Lord, I will repay," etc., and it cannot be otherwise than that he who enters upon it shall run the risk of doing much against God and man which a Christian conscience cannot approve. . . . Now to make one's self a judge and execute judgment upon others is certainly wrong, and the wrath of God will not suffer it to go unpunished. . . . Accordingly, if, as you write, you desire my advice, it is this: Accept terms of peace wherever they can be obtained, and rather suffer injury in possessions and honor, than prosecute further an undertaking in which you must make yourself responsible for the sins and villainy of all who may follow your fortunes.[56]

Luther warned the erring conscience by disclosing the burden of guilt that flows from further sinning. This was his message to Hans Kohlhase: "But you ought to consider what a grievous burden your conscience will have to carry if you knowingly bring ruin upon so many people, as you have no right to do."[57] The worst experience in life, for Luther, is a burdened conscience. So the greatest deterrent to a life of sin is the possibility of heaping the burden of guilt upon one's own conscience.

Once exposed and warned, Luther sought to cast out the evil conscience. Luther derived from Isaiah 36 "what counsel and help should be given to tempted and timid consciences." His counsel—at times the best response to temptation is to refuse to obsess over it: "The more one worries himself and quarrels with them, the more they press upon him and harass him."[58] Horrible results occur if we do not learn the art of despising and casting out evil thoughts and replacing them with pure thoughts of Christ's grace: "I have known many such, who, when very great and sudden temptations have assailed them, did not understand the art of despising and casting out these thoughts, and in consequence lost their minds and became violently insane; and some, when their minds had become too severely strained by these startling thoughts, took their own lives."[59]

So instead, "as these thoughts came of themselves, so he should let them go of themselves again, and only not give himself up to them."[60] Rather than obsessing on the temptations to sin, "one should therefore banish from his mind and heart the grievous thoughts of sin and of the wrath of God, and cherish the very opposite thoughts."[61] Do not focus on the fleshly passions; rather fix your mind on Christ's gospel of grace.

Timeless Truth for Life and Ministry Today

If we are to offer Luther-like pastoral reconciling, then like Luther we must apply Christ's gospel of grace to the conscience. Put in today's language, we must enlighten people to the daily significance of the gospel indicatives—what Christ has already done for us and whose we are in Christ. Victory over temptation begins when we are taught by the grace of Christ to say "No" to unrighteousness and "Yes" to Christlikeness (Titus 2:11–13). Victory over Satan's condemnation when we have given into temptation begins when we are taught by the grace of Christ that there is therefore now no condemnation to those who are in Christ Jesus (Romans 8:1).

We can condense Luther's practice of reconciling with this tweet-size summary:

> Grace is Christ's prescription for our disgrace—forgiving medicine for sin, preventative medicine for victory over temptation, and cleansing medicine for victory over Satan's condemnation.

For Luther, a right relationship with God served as the foundation of the Christian life. By grace through faith we bask in our gracious Father's love. Reconciling turned us upward to God in loving worship. Upon that foundation, Luther sought to build a life of faith active in love. Reconciling and guiding turn us outward toward others in loving ministry for God's glory.

If reconciling applies the daily significance of the gospel indicatives, then in guiding Luther applied the daily significance of the gospel indicatives and imperatives—how the Spirit empowers us to live out who we already are in Christ. Luther did not simply teach that sanctification is the art of getting used to our justification.[62] Instead, he counseled that sanctification is the art of applying our justification, reconciliation, regeneration, and redemption through faith active in love. Chapter 10 develops this more robust perspective of sanctification as it unpacks Luther's theology of guiding pastoral care.

CHAPTER TEN

FAITH ACTIVATES LOVE:
LUTHER'S THEOLOGY OF GUIDING

FROM JANUARY 1 to December 31, 1531, Luther faced personal sickness, the life-threatening illness of his mother, ongoing persecution, and the daily burdens of overseeing the burgeoning growth of the churches in the Reformation movement. Adding to these external stresses, Luther's experienced ongoing internal battles with *anfechtungen*. In the midst of these external pressures and internal temptations, Luther delivered his lectures on Galatians at the University of Wittenberg—lectures which became his *Commentary on Galatians*. Luther's lectures were an opportunity to preach the gospel to himself. Speaking of Galatians 3:1 and Satan's bewitching deceptions, Luther told his students, "To tell the truth, he sometimes assails me so mightily and oppresses me with such heavy cogitations, that he utterly shadows my Savior Christ from me and, in a manner, takes Him out of my sight."[1] As we saw in chapter 1, Satan was attempting to crop Christ out of Luther's picture.

In lecturing his students on Galatians, Luther told of a man who took his own life because Satan had imprinted on his imagination the image of Christ accusing him before God. Because Luther knew he was not alone in being tempted by Satan to doubt Christ's grace, he constantly sought to bring Christ and his grace back into the picture: "So we also labor by the Word of God that we may set at liberty those that are entangled, and bring them to the pure doctrine of faith, and hold them there. . . . The Scripture does not set forth Christ as an accuser, a judge, or a tempter, but as a reconciler, a mediator, a comforter, and a throne of grace."[2] For Luther, the greatest threat to empowered Christian living was a darkened understanding of Christ and our identity in Christ.

Therefore, nothing was more important to Luther than reminding God's children to remind themselves that they were indeed God's children. Speaking of Galatians 1:4 ("Who gave himself for our sins"), Luther challenged his students to personalize the gospel:

> But weigh diligently every word of Paul, and specially mark well this pronoun, "our." You may easily believe that Christ the Son of God was given for the sins of Peter, of Paul, and of other saints, whom we account to have been worthy of this grace; but it is a very hard thing that you who judge yourself unworthy of this grace should from your heart say and believe that Christ was given for your own invincible, infinite, and horrible sins.[3]

Preaching the gospel to ourselves is hard work. We are to weigh diligently and we are to labor diligently:

> Labor diligently . . . when your conscience is thoroughly afraid with the remembrance of your sins past, and the devil assails you with great violence, going about to overwhelm you with heaps, floods, and whole seas of sins, to terrify you and to drive you to despair; that then I say, you may be able to say with sure confidence: Christ the Son of God was given, not for the righteous and holy, but for the unrighteous and sinners.[4]

How can we defeat such devilish deception? Luther counsels "devil craft"—the art of using God's sufficient Word to overcome the devil's cunning lies:

> Let us therefore arm ourselves with these and like verses of the Holy Scriptures, that we may be able to answer the devil (accusing us, and saying: You are a sinner, and therefore you

are damned) in this sort: "Christ has given Himself for my sins; therefore, Satan, you shall not prevail against me when you go about to terrify me in setting forth the greatness of my sins, and so to bring me into heaviness, distrust, despair, hatred, contempt and blaspheming of God. As often as you object that I am a sinner, you call me to remembrance of the benefit of Christ my Redeemer, upon whose shoulders, and not upon mine, lie all my sins; for 'the Lord hath laid on him the iniquity of us all,' and 'for the transgression of people was he stricken' (Isaiah 53:6, 8). Wherefore, when you say I am a sinner, you do not terrify me, but comfort me above measure."[5]

Satan seeks to keep Christians from living out their Christian life by convincing them that they are not even Christians. Luther defeats Satan's lie with gospel truth—with faith in Christ's grace. How then shall we live once we receive gospel comfort? For Luther, we are not simply getting used to our complete salvation. We are applying it—living out our faith in Christ's grace active in love:

When I have Christian righteousness reigning in my heart, I descend from heaven as the rain makes fruitful the earth; that is to say, *I do good works*, how and wheresoever the occasion arises. If I am a minister of the Word, I preach, I comfort the brokenhearted, and I administer the sacraments. If I am a householder, I govern my house and family well, and in the fear of God. If I am a servant, I do my master's business faithfully. To conclude, whoever is assuredly persuaded that Christ alone is his righteousness, does not only cheerfully and gladly work well in his vocation, but also submits himself through love to the rulers and to their laws.[6]

Luther's Guiding Counsel and Progressive Sanctification

Luther's insights from Galatians provide us with an outline of his theology of guiding. First, Luther enriched the focus of guiding. In church history, guiding was always connected with progressive sanctification and growth in grace. However, at times historic guiding narrowed its focus to wisdom principles for Christian decision-making. While Luther shared biblical wisdom principles (as chapter 11 will explore), he exponentially deepened guiding by refocusing on progressive sanctification with an emphasis on the state of mind of the person being guided.

Luther's lectures on Galatians explained that we cannot effectively guide Christians who doubt their standing before God. Knowing that Satan sought to crop the Christ of the cross out of the picture, Luther focused his guiding on mind renewal for relationship renewal. Luther's guiding was not just about wisdom principles or mind renewal, but Luther focused specifically on relationship renewal—a renewed understanding of our relationship to God in Christ. Luther built his pastoral guiding on the foundation of the gospel meta-narrative of who God is in Christ, what God has done in Christ, and who we are in Christ.

Second, Luther enriched the approach to guiding, tying it directly to a comprehensive theology of progressive sanctification. In developing a theology of sanctification, some in church history and some today stress gospel indicatives while others stress gospel imperatives.

In the gospel indicative approach, sanctification is often defined as the art of getting used to our justification. This approach highlights what Christ has done for us, our position in Christ, and our identity in Christ. In this view, sanctification entirely or almost exclusively involves the work of God where our only role is to remember and re-believe what God has already done for us in the gospel (gospel indicatives). We might label this the *Let Go and Let God* approach, where we are more passive and inactive as we rest in the realities of the gospel.

In the gospel imperative approach, sanctification is often described as the active process of putting off and putting on. In this approach, sanctification, while initially the work of God, primarily involves our active effort to change as we obey the commands of God (gospel imperatives). This approach highlights how we are to live out our Christianity. We might label this the *Try Harder* approach, where our focus is less on our position in Christ and more on our obligation to Christ, less on our identity in Christ and more on working for Christ, less on passively resting in Christ and more on our active effort to be like Christ, and less on Christ's empowering grace and more on our human effort.

While clearly highlighting the necessity of guiding Christians into an understanding of their identity in Christ—gospel indicatives, Luther never stopped there. He understood the Christian's ongoing need for admonition and for Spirit-empowered putting off and putting on—gospel imperatives. Luther consistently sought to enlighten, encourage, and empower Christians to live out gospel imperatives in light of gospel indicatives. Luther's guiding pastoral counseling defined progressive sanctification as freely and joyfully living out our justification, reconciliation, regeneration, and redemption through faith active in love.

Third, Luther enriched the goal of guiding. In the religious culture of his day, guiding sought to help people to become more holy (progressive sanctification) by doing holy tasks like praying, fasting, and other spiritual disciplines. While granting a role for spiritual disciplines, Luther's guiding highlighted a relational theology in which the essence of progressive sanctification involves encountering God's love in Christ and living out that love toward others.

Luther's guiding was gospel-centered and neighbor-centered because he sought to empower Christians to apply their faith in Christ's grace by loving others for and like Christ. Luther sought to guide Christians into Christlikeness by living out who they already were in

Christ and by giving love to others out of the overflow of the love they have from Christ. Faith activates love.

Luther's Focus for Guiding: Mind Renewal about Relationship Renewal

Luther's theology of guiding is much like Peter's theology of progressive sanctification in 2 Peter 1. Peter starts with mind renewal for relationships renewal—envisioning the recipients of his letter as recipients of Christ's righteousness resulting in grace from Christ and peace with God (2 Peter 1:1–2). Peter next highlights the work of Christ and believers' identity in Christ: "His divine power has given us everything we need for life and godliness through our knowledge of him who called us by his own glory and goodness. Through these he has given us his very great and precious promises, so that through them you may participate in the divine nature and escape the corruption in the world caused by evil desires" (2 Peter 1:3–4).

But Peter does not stop here. He continues by directing Christians to live out their faith active in love. They are to make every effort to add to their faith Christlike characteristics—the pinnacle of which is love (2 Peter 1:5–7).

Peter emphasizes the connection between gospel imperatives and gospel indicatives with the transitional statement, "for this very reason" (2 Peter 1:5). Because you are new creations in Christ (gospel indicatives), make every effort to put off the old way and to put on the new way so that you will be effective and productive in your knowledge of Christ (gospel imperatives).

Gospel Memory Aids for Gospel Amnesia

Peter and Luther align in their commitment to gospel memory aids for gospel amnesia. The Christian who fails to progress in sanctification is "nearsighted and blind, and has forgotten that he has been cleansed from his past sins" (2 Peter 1:9). Luther and Peter agree:

to Christians suffering from gospel amnesia, biblical counselors prescribe gospel memory aids to renew the mind about our renewed relationship with God through Christ:

> So I will *always remind you* of these things, even though you
> know them and are firmly established in the truth you now
> have. I think it is right to *refresh your memory* as long as I live
> in the tent of this body, because I know that I will soon put
> it aside, as our Lord Jesus Christ has made clear to me. And I
> will make every effort to see that after my departure you will
> *always be able to remember* these things. (2 Peter 1:12–15,
> emphasis added)

Luther taught that not only can we forget these truths; we also
can forget how to apply these truths in the midst of Satan's temptations. Speaking again of Galatians 1:4 ("Who gave himself for our
sins"), Luther explained to his students:

> These things, as touching the words, we know well enough
> and can talk of them. But in practice and in the conflict,
> when the devil goes about to pluck the word of grace out
> of our hearts, we find that we do not yet know them as we
> should. He who at that time can define Christ truly, and can
> magnify Him and behold Him as his most sweet Savior and
> high priest, and not as a judge, this man will overcome all
> evils, and is already in the kingdom of heaven. But to do this
> in the conflict is of all things the most hard. I speak this by
> experience.[7]

What is Luther's sanctification process for overcoming all evils? It
is defining Christ truly, magnifying him, and beholding him in all his
amazing grace and awesome goodness. The Spirit empowers us to win
our battle with sin as we return to our first love for Christ, remember
our first awe of Christ, and recall Christ's eternal grace to us.

Cropping Christ's Grace Back into the Picture

Luther developed this idea more fully when he explained Galatians 4:19 ("My dear children, for whom I am again in the pains of childbirth until Christ is formed in you.") to his students:

> Now, the form of a Christian mind is faith or the confidence of the heart that lays hold on Christ and cleaves to Him alone, and to nothing else. The heart being furnished with this confidence, or assurance, that for Christ's sake we are righteous, has the true form of Christ. Now this form is given by the ministry of the Word. . . . For the Word comes from the mouth of the Apostle or minister, and enters into the heart of him who hears it. There the Holy Ghost is present, and imprints the Word in the heart, so that it consents to it. Thus every godly teacher is a father who engenders and forms the true shape of a Christian mind by the ministry of the Word.[8]

Christ is formed in us as we preach the gospel to one another, reminding each other of our reconciled relationship with God through Christ: "When Satan leads me to the law, I am damned, but if I can take hold of the promise I am free. Peter said, 'Grow in the knowledge of Christ.' This isn't a knowledge of the law . . . but it is the knowledge that Christ is the most just and most merciful One, in whom alone we dwell. Satan clouds this basic knowledge in our hearts in a remarkable way and causes us to trust an earthly friend more than Christ."[9]

Knowing Luther, it should come as no surprise that the grace-content of our gospel reminders are meant to counteract the works-content of Satan's condemning lies:

> Christ, according to the proper and true definition, is no Moses, no lawgiver, no tyrant, but a mediator for sins, a free giver of grace, righteousness, and life; who gave Himself, not for our merits, holiness, righteousness and godly life, but for our sins. If He gave Himself to death for our sins, then undoubtedly He

is no tyrant or judge who will condemn us for our sins. He is no caster-down of the afflicted, but a raiser-up of those who are fallen, a merciful reliever and comforter of the heavy and brokenhearted. Otherwise Paul would be lying when he says: "Who gave Himself for our sins."[10]

Luther again admonished his students and all Christians to personalize the gospel truth that defines Christ as the one who gave himself for our sins: "Learn this definition diligently, and especially so exercise this pronoun 'our,' that this one syllable being believed may swallow up all your sins; that is to say, that you may know assuredly, that Christ has taken away the sins, not of certain men only, but also of you. Believe that Christ was not only given for other men's sins, but also for yours."[11]

Why is mind renewal about our reconciled relationship to God so important for Luther? How do these gospel reminders relate to guiding one another in the progressive sanctification journey? The troubled conscience that doubts it is at peace with God is in too much spiritual-relational turmoil to receive general wisdom principles. It first must receive the ultimate wisdom principle of grace and peace, what Luther calls the "highest wisdom of Christians."[12] If the goal of guiding is empowering Christians to love their neighbor, then the enemy of that goal is the failure to receive God's love—his grace and peace:

These two words, *grace and peace*, comprehend in them whatever belongs to Christianity. Grace releases sin, and peace makes the conscience quiet. The two fiends that torment us are sin and conscience. But Christ has vanquished these two monsters, and trodden them underfoot, both in this world, and in that which is to come. Moreover, these two words, *grace and peace*, contain in them the whole sum of Christianity. Grace contains the remission of sins; peace a quiet and joyful conscience.[13]

Luther's theology of biblical guiding teaches that the Spirit empowers us to love one another as we enlighten one another to God's love for us in Christ.

Luther drove this biblical guiding principle home further and deeper when he exegeted Galatians 4:6, which he translates as "crying Abba, Father." Luther wrote, "Paul might have said: 'God sent the Spirit of His Son into our hearts, calling, Abba, Father.' But he says, 'crying Abba, Father,' that he might show and set forth the temptation of a Christian, who yet is but weak, and weakly believes."[14]

Luther counseled us that before we counsel a brother or sister to love like the Father, we must first counsel them to grasp the Father's love. When tempted to sin, condemned by Satan, and confused about life, Luther explained that sometimes all we can utter is "Ah, Father!" But what power is in that word "Father":

> This is but a little word, and yet it comprehends all things. The mouth speaks not, but the affection of the heart speaks after this manner. "Although I am oppressed with anguish and terror on every side, and seem to be forsaken and utterly cast away from your presence, yet am I Your child, and You are my Father for Christ's sake; I am beloved because of the Beloved." Wherefore, this little word "Father," conceived effectually in the heart, passes all the eloquence of Demosthenes, Cicero, and of the most eloquent rhetoricians that ever were in the world.[15]

Luther personalized this practice of mind renewal for relationship renewal: "Apart from the forgiveness of sins I can't stand a bad conscience at all; the devil hounds me about a single sin until the world becomes too small for me, and afterward I feel like spitting on myself for having been afraid of such a small thing." What is Luther's only hope? "So only the knowledge of Christ preserves me. . . . This is what knowledge of Christ means: by his death has been won the victory over death."[16]

When a counselee or parishioner comes to us doubting their reconciled relationship, like Luther, we counsel them to cling to the promise of Scripture: "Let us learn, therefore, in great and horrible terrors, when our conscience feels nothing but sin and judges that God is angry with us, and that Christ has turned his face from us, not to follow the sense and feeling of our own heart, but to stick to the Word of God."[17] If the greatest threat to empowered Christian living is a darkened understanding of Christ and our identity in Christ, then the most profound wisdom we can share with one another involves enlightening each other to biblical truth (mind renewal) about our reconciliation in Christ (relational renewal).

Luther's Approach to Guiding: Imperatives Founded on Indicatives

If we were to stop at Luther's focus for guiding, we might assume that Luther defined progressive sanctification as the art of getting used to our justification and reconciliation. However, Luther's approach to progressive sanctification involved applying our justification, reconciliation, regeneration, and redemption by living out gospel imperatives.

Luther consistently ministered to Christians by counseling the gospel to them—the gospel indicatives of who God is in Christ, of who they are in Christ, and of the implications of the cross and resurrection of Christ. In a parallel manner, Luther insisted on ministering to Christians by counseling via gospel imperatives—counseling Christians to live out the gospel imperatives in light of the gospel indicatives. Luther's approach to guiding and progressive sanctification was not an either/or approach; it was a both/and approach—gospel imperatives and gospel indicatives.

Preaching Gospel Imperatives to Christians

Luther was both/and because the Scriptures are both/and. Luther's sermon on Ephesians 4:22–28 is just one of many clear examples of Luther's consistent connection of gospel imperatives with gospel indicatives: "Here again is an admonition for Christians to follow up their faith by good works and a new life." Luther continued by explaining that though Christians have forgiveness of sins (gospel indicatives), "the old Adam still adheres to their flesh and makes himself felt in tendencies and desires to vices physical and mental." So, does the Christian simply let go and let God? Simply rest on the gospel indicatives? No. Christians must "offer resistance" and receive admonition. Luther exhorted, "Yea, even those who gladly hear the Word of God, who highly prize it and aim to follow it, have daily need of admonition and encouragement, so strong and tough is that old hide of our sinful flesh."[18]

It is common to hear that the gospel is not just a message of salvation to the non-Christian, but also a continuous message for Christians. At times we hear that as if it means, *only gospel indicatives are for Christians.* However, Luther, commenting on Paul in Ephesians 4, saw the necessity of gospel imperatives for Christians:

Therefore, the Gospel ministry is necessary in the Church, not only for the instruction of the ignorant, but also for the purpose of awakening those who know very well what they are to believe and how they are to live, and admonishing them to be on their guard daily and not to become indolent, disheartened or tired in the war they must wage on this earth with the devil, with their own flesh, and with all manner of evil.[19]

Luther tenaciously admonished believers with gospel imperatives because this is Paul's pattern: "For this reason Paul is so persistent in his admonitions that he actually seems to be overdoing it. He proceeds as if the Christians were either too dull to comprehend or so inattentive and forgetful that they must be reminded and driven." The gospel indicatives alone are not enough, because knowing who we are in Christ is not enough: "The apostle well knows that though they have made a beginning in faith and are in that state which should show the fruits of faith, such result is not so easily forthcoming." In other words, the fruit of righteousness does not blossom by doctrine alone, as Paul and Luther say next: "It will not do to think and say: Well, it is sufficient to have the doctrine, and if we have the Spirit and faith, then fruits and good works will follow of their own accord. For although the Spirit truly is present and, as Christ says, willing and effective in those that believe, on the other hand the flesh is weak and sluggish. Besides, the devil is not idle, but seeks to seduce our weak nature by temptations and allurements."[20] The great preacher of the doctrine of gospel indicatives insisted that we must add gospel imperatives to our ministry to our brothers and sisters in Christ.

Luther could not be clearer about his both/and ministry: "So we must not permit the people to go on in their way, neglecting to urge and admonish them, through God's Word, to lead a godly life." Nor could Luther be clearer about what happens when we fail to follow gospel indicatives with gospel imperatives:

> What would be the result if we were no more urged and admonished but could go on our way thinking, as many self-satisfied persons do: I am well acquainted with my duties, having learned them many years ago and having heard frequent explanations of them; yea, I have taught others? It might be that one year's intermission of preaching and admonition would place us below the level of the heathen.[21]

Luther's language is not the language of just getting used to our justification. It is the language of exhorting one another to apply our complete salvation in our daily Christian lives.

Luther believed that because Christ already changed us (regeneration and redemption), our lives should progressively change: "Therefore you must by all means put off the old man and cast him far from you. . . . For glorying in the grace of God and the forgiveness of sin is inconsistent with following sin—remaining in the former old un-Christian life and walking in error and deceitful lusts."[22] Luther counseled Christians this way because Paul counseled believers this way: "Now, this exhortation in itself is simple and easy of comprehension. The apostle is but repeating his exhortations of other places—on the fruits of faith, or a godly walk—merely in different terms. Here he speaks of putting away the old man and putting on the new man, of being 'renewed in the spirit of your mind.'"[23]

Whether we call it progressive sanctification, growth in grace, daily Christian living, the fruits of faith, a godly walk, or putting off and putting on—Paul and Luther both practiced the personal ministry of the Word through linking gospel imperatives to gospel indicatives.

Connecting Gospel Indicatives and Gospel Imperatives

Luther connected gospel indicatives and gospel imperatives by emphasizing mind renewal about who God is in Christ. The right image of who God is leads to rightly imaging God in how we live: "Having put away the old man, the apostle exhorts us further to put on the new man, that day by day we may grow as new creatures." And how does this occur? "This is effected by first being delivered from error—from the erroneous thoughts and ideas incident to our corrupt nature with its *false conceptions of God*."[24] The foundation for putting off the old man and putting on the new man (gospel imperatives) is putting off false conceptions of God (gospel indicatives).

We build on this foundation by putting on new conceptions of God revealed in Christ—being renewed in the spirit of our mind. By "constantly growing and becoming established in that true conception and clear knowledge of Christ begun in us, in opposition to error and idle vaporings . . . the heart is illumined unto righteousness and holiness, wherein man follows the guidance of God's Word and feels a desire for a godly walk and good life."[25] Knowing who God is in Christ (gospel indicatives) fuels our desire for godliness and empowers us for godly living (gospel imperatives).

Luther also connected gospel indicatives and gospel imperatives by emphasizing mind renewal about who we are in Christ. The right image of ourselves as new creations in Christ leads to rightly imaging God in how we live: "They who are regenerate and renewed by the Holy Ghost to a heavenly righteousness and to eternal life, are given a new light, a new flame, new and holy affections (as the fear of God), true faith and assured hope. There begins in them also a new will. And this is to put on Christ, truly, according to the gospel."[26] Once Christians begin to truly understand the new person they are in Christ, they begin to live out who they already are—to chisel out and reveal the new person from the inside out.

Our salvation creates a new identity in Christ. In Christ, we are forgiven ones (justification), sons and daughters (reconciliation), saints (regeneration), and victors (redemption). Gospel imperatives are encouragements and exhortations to live out our new identity—to express in daily relationships who we already are in inner reality. As Kolb explains, "Passive righteousness [gospel indicatives] is what makes people who they are at their core, their fundamental identity. The Creator gives them this identity, and from it proceeds their character. Their character shapes their decisions and actions, which constitutes the active the active righteousness [gospel imperatives], the actions that God designed them to perform."[27]

Additionally, Luther connected gospel indicatives and gospel imperatives by emphasizing mind renewal about what Christ has done for us. The right image of Christ's amazing grace leads to rightly imaging God in how we live: through faith in Christ we "begin again to have a joyful and confident heart toward God." Through reconciliation and justification we are "comforted by his grace." The result? "Accordingly they are disposed to lead a godly life in harmony with God's commandments and to resist ungodly lusts and ways. These begin to taste God's goodness and loving kindness"[28] and thus are motivated to live for the glory of God. Changed (regeneration and redemption) and accepted (justification and reconciliation) by grace, we are stirred by gospel gratitude to lead a godly life, saying *No* to unrighteousness and *Yes* to righteousness for God's glory.

Luther's Goal in Guiding: Faith Activates Love

Luther maintained the conviction that the conscious awareness of being loved by God the Father through Christ the Son was the only power capable of changing us. As John writes, "We love because he first loved us" (1 John 4:19); "Everyone who loves has been born of God and knows God" (1 John 4:7). This is why Luther, the pastoral counselor, focused on moving people to an encounter with God's love in Christ, applying John's word, "And so we know and rely on the love God has for us. God is love. Whoever lives in love lives in God, and God in him" (1 John 4:16).

Christ's grace not only forgives us (justification and reconciliation); it also changes us (regeneration and redemption). That change is in the direction of outward-focused, Christlike, sacrificial love for others: "Dear friends, let us love one another, for love comes from God" (1 John 4:7). Luther's guiding ministry was gospel-centered and neighbor-centered. Luther guided Christians to grasp the infinite richness of Christ's love and then to love others out of the abundance of grace they received from Christ. Faith activates love.

The Heresy of Inactive Faith

When the doctrine of faith without works is misunderstood, Christians can be tempted simply to bask in all this love and become so heavenly minded that they are of no earthly good—inactive faith instead of faith active in love.

This theoretical misunderstanding of Luther's teaching became a reality for one of his prized students, John Agricola. Agricola of Eisleben (1494–1566) was a student of Luther and became a faithful friend. He graduated with a Master of Arts degree from the University of Wittenberg in 1518; in 1519 he accompanied Luther to the

Leipzig Disputation; in 1520 he married. From 1525–1535, Agricola became a well-known preacher and reformer in Eisleben.

On September 11, 1528, Luther penned a letter to Agricola asking for information about a rumor to the effect that John was teaching a faith that does not produce works. In Luther's words, "The story goes that you are starting to affirm and fight for a new doctrine, namely, that faith can exist without good works." Luther then explained that he is writing "to admonish you in all seriousness to watch Satan and your own flesh," and to please "accept this warning with good will, since you know from what kind of heart it comes. And further please report to me on the status of this matter." Luther then noted how shocked he was when other followers fell away from the truth and how concerned he was that his most intimate friend, Agricola, might also fall away from the truth.[29]

Luther was deeply concerned about the false doctrine of inactive faith, in part, because he was commonly charged with teaching faith that did not yield works. In his lectures on Galatians, Luther noted that even the world "charges that the gospel is a seditious doctrine that . . . abolishes laws, corrupts good manners and sets men at liberty to do what they want . . . calling it the greatest plague that can be in the whole earth."[30]

Luther reserved his deepest concern for how Satan shrewdly twists and distorts gospel faith. Lecturing on Galatians 5:13 ("for, brethren, ye have been called to liberty; only use not liberty for an occasion to the flesh, but by love serve one another"[31]), Luther informed his students of Satan's schemes: "This evil is common and the most pernicious of all others that Satan stirs up in the doctrine of faith. In many he turns this liberty, wherewith Christ has made us free, into the liberty of the flesh." Luther noted how Jude also protests this doctrinal distortion, "There are wicked men crept in unawares, turning the grace of our God into lasciviousness."[32]

The flesh also is utterly ignorant of the doctrine of grace: "There-fore, when it hears the doctrine of faith, it abuses and turns it into wantonness. If we are not under the law, it says, then let us live as we please, let us do no good, let us give nothing to the needy, let us not suffer any evil, for there is no law to constrain us."[33]

The world, the flesh, the devil, and even the church (Agricola) all conspire against a balanced, comprehensive understanding of the relationship between faith and works: "Wherefore there is danger on either side. If grace or faith is not preached, no man can be saved; for it is faith alone that justifies and saves. On the other side, if faith is preached, some will understand the doctrine of faith carnally and draw the liberty of the spirit into the liberty of the flesh."[34]

Luther's preached the same message to the world, the flesh, the devil, and the church: *don't use gospel liberty for gospel license but for gospel love.* He wrote, "We teach our brethren with singular care and diligence by the example of Paul, that they think not this liberty of the Spirit, purchased by the death of Christ, is given to them that they should make it an occasion of carnal liberty, but that they should serve one another through love."[35]

Faith Never Takes a Holiday

Before explaining the role of works of love, Luther ensured that people understood the relationship between faith and works: "The apple makes not the tree, but the tree makes the apples. So faith first makes the person who afterwards brings forth works. . . . Christians are not made righteous by doing righteous things, but being made righteous by faith in Christ, they do righteous things."[36] And, "We must first of all to believe, and so through faith to perform the law. We must first receive the Holy Ghost, through whom we, being en-lightened and made new creatures, begin to do the law, that is to say, to love God and our neighbor."[37]

Speaking of Galatians 3:12, Luther added, "By this distinction Paul separates charity from faith and teaches that charity justifies not, because the law helps nothing to justification. Faith alone justifies and quickens; and yet it stands not alone, that is to say, it is not idle. Works must follow faith, but faith must not be works, or works faith. The bounds must be rightly distinguished one from the other."[38]

Lecturing on Galatians 5:6, Luther again presented his perspective on the relationship between faith and works:

> On the left hand he shuts out the Jews, and all such as will work their own salvation, saying, "In Christ neither circumcision," that is to say, no works, no worshiping, no kind of life in the world, but faith alone without any trust in works avails. On the right hand he shuts out all slothful and idle persons who say: "Let us only believe and do what we please. Not so, you enemies of grace," Paul says. It is true that only faith justifies, but I speak here of faith which, after it has justified, is not idle, but occupied and exercised in working through love.[39]

We are not saved by works, but we are saved to do good works.

But what are those good works? What does active faith look like? Recall that in the religious culture of Luther's day the works of faith were identified as holy tasks like praying and fasting. Typically, people thought, *the most holy people were those who separated themselves from the world—monks, nuns, and hermits.* This was not Luther's perspective: "A woman suckling an infant or a maid sweeping a threshing floor with a broom is just as pleasing to God as an idle nun."[40]

Christian living is not about rites and rituals, but relationships. Speaking of Galatians 5:14 ("For the entire law is fulfilled in keeping this one command: 'Love your neighbor as yourself.'"), Luther told his students, "It is as if he said: You are drowned in your superstitions and ceremonies concerning places and times, which profit neither yourselves, nor others; and in the meanwhile, you neglect charity which you ought to have kept. What madness is this? So says

Jerome: We wear and consume our bodies with watching, fasting, labor, etc., but we neglect charity, which is the only lady and mistress of works."[41] As Tappert explains, for Luther, "The aim is not to get people to do certain things—fasting, going on a pilgrimage, becoming a monk, doing 'good works,' even receiving the Sacrament—so much as it is to get people to have faith and to exercise the love which comes from faith."[42]

For Luther, and for Paul in Galatians 5:6, the work of faith is love: "Paul therefore in this verse sets forth the whole life of a Christian, namely, that inwardly it consists in faith towards God, and outwardly in charity and good works towards our neighbor."[43] Luther's entire summation of the Christian life is faith working by love: "In this verse Paul is not declaring what faith is nor what justification is, but what the Christian life is."[44]

Luther entitled the first 344 pages in his commentary on Galatians, "The Doctrine of the Gospel." The last sixty pages he entitled, "The Doctrine of Good Works." This is Luther's and Paul's gospel indicative and gospel imperative. It is their faith active in love. As Luther said in his introduction "The Doctrine of Good Works:"

> Now follow exhortations and precepts of life and good works. For it is the custom of the Apostles, after they have taught faith and instructed men's consciences, to add precepts of good works, whereby they exhort the faithful to exercise the duties of charity one toward another. . . . In order that it might appear that Christian doctrine does not destroy good works, or fight against civil ordinances, the Apostle also exhorts us to exercise ourselves in good works and in an honest outward behavior, and to keep charity and concord one with another.[45]

In *The Freedom of the Christian*, Luther developed his thinking further: "Works are not the true possession by which one becomes just and righteous before God, but do them freely out of love, for nothing, in order to please God, having sought nothing else in them and having regarded them in no other way than that God is pleased, for whose sake one gladly does one's very best."[46]

This is similar language to what Luther uses to introduce Romans 12 and following: "Then he describes the outward conduct of Christians, under spiritual government, telling how they are to teach, preach, rule, serve, give, suffer, love, live, and act toward friend, foe and all men. These are the works that a Christian does; for, as has been said, faith takes no holiday."[47]

Salvation in Christ (gospel indicatives) frees, empowers, and motivates us through faith to serve others in love (gospel imperatives). Progressive sanctification is faith active in love—exercising the love that comes from faith in the grace of Christ.

Timeless Truth for Life and Ministry Today

If we are to provide Luther-like pastoral guiding, then like Luther we must defend a robust, gospel-centered theology of progressive sanctification. Rather than starting with specific wisdom principles for particular situations, Luther targeted the heart through mind renewal. He laid the foundation through mind renewal for relationship renewal: the right understanding of our standing before God empowers us to win our battle with sin as we return to our first love for Christ, remember our first awe of Christ, and recall Christ's eternal grace to us.

Luther built on this foundation through emphasizing: (1) mind renewal about who God is in Christ: the right image of who God is leads to rightly imaging God in how we live; (2) mind renewal about who we are in Christ: the right image of ourselves as new creations in Christ leads to rightly imaging God in how we live; and (3) mind renewal about what Christ has done for us: the right image of Christ's amazing grace leads to rightly imaging God in how we live.

Luther crowned his sanctification project with mind renewal about our relationships to one another: a faith image of God's relationship to us in Christ leads to active love toward others that flows from and reflects the love of Christ.

Luther's theology of guiding in this chapter can be summarized with this tweet-size synopsis:

Progressive sanctification involves living out our justification, reconciliation, regeneration, and redemption (gospel indicatives) through faith active in love (gospel imperatives).

How do we empower and equip one another to live out our faith in God in love for others? Luther teaches us in chapter 11.

CHAPTER ELEVEN
FAITH ACTIVE IN LOVE:
LUTHER'S METHODOLOGY OF GUIDING

THE DATE was November 6, 1530. Because of his close relationship with Jerome Weller, Luther signed his letter, "Thy Martin Luther." Luther wrote to Weller because he was so despondent about his Christian life that he was ready to give up.

Luther launched his letter of spiritual guidance with words that might at first glance seem trite or perfunctory, but upon a second look are rich with guiding wisdom: "Grace and Peace in Christ. My dearest Jerome."[1] "Grace and Peace" should sound familiar. They are the words that Luther lectured his students about from Galatians 1:3. They are not just a salutation. They are salvation reminders—justification (grace) and reconciliation (peace). Imagine the power of hearing those words when you have felt defeated: "You say that the temptation is heavier than you can bear, and you fear that it may so break you down and crush you that you may fall into despair and blasphemy."[2] Into this darkness, Luther greeted his friend with "Grace and Peace." Experience the power of hearing those words from one of the most famous Christians in the world who calls you, "My dearest Jerome."

Ever the spiritual diagnostician, Luther quickly identified the root source of Jerome's feelings of spiritual defeat: "You should firmly believe that this your temptation comes from the devil, and that he vexes you so because you believe on Christ." Luther not only exposes the source of Weller's temptation, he reveals the devil's schemes: "I understand this wile of the devil. If he is unable to cast his victim to the ground at the first assault of temptation, he attempts by persisting to so weary and weaken him that he may fall and acknowledge himself beaten."[3]

Then, in the spirit of 2 Corinthians 10:3–7, Luther guided Weller to take every thought captive to obedience to Christ: "You must, then, make an earnest effort to boldly despise these thoughts suggested by the devil." And, Weller must do so with the people of God: "Then look about for some one with whom you can talk. By all means avoid loneliness; for it is just when you are alone that he sets his snares and catches you."[4]

Next, Luther shared some good, old-fashioned counselor self-disclosure: "I will tell you what was my experience when I was just about your age." Luther took Weller back to Luther's days in the monastery when he faced similar temptations to despair and sought the guidance and counsel of his spiritual mentor, Dr. Staupitz. Rather than directly addressing Luther's current despair, paradoxically, Staupitz cast a vision of Luther's future faith active in love: "You do not know, Martinus, how useful and necessary this temptation is for you. God does not exercise you thus for nothing. You will see that he wants your service to accomplish some great things." Luther then told Weller, "And so it has turned out; for I can say without boasting that I have become a great doctor, which, at the time when I was enduring this temptation, I would never have thought possible."[5] Picture it. Luther was at the end of his progressive sanctification rope, and Staupitz helped Luther to envision the other end of the rope—God's future plans to use Luther mightily.

As a skilled biblical counselor, Luther moved from his story and God's story back to God's story and Weller's story: "Just so it will no doubt be with you. You will become a great man." Wow! Languishing in the pit of spiritual despair, Luther raised Weller up to the mountaintop of future vision: "Only see to it that you keep up good courage meanwhile, and bear yourself bravely, fully convinced that such words, especially when they come from such learned and great men, are like oracles and prophecies."[6] Like Paul with Timothy in 2 Timothy 1:3–8, Luther took timid Jerome and fanned into flame the gift of God within him through casting a vision of God's story invading Weller's story.

To envisioning, Luther added encouraging: "Take courage, therefore, and cast these deceptive thoughts utterly away from you."[7] Luther encouraged—planted courage within, fans into flame, stirs up.

Luther ended like he began—with Christ's gospel of grace. He sandwiched gospel indicatives around gospel imperatives. When Satan tempts us to despair, we do not look ultimately to our self, but ultimately and always to Christ: "When the devil casts up to us our sin, and declares us worthy of death and hell, we must say: 'I confess that I am worthy of death and hell. What more have you to say?' 'Then you will be lost forever!' 'Not in the least: for I know One who suffered for me and made satisfaction for my sins, and his name is Jesus Christ, the Son of God. So long as he shall live, I shall live also.' Thy Martin Luther. Nov. 6, 1530."[8]

Luther's Guiding Practice: Pilgrim's Sanctification Progress

The preceding vignette outlines how Luther guided people to make wise, Christlike decisions, and it demonstrates how Luther equipped Christians to grow in Christlikeness on their Christian journey—pilgrim's sanctification progress. As with sustaining, healing, and reconciling, Luther started with a two-fold vision: who is Christ in the sanctification process and who are we in Christ in the guiding journey? Luther found it futile to guide a defeated, tortured conscience toward any fruitful decision-making. And he found it ineffective to help Christians live like Christ when they failed to understand God-in-Christ and themselves-in-Christ.

As we saw in chapter 10, Luther did not stop with gospel indicative reminders. He consistently moved to gospel imperatives in the form of encouraging and empowering Christians to live out their faith active in love. Luther also exposed Satan and his schemes—devil craft. Our progressive sanctification journey is a spiritual conflict that we fight in Christ's strength against the world, the flesh, and the devil.

What we do not witness in the preceding vignette is Luther's final step in the guiding process. I call this stage "decision-making and the will of God." Luther enriched and deepened guiding, making it first and foremost about Christlikeness as he targeted the growth in grace of the heart, mind, and conscience. Having targeted the heart, Luther then envisioned, encouraged, and empowered Christians to understand God's will on their faith-active-in-love journey.

Hiltner describes guiding with the analogy of trekking through the North Woods with an experienced guide. Expanding this analogy, we can survey the map Luther used as he guided Christian pilgrims on their sanctification journey.

- Exercising the Christian's Renewed Heart: Target the Inner Person
  » Enlightening the Eyes of the Heart to Christ Our Victor
  » Envisioning the Christian as a Victor in Christ: The Freedom of the Christian
  » Encouraging and Exhorting Christians to Live Out Their Victory through Christ
- Exposing the Christian's Spiritual Conflict: Practice Devil-Craft
- Equipping Christians for Daily Life: Impart the Counsel of the Gospel
  » The One True North: Faith Active in Love
  » The Three Guideposts of Relationships: Realms of Human Relationships
  » The Four Compass Points of Responsibility: Arenas of Vocational Callings

Exercising the Christian's Renewed Heart

Continuing the imagery of the Christian life as a trek in the North Woods, the last desire an experienced guide has is to lead someone up arduous terrain if the person has a bad heart, a heart that is out of shape spiritually. So, when Christians with a tortured conscience came to Luther for guidance, we do not witness him telling them what decisions to make. Instead, he targeted their renewed heart, the inner person who is a new creation in Christ. As babes in Christ with a new but not always strong heart, Luther sought to exercise the heart, mind, and conscience. To use today's language, Luther was not only a guide; he was also a personal trainer. Or, to use another modern analogy, Luther was a spiritual cardiologist, prescribing a healthy heart regimen that helped Christians to grow from neo-natal saints (babes in Christ—1 Peter 2:2) to *nikao* saints (victors in Christ—Romans 8:37).

This portrait of Luther's guiding is not just a modern perspective looking back 500 years on Luther. Consider Martin Bucer's perspective on pastoral care from his work *Concerning the True Care of Souls*, written in 1538. Influenced by Luther, Bucer saw guiding as the art of equipping Christians to grow whole and strong in their Christian faith and then urging them to move forward in all good—faith active in love.[9] Guides are shepherds who focus first on the spiritual welfare and health of Christians before focusing on specific Christlike decision-making.

Enlightening the Eyes of Our Heart to Christ Our Victor

For sustaining, Luther pointed suffering Christians to Christ the Comforter. In healing, Luther showed hurting Christians Christ the Resurrection and the Life. With reconciling, Luther directed despairing Christians to Christ the gracious, forgiving Savior. In guiding, Luther proclaimed to defeated Christians Christ the Victor.

Many times Luther blended several of these images. This was the case in his letter to his mother. Learning of her serious illness, Luther wrote not only to console her by pointing her to Christ the Comforter, but also to strengthen and guide her by directing his mother to Christ the Victor over the world, the flesh, Satan, sin, and death:

"Christ says, 'Be of good cheer; I have overcome the world.' If he has overcome the world, surely he has also overcome the sovereign of this world with all his power."[10]

Luther then teaches his mother how to apply Christ's victory to her life situation through gospel self-counsel:

> Let us in opposition to this lift up our hearts and say: "Behold, dear soul, what are you doing? Dear death, dear sin, how is it that you are alive and terrify me? Do you not know that you have been overcome? Do you, death, not know that you are quite dead? Do you not know the One who says of you: 'I have overcome the world?' It does not behoove me either to listen to your terrifying suggestions, or heed them. Rather, I should listen to the comforting words of my Savior: 'Be of good cheer, be of good cheer; I have overcome the world.' He is the victor, the true hero, who gives and appropriates to me his victory with this word: 'Be of good cheer!'"[11]

In the greatest trial of life, Luther cropped Christ the Victor, Christ the true Hero, back into the picture of his mother's soul. She was not only to know this, she was to reckon on this and appropriate this victory in her own life.

When the Christian pilgrim is on a trail marked, "Death," we need guides who will direct us to the one who is the Victor over death. As Luther reminded his mother: "For he who has begun his work in you will also graciously complete it. . . ." We are helpless without Christ's victorious help: "We are unable to accomplish anything against sin, death, and the devil by our own works." So what are we to do? "Therefore, another appears for us and in our stead who definitely can do better; he gives us his victory, and commands us to accept it and not to doubt it."[12] Our victory in our sanctification journey lies in Christ our Victor.

Envisioning the Christian as a Victor in Christ

Through faith we are not only forgiven (justification) and welcomed home (reconciliation); we are also made new (regeneration)
and empowered (redemption). Luther wrote, "Faith, however, is a divine work in us. It changes us and makes us to be born anew of God
(John 1); it kills the old Adam and makes altogether different men, in
heart and spirit and mind and powers, and it brings with it the Holy
Ghost."[13]

For Luther, regeneration/redemption by faith is a doctrine for
daily Christian life. Thus, Luther immediately added, "Oh, it is a living, busy, active, mighty thing, this faith; and so it is impossible for
it not to do good works incessantly. It does not ask whether there
are good works to do, but before the question rises; it has already
done them, and is always at the doing of them."[14] Luther's guiding
was more than techniques, steps, and principles. He was far more
concerned with renewing the mind so that a new lifestyle emerges—
faith active in love. The gospel informs and influences how Christians
think about themselves—new victorious creations in Christ—in order to shape how Christians live out their faith. As we saw in chapter
2, nowhere does Luther communicate this with more passion than in
his Preface to Romans:

> Faith is a living, daring confidence in God's grace, so sure and
> certain that a man would stake his life on it a thousand times.
> This confidence in God's grace and knowledge of it makes
> men glad and bold and happy in dealing with God and all
> His creatures; and that is the work of the Holy Ghost in faith.
> Hence a man is ready and glad, without compulsion, to do
> good to everyone, to serve everyone, to suffer everything, in
> love and praise to God, who has shown him this grace; and
> thus it is impossible to separate works from faith, quite as
> impossible as to separate heat and light fires.[15]

We are free through faith to serve one another in love—this is the vision toward which Luther guided Christian pilgrims.

This vision of the free and empowered Christian originates in the gospel, and it is nurtured by the gospel:

> Nothing else in heaven and on earth can make the soul alive, righteous, free, and Christian besides the gospel, the word of God preached by Christ. As Christ himself says in John 11:25, "I am the resurrection and the life. Those who believe in me . . . will live and . . . never die." Likewise, John 14:6, "I am the way, and the truth, and the life." Again in Matthew 4:4, "One does not live by bread alone, but by every word that comes from the mouth of God." So we can now be sure that the soul can do without all things except the word of God, and without the word of God, nothing can help it. And if it has the word of God, it needs nothing else; it has everything it needs in the word.[16]

In *The Freedom of a Christian*, Luther further highlighted the vision of the Christian's victorious identity in Christ:

> Now let us see what other things we have in Christ and what a great blessing true faith is. . . . Now as Christ has the right of the firstborn with their honor and dignity, he then shares it with all his Christians, so that by faith they all also become rulers and priest with Christ, as St. Peter says in 1 Peter 2:9, "You are a chosen race, a royal priesthood." What then happens is that through faith a Christian person is lifted up so high over all things as to become a sovereign over all things spiritually, for nothing at all can now harm that one's salvation. . . . Above and beyond that, we are priests, which is far more than being a king or queen, because the priesthood makes us worthy to stand before God and to intercede for others. . . . Who can even imagine, therefore, how high the honor and status of the

Christian person is? Through one's dominion one has power over all things, and through one's priesthood one has power over God, because God does what one asks for and desires.[17]

What is the nature of our victorious identity in Christ? We are rulers and priests with dominion and power. And what difference does it make for us when we become aware of this spiritual reality? Faith is guided and guarded, sustained and strengthened:

> Yet Christ should and must be preached so that faith is engendered and sustained in you and me. This faith is awakened and sustained when I am told why Christ came, how to benefit and have my needs fulfilled by him, and what he brought and gave me. This occurs when a person correctly explains the Christian freedom that we have from Christ and that we are rulers and priests, having power over all things, and that all we do is pleasing and acceptable in the eyes of God and is heard by God.[18]

I call Luther's focus our "universal identity in Christ"—what is true of every Christian. We are victors, rulers, priests, and so much more in Christ. In Luther's letters, he not only focused on individuals' universal identity, he also very specifically helped them envision their unique identity in Christ. We saw this already with his oracle to Jerome Weller, "You will become a great man."

Luther evidences a similar focus in his letter to Elector John, written on May 20, 1530. The Elector John was attending the Diet of Augsburg at the time. Luther wrote a personal letter of pastoral counsel dedicated to strengthening the Elector by envisioning and affirming specific ways in which the Elector was living out his new identity in Christ.

As an understanding counselor, Luther began by empathizing with the Elector and his difficult situation: "Your Electoral Grace is now, and has to be, in a tireless situation. May our dear Father in heaven help Your Electoral Grace to remain steadfast and patient in

God's grace which he gives us so abundantly."[19] Luther then transitioned from sustaining empathy to guiding envisioning: "none of the raging sovereigns and enemies can find any fault with Your Electoral Grace . . . for they know your Electoral Grace to be a blameless, peaceful, devout, and faithful sovereign."[20]

Luther next progressed even further by expressing God's vision of the Elector:

> Truly, Your Electoral Grace's territory is a beautiful paradise for such young people; there is no other place like it in all the world. God has erected this paradise in Your Electoral Grace's land as a token of his grace and favor for Your Electoral Grace. It is as if he should say: "To you, dear Duke John, I entrust my most precious treasure, my pleasant paradise, and ask you to preside over it as father. I place it under your protection and government, and I give you the honor of being my gardener and caretaker. This is most certainly true, for the Lord God, who has set Your Electoral Grace over this territory to be its father and helper, feeds all the people through Your Electoral Grace's office and service, and they all must eat of Your Electoral Grace's bread."[21]

That's specific envisioning: the Elector John is God's gardener and caretaker and God's people's father and helper.

Encouraging and Exhorting Christians to Live Out Their Victory through Christ

In light of the Elector John's unique identity in Christ, Luther exhorted the Elector to continue to serve God by assuring that the gospel is cultivated and preserved in his territory. This was no easy task, given the external struggles with Electors from other territories and given the internal temptations from Satan. As Luther acknowledged, "I am sorry that Satan is trying to disturb and trouble Your Electoral Grace's heart." Luther continued, "I know him very well, and I know how he is used to tossing me around. He is a doleful, sour spirit who cannot bear to see anyone happy or at peace, especially with God."[22] Luther then combined envisioning and encouraging: "How much less will he [Satan] be able to endure it that Your Electoral Grace is of good courage, since he knows very well how much we depend on Your Electoral Grace."[23]

After the Diet of Worms, Luther was forced into hiding. In a letter written on May 12, 1521, in the aftermath of the Diet, Luther encouraged and exhorted Philip Melanchthon to be steadfast and to continue the fight for the gospel: "You, therefore, as minister of the Word, be steadfast in the meantime and fortify the walls and towers of Jerusalem until the enemy also attack you. You know your call and your gifts. I pray for you as for no one else, if my prayer can accomplish something—which I do not doubt. Return, therefore, this service so that we carry this burden together."[24] If Melanchthon saw Luther as a warrior for the faith, then Luther more than returned the favor by envisioning Philip as very much his equal in standing firm and strong for the gospel.

Two weeks later, on May 26, 1521, Luther wrote Melanchthon again. He began by playfully teasing and chiding Philip to practice what they both preach: "Come on, let's test at least once a small part of Christ's teaching, since things have come to pass this way at the call of God and not through our doing." He then envisioned, encouraged, and exhorted Melanchthon: "Even though I should perish, the gospel will not lose anything. You surpass me now in teaching the gospel and succeed me as Elisha followed Elijah with a double portion of Spirit—which may the Lord Jesus graciously bestow upon you."[25] Imagine Philip's renewed courage when his mentor cast a vision of him as Luther's Elisha!

Luther also exhorted his wife, Katy, to live out the truth. Luther was away in Eisleben for an extended time for ministry and received word that Katy was worried about him. He wrote to her on February

10, 1546, asking, "Is this the way you learned the Catechism and the faith?" Instead, Luther exhorted her to live the gospel: "Pray, and let God worry. You have certainly not been commanded to worry about me or about yourself. 'Cast your burden on the Lord, and he will sustain you,' as is written in Psalm 55 and many more passages."[26] Luther never settled for faith without love because Christians are spiritual pilgrims and pioneers, not settlers. So Luther always spurred Christians on toward love and good deeds—faith active in love.

Exposing the Christian's Spiritual Conflict

If we are traveling the North Woods, we would expect that our guide be familiar with the dangers peculiar to the region. Luther, as an experienced spiritual director, knew all about the enemy of the faith. If guiding is about making confident, Christlike choices inspired by a daring faith in Christ's grace, then the greatest threat to the pilgrim's progress is Satan's assaults on the conscience. If faith active in love encapsulates mature Christian living, than doubt inactive in shame encapsulates Satan's scheme.

Luther was not alone in exposing the demonic dangers that line the sanctification path. Throughout the history of Christian guiding, soul physicians practiced devil craft—the shared discovery of biblical principles for defeating Satan's works-based narrative. John Bunyan's autobiography, *Grace Abounding to the Chief of Sinners*, exemplified this belief in the art of devil craft. Bunyan tells how he withdrew from a certain spiritual guide who knew nothing about devil craft and was, therefore, of little use when Satan was spewing his bile and ire:

> About this time I took an opportunity to break my mind to an ancient Christian, and told him all my case; I told him also, that I was afraid I had sinned the sin against the Holy Ghost; and he told me, he thought so too. Here, therefore, I had but cold comfort; but talking a little more with him, I found him, though a good man, a stranger to much combat

with the devil. Wherefore I went to God again, as well as I could, for mercy still.[27]

Luther and Bunyan were simply disciples of Paul. The Corinthians refused to forgive, comfort, and reaffirm their love for a repentant brother in Christ. Instead, they allowed him to be overwhelmed by excessive sorrow. Paul explained that such behavior aligned with Satan who seeks to outwit us when we are unaware of his schemes—the craftiness of the devil whose prime directive is to overwhelm the conscience with guilt, sorrow, and shame (2 Corinthians 2:5–11).

In his cunning craftiness, the devil sought not only to condemn the believer, but even more insidious, Satan sought to condemn God! In his exposition of Genesis 3, Luther notes:

> We shall find that this was the greatest and severest of all temptations; for the serpent directs its attack at God's good will and makes it his business to prove from the prohibition that God's will towards man is not good. Therefore Satan here attacks Adam and Eve in this way to deprive them of the Word and to make them believe his lie after they have lost the Word and their trust in God.[28]

Luther waged unremitting warfare against the devil. Perhaps Luther's most succinct summations of devil craft are his many interactions with Jerome Weller: "The devil can fashion the oddest syllogisms. For example. 'You have sinned; God is wrathful toward sinners; therefore, despair.'"[29] When the mind is inundated with such spiritual despair, it is impossible to guide a Christian pilgrim toward confidence Christlike choices.

Luther based his practice of devil craft on Paul's spiritual warfare strategy: "For though we live in the world, we do not wage war as the world does. The weapons we fight with are not the weapons of the world. On the contrary, they have divine power to demolish strongholds. We demolish arguments and every pretension that sets itself up against the knowledge of God, and we take captive every thought to make it obedient to Christ" (2 Corinthians 10:3–5).

Luther's practice was to expose Satan as the ultimate source of a distraught conscience. Recall Luther's biblical counsel to Jonas of Stockhausen: "have no doubt that such thoughts, being contrary to the will of God, are most certainly hurled and driven by force into your heart by the devil."[30] Luther externalized the source of mental anguish. This is wise and vital counsel because we can begin to think and feel that the source of our despondent thoughts is God's Spirit convicting our spirit. We mistake worldly sorrow that leads to death with godly sorrow that brings life (2 Corinthians 7:7–13).

Our brain begins to have a mind of its own, and Satan's condemning narrative seems as if it is eternal reality. So Luther turned Jonas away from self-trust: "It is reported to me by good friends that the wicked enemy is sorely assailing you with disgust of life and desire for death. O, my dear friend, now it is high time that you should give up trusting your own thoughts and following them."[31]

So, where should Jonas turn if he cannot trust his own thinking? Luther prescribed three remedies: trust the Word of God, the people of God, and the Son of God. With Jonas, Luther shared examples from Christ, Elijah, Jonah, and other prophets, and then exhorted: "To such words and examples, as the words and admonitions of the Holy Spirit, you must give honest heed, rejecting and casting out the thoughts that lead you to oppose them."[32]

Jonas should also turn to the people of God. After telling Jonas not to trust his own thoughts, Luther exhorts Jonas to "listen to other people who have escaped from the power of this temptation. Press you ear close to our lips, and let our word go straight down into your heart, and God will comfort and strengthen you through our word."[33] The very day that Luther wrote to Jonas, he sent a dispatch to Jonas' wife in which he emphasized the need for God's people: "But let me urge you not to leave your husband alone for a single moment . . .

Solitude is real poison for him, and the devil therefore tries to keep him alone."[34]

Of course, the ultimate person who can defeat Satan's lies is Christ. In his concluding words to Jonas, Luther wrote, "I herewith commend you to our dear Lord, the only Saviour and true Conqueror, Jesus Christ. May he gain his victory and celebrate his triumph over the devil in your heart."[35] It is no accident that Christ's conquest over the devil is the central motif in "A Mighty Fortress Is Our God":[36]

> And though this world, with devils filled, should threaten to undo us,
> We will not fear, for God hath willed His truth to triumph through us;
> The Prince of Darkness grim, we tremble not for him;
> His rage we can endure, for lo, his doom is sure,
> One Little word shall fell him.[37]

Luther was a good shepherd. He targeted the heart, strengthening the inner person so that they are spiritually prepared and equipped for the guiding journey. Luther was an experienced shepherd. He practiced devil craft, exposing the wolf in sheep's clothing who seeks to obstruct the path on pilgrim's sanctification journey. Having addressed the internal issue (the heart) and the external enemy (the devil), Luther was now reading to equip Christians to make confident Christlike choices focused on faith active in love.

Equipping Christians for Daily Life

In his guiding ministry, Luther practiced the adage, *give a man a fish and you feed him for a day; teach a man to fish and you feed him for a lifetime.* James Propst had written Luther seeking his counsel. After some delay, Luther responded, "I think that you do not need my letters, since in other ways you have been so richly endowed by God as to be able to guide and console both yourself and all others in this very evil age."[38] This was Luther's goal—to equip God's people with wisdom from God's Word so that they could make assured decisions about God's will.

This was also Luther's approach in a letter to Lazarus Spengler who was to adjudicate a court case regarding four suspects. He forwarded to Luther some records of the investigation and asked Luther for advice regarding the treatment of these four defendants. In the middle of Luther's response, he shared some brief biblical principles; however, he did not tell Spengler exactly what to do. Instead, Luther started and ended his letter to Spengler by drawing out Spengler's wisdom. Luther began by labeling him "prudent and wise" and then affirmed and validated Spengler's walk with Christ by expressing that he was "pleased that Christ is so active among you." He ended his letter simply stating, "No doubt, you gentlemen will know how to proceed in that situation."[39]

Rather than pointing people to the "counsel of Luther," the Reformer guided people to the "counsel of the gospel"—a phrase Luther penned in a letter to Melanchthon,[40] who was seeking Luther's counsel regarding the role of the government and Christians in governmental authority. Luther explained that in this matter, as in many other topics, the Bible directly addresses some issues, while remaining silent on others. When the Bible clearly speaks, we have distinct direction. But in other cases, when the Bible does not give direct commandments, how is the Christian to make informed, free decisions? In those situations, Christians must apply the "counsel of the gospel"—wisdom for making daily life decisions based upon the implications of the Bible's grand redemptive narrative.[41] Luther imparted to people the counsel of the gospel by guiding them toward the one true north of faith active in love, by directing them to three guideposts of relationships, and by focusing them on four compass points of human responsibility.

The One True North: Faith Active in Love

What does it mean to be godly and to express our faith in God active in love for others? In a table talk recorded in 1533, Luther succinctly captured the relationship between faith and love: "Concerning the verse in Galatians 5:6, 'faith working through love,' we also say that faith doesn't exist without works. However, Paul's view is this: Faith is active in love, that is, that faith justifies which expresses itself in acts. . . . Faith comes first and then love follows." Luther concluded with this summary: "But this, he says, is what counts: 'Believe in me and be godly.'"[42]

Luther's depiction of godliness and faith active in love is very earthy, very real, very day-by-day, as Luther indicated in his lecture on Galatians 5:14, "For all the law is fulfilled in one word, even in this: Thou shalt love thy neighbor as thyself." Luther continued:

> To serve one another through love, that is, to instruct him who goes astray, to comfort him that is afflicted, to raise up him that is weak, to help your neighbor by all means possible, to bear with his infirmities, to endure troubles, labors, ingratitude and contempt in the Church and in civil life, to give honor due to your parents, to be patient at home with a froward wife and an unruly family: these are works which reason judges to be of no importance. But indeed they are such works that the whole world is not able to comprehend the excellence and worthiness thereof.[43]

For Luther, spirituality, godliness, progressive sanctification, daily Christian living—whatever the label—involved faith active in love within the household of the world. He did not disassociate faith from daily living. Each Christian was called on to be a taste of Christ (his love and grace) to his neighbor. Each Christian, motivated by the Father's great grace, was to be a great giver of grace to others. "Thus, Christians, even if completely free, become willing servants once again in order to help the neighbor, walking alongside and dealing with each neighbor the way God through Christ dealt with them—and all for nothing, looking for nothing in return except God's good pleasure."[44]

Luther then explained the mindset behind such ministry:

> They think: "Well, all right. My God, through Christ, out of sheer compassion, purely and freely, gave me, an unworthy and damned person, without my deserving it, the full riches of all righteousness and salvation, so that from this point forward I need nothing more than to believe it is so. Aye, to such a Father, who has inundated me with abundantly overflowing possessions, I shall, freely, cheerfully, and for nothing in return, do what well pleases him and in relation to my neighbor also become a Christ, the way Christ became for me, and do nothing else than what I see is necessary, useful, and a blessing to my neighbor, since through my faith I already have enough of everything I need in Christ." Look this is how love and pleasure for God flow out of faith and how out of love flows a free, willing, and cheerful life, lived freely, serving the neighbor for nothing.[45]

Luther envisioned the gospel creating "real Christians"[46] who through faith in Christ's grace were turned outward in love toward others—free through faith to serve others in love. The creation of these real Christians took precedence over other agendas. Luther transformed "piety," the German word *Frommigkeit*, "from a term for general upright and honorable living to a designation for living a life of faith in God that produces love and service to others."[47] This was Luther's target, his destination, his due north—faith active in love. The North Pole for all decision-making revolved around whether an action was indicative of gospel faith in God expressing itself in gospel love for others.

The Three Guideposts of Relationships

In specific situations, what does faith active in love look like? If the Bible does not offer a specific command in a given relationship, how does a Christian decide what actions best exemplify faith active in love? Luther addressed these questions by proposing three relational guideposts connected to a person's relationship to God, others, and self.[48]

- **The Guidepost of Faith in Relationship to God**—The "Law" of Faith: In this situation, what action/attitude would be indicative of faith in God's grace? In this situation, what response would evidence faith in and reliance upon Christ?
- **The Guidepost of Love in Relationship to Others**—The "Law" of Love: In this situation, what action/attitude would be indicative of love for my neighbor? In this situation, what response would evidence Christlike love for others? What would it look like to serve my neighbor in love?
- **The Guidepost of Conscience in Relationship to Self**—The "Law" of Conscience: In this situation, what action/attitude would enslave or free my conscience? In this situation, is participation in this contrary to my conscience?

When faced with a decision, Luther encouraged people to ask these three types of questions: Is this indicative of faith in God's grace? Is this indicative of love for God's people? Is participation in this contrary to my conscience? Luther taught that the wise, spiritual conscience could use these questions to ascertain direction and to experience confidence and freedom to live a life of faith active in love.

Although Luther held unwavering views about those doctrinal issues of which he had become convinced, he also believed that there was a great realm of freedom outside those doctrines. Within this realm of freedom, the believer was enlightened by the Scriptures and empowered by the Spirit to wisely ask and answer decision-making questions related to the guideposts of faith, love, and conscience. When Christ died, he granted people grace which cleansed sinful souls; and he also granted the Holy Spirit as the divine Counselor who directs souls: "Christ did not only earn *gratia*, 'grace,' for us, but also *donum*, 'the gift of the Holy Spirit.'"[49] All believers have dwelling within them the Holy Spirit who guides them into all truth. Because of this, Christians can make confident decisions. Their consciences are free and liberated to decide how to live their lives based upon their biblical interpretation of the scriptural guideposts of faith, love, and conscience.

Luther often combined these decision-making guideposts, such as when he connects faith and conscience in his commentary on Romans: "Everything that is not of faith is sin, because it goes counter to faith and conscience; for we must beware with all possible zeal that we may not violate our conscience."[50] Luther taught that Christians should act out of faith because faith and trust in God produced freedom and peace. When a potential decision brought with it great doubt, then faith was absent, and the best course was not to act in that matter. Luther's guiding suggested that people should never do what is contrary to the conscience, even in areas of freedom.

Christoph Jorger, an officer at Vienna, had attended the religious services of the Catholic Church, and had thereby given offence to the adherents of the Reformation. He asked Luther for advice. Luther's reply illustrates the importance of the conscience in decision-making:

> First of all, since you find your conscience burdened in this matter, you can find no better advisor nor doctor than just that very conscience of yours. Why do you wish to live in such a way that your conscience shall be all the while biting and lashing you and leaving you no rest? That would be indeed, as they used to say, to live in a forecourt of hell. Therefore, if your conscience is restless and uncertain in this matter, try by all means to free yourself from this restlessness,

for it works against faith, which tends to make the conscience ever more secure and firm.[51]

Luther frequently connected and combined the guideposts of faith and love, as he does at the end of *The Freedom of a Christian*, saying, "Out of all these things the conclusion follows that Christians do not live in themselves but in Christ and in their neighbor—in Christ through faith and in the neighbor through love. Through faith one ascends above oneself into God. From God one descends though love again below oneself and yet always remains in God and God's love."[52]

On February 12, 1544, Luther responded to a letter in which George Spalatin had sought advice about the fixing of fair prices for grain. Luther explained that there is no "dot," no one black and white answer. Instead, we must use the law of love, combined with the law of conscience: "Your questions concerning usury with grain cannot be settled by any certain rule on account of the great variations in times, places, persons, circumstances, and cases. Therefore, the matter must be left to individual conscience; every man, confronted by natural law, must ask, Would you that others should do to you what you do to them?"[53]

The Four Compass Points of Responsibility

Luther added an additional category to his Christian guiding: the four compass points of vocational responsibility. Scholars have variously described these as vocations, callings, estates, offices, duties, and stations.[54] In the culture of Luther's day, vocation was typically reserved for a religious vocation such as priest, monk, or nun. Luther exponentially expanded the concept by explaining that every Christian has multiple arenas of responsibility before God. Luther summarized these as home, work, community, and the church. God's Word and the three guideposts provide direction for how Christians are to live out their calling in each arena. Spirituality, for Luther, involved faith active in love within these four households of the world.

For Luther, vocation involved learning how to live the Christian life in the world, but not of the world. The maturing Christian increasingly learns how to be sensitive to and respond to God's calling in every dimension of life, including what seems most ordinary. Veith describes Luther's understanding of vocation as sparking "a reformation of Christian spirituality."[55]

Luther wanted Christians to "guide themselves" by asking questions such as: What are my home, work, community, and church relationships like? In these areas of responsibility, am I doing those things that are indicative of faith in Christ? In these areas of responsibility, am I doing those things that are indicative of love for others? In these areas of responsibility, am I doing anything that is contrary to my conscience? Luther applied his doctrine of vocation succinctly, powerfully, and practically:

> A man is to live, speak, act, hear, suffer, and die for the love and service of his wife and child, the wife for the husband, the children for the parents, the servants for their masters, the masters for their servants, the government for its subjects, the subjects for their government, each one for his fellow man, even for his enemies, so that always one is the other's hand, mouth, eye, foot, even heart and mind.[56]

Luther's guiding sought to equip people to live wise and loving lives in each of these four communal estates. The Reformer believed that many of life's difficulties would resolve if Christians would live all of life, especially communal life, *coram Deo*: "God wants no lazy idlers. Men should work diligently and faithfully, each according to his calling and profession, and then God will give blessings and success."[57]

Vocation brings the Christian life into the ordinary world of our everyday living. Luther wrote:

> If you are a manual laborer, you find that the Bible has been put into your workshop, into your hand, into your heart. It

teaches and preaches how you should treat your neighbor. Just look at your tools—at your needle or thimble, your beer barrel, your goods, your scales or yardstick or measure—and you will read this statement inscribed on them. Everywhere you look, it stares at you. Nothing that you handle every day is so tiny that it does not continually tell you this, if you will only listen.[58]

In Luther's picture, Christians are on a journey carrying a map headed toward the pole of faith active in love. They also have an internal guide—the Holy Spirit who works through the Word of God. God also directs people through the three geographic markers of the realms of relationships—the guideposts of faith, love, and conscience. And God guides us though the four compass points of our arenas of responsibility. Luther's guiding sought to equip people to apply these guideposts and compass points to specific relational and vocational situations where the Word gave no clear direction. He attempted to advise people how to live out the consequences of faith with a free conscience by loving their neighbors in all of life's complexities in all of life's callings.

Timeless Truth for Life and Ministry Today

In *The Hobbit*, in a chapter entitled "A Short Rest," Tolkien describes Rivendell, the place the hobbits and their traveling companions sought lodging in the midst of their journey:

All of them, the ponies as well, grew refreshed and strong in a few days there. Their clothes were mended as well as their bruises, their tempers and their hopes. Their bags were filled with food and provisions light to carry but strong to bring them over the mountain passes. Their plans were improved with the best advice. So the time came to midsummer eve, and they were to go on again with the early sun on midsummer morning.[59]

If we are to provide Luther-like pastoral guiding, then we need to follow a Rivendell-like approach to ministry. What happened at Rivendell captures Luther's robust guiding process. For Luther, guiding was all about the heart—empowering Christians to grow refreshed and strong in grace. Luther ministered to the heart so that Christians were strengthened for the rest of their journey—a journey that involved being ambassadors of Christ's love in action. Strong hearts prepared for faith active in love were then helped along their journey with the best advice—advice focused on wisdom principles built around biblical guideposts and scriptural callings.

We can condense Luther's methodology of guiding with this tweet-size summary:

Christian pilgrims progress in their sanctification journeys by exercising their hearts in the gospel victory narrative—trekking toward the gospel pole of faith active in love.

CONCLUSION

HOW IS MARTIN LUTHER REFORMING YOUR LIFE AND MINISTRY?

I INTRODUCED our journey into Martin Luther's pastoral counseling by acknowledging his impact upon my life and ministry. We will conclude our trek together by applying what we have learned about Luther.

Whenever I teach, I always ponder two questions: *What? So what?* The first question highlights the biblical content of what has been taught and learned. The second question emphasizes the personal life and ministry application of the content—so what difference does all of this make? To ensure that people address the practical implication question, at the end of a lesson, seminar, or sermon, I will often ask people, "Based upon what we've just learned together, what one or two primary applications would you make to your life? What one or two central applications would you make to your ministry to others?"

I would like to encourage you to do the same. Based upon what you have learn from Martin Luther in *Counseling Under the Cross,* what one or two main applications is God calling you to make in your life? What one or two primary applications is God calling you to make in your ministry to others? To answer those questions, perhaps a review would be helpful.

The "What?" Question: Revisiting Our Tweet-Size Summaries

To refresh our memories of what Martin Luther has taught us, here is a review of our summaries from each chapter.

- Chapter 1: Terrified before God: Luther's Spiritual Trials
  » We desperately need counseling under the cross because Satan's seeks to crop the Christ of the cross out of our picture so we'll flee from the Father and entrust ourselves to anyone but God.
- Chapter 2: Peace with God: Luther's Cross-Shaped Theology
  » The Christ of the cross transformed Luther the man terrified before God into Luther the man at peace with God.
- Chapter 3: Counseling Through the Lens of the Cross
  » In order to comprehensively view and competently use the Bible in biblical counseling, we must view life through the lens of Christ's gospel victory narrative.
- Chapter 4: Suffering and the Trial of Faith: Luther's Theology of Sustaining
  » When life is bad, we defeat satanic doubts about God's goodness by facing our suffering face-to-face with God in the face of Christ.
- Chapter 5: Gospel-Centered Comfort for Suffering: Luther's Methodology of Sustaining
  » The human comforter is a sorrow sharer who points people to the supreme Comforter by incarnationally entering the sufferer's earthly story.
- Chapter 6: The Spiritual Significance of Suffering: Luther's Theology of Healing
  » God's good heart always produces good purposes in our suffering: he sometimes chooses to cure us; he always chooses to mature us. God uses suffering to form and transform us.
- Chapter 7: Christ's Gospel Medicine for Suffering: Luther's Methodology of Healing
  » When suffering tempts us to despair, we prescribe Christ's gospel medicine of healing hope—reconciled relationships, renewed minds, and revived courage.

- Chapter 8: The Spiritual Anatomy of the Soul: Luther's Theology of Reconciling
  » Daily behold in Christ's gospel mirror your gracious Father saying to you: "Forgiven! Welcome home! Saint! Victor!"
- Chapter 9: Christ's Grace Prescription for the Soul: Luther's Methodology of Reconciling
  » Grace is Christ's prescription for our disgrace—forgiving medicine for sin, preventative medicine for victory over temptation, and cleansing medicine for victory over Satan's condemnation.
- Chapter 10: Faith Activates Love: Luther's Theology of Guiding
  » Progressive sanctification involves living out our justification, reconciliation, regeneration, and redemption (gospel indicatives) through faith active in love (gospel imperatives).
- Chapter 11: Faith Active in Love: Luther's Methodology of Guiding
  » Christian pilgrims progress in their sanctification journey by exercising their heart in the gospel victory narrative by trekking toward the gospel pole of faith active in love.

The "So What?" Question: How *Counseling Under the Cross* Has Impacted Us

Whenever I ask the "So What?" question, I always answer it too. If it is a seminar, people often say, "But you've taught this material dozens of times. It doesn't impact you each time, does it?" Actually, if I am open to and engaged with my material, I am impacted each time I teach any topic related to the Bible, biblical counseling, or church history.

This is true of my recent reworking of the material for *Counseling Under the Cross*. This book began as my PhD dissertation written in 1997. It has the academic title of "Spiritual Care in Historical Perspective: Martin Luther as a Case Study in Christian Sustaining,

Healing, Reconciling, and Guiding." (Isn't *Counseling Under the Cross* a better title?) Because of the topic, my dissertation was not necessarily the "dry-as-dust" academic tome that people think of when they hear about someone's doctoral dissertation. Plus, I had been writing, speaking, preaching, and teaching using quotes and concepts from Luther for two decades since I wrote my dissertation. So, I assumed it would take me about one day per chapter to rewrite my dissertation manuscript into the book you now hold in your hands.

I was mistaken. It took me close to a week per chapter over the course of two years to turn my dissertation into this book. Why? First, because I wanted it all to be fresh for me. Second, because I love studying Luther, I ended up doing as much new research as I had done two decades ago. Third, because I'm not the same person, counselor, and writer today that I was twenty years ago, this is truly new material for me—this is not a rewrite, but a fresh writing of Luther's pastoral counseling. So, yes, this material has been impacting my life and ministry—not just from twenty years ago, but for the past two years.

Luther's Impact on Our Personal Lives

In my personal life, writing *Counseling Under the Cross* reminded me of what I always share with my counselees: "God gives us permission to grieve." Luther grieved deeply the loss of his daughter, his mother, and his father. His faith in Christ did not eliminate grief. Instead, it allowed parent-Martin and son-Martin to take his deep grief to a God who has a good and compassionate heart. In the past two weeks, I have experienced two significant losses. Researching Luther reminds me that God has given me permission to grieve, to lament, to cling to Christ in my suffering.

Also in my personal life, Luther reminds me that though we always want to strive to grow in Christ (progressive sanctification), the counselor, pastor, spiritual friend will never be perfect this side of heaven. If you track the chronology of the vignettes about Luther's spiritual trials—his *anfechtungen*—you will detect that he struggled with spiritual doubts about God's grace to him long after his salvation by grace alone through faith alone in Christ alone. Luther's theology did not prevent him from struggling spiritually. Luther's theology did not lead to instant glorification or even instant sanctification. While this is no excuse to sin, it has been a reminder to me that my life is a progressive sanctification journey. I do not have to wait until I am perfect as a person to be a biblical counselor. Instead, God calls me every day, every second, to cling to his grace for ongoing forgiveness and for daily sanctification.

Luther has impacted me personally in the area of suffering by his fresh reminders of God's compassion. Luther has impacted me personally in the arena of sin and sanctification through his fresh reminders of God's grace and peace.

How about you? After reading eleven chapters of *Counseling Under the Cross* what difference is Luther's life making in your life?

Luther's Impact on Our Ministry

In my biblical counseling ministry, writing *Counseling Under the Cross* has reminded me of the importance of seeing every counseling contact as an audience with at least four persons: the counselee, the human counselor, the divine Counselor (God through his Spirit and his Word), and the anti-counselor—Satan. Throughout this book, you have read a lot about Luther and Satan. Luther battled against Satan's continuous attempts to crop Christ and his grace out of Luther's mental picture. One of the greatest lessons I am learning from Luther is my calling as a biblical counselor to crop Christ back into the mental and relational universe of my counselees. Satan lies. He condemns. He seeks to blind us to God's good heart. This has been his strategy since Genesis 3. Through studying Luther's pastoral counseling ministry, I am motivated more than ever to help counselees to grasp together with all the saints the infinite love, grace, and peace of God in Christ.

Also in my counseling ministry, Luther is reminding me not only of the sufficiency of Scripture, but of the relevancy, profundity, and authority of Scripture. This book could just as easily have been titled *Counseling the Word*. In fact, *Counseling Under the Cross* and *Counseling the Word* communicate the same message because for Luther the Word of God is the gospel victory narrative of Christ. "Sufficiency of Scripture" is not some buzz word of the modern biblical counseling movement. "Sufficiency of Scripture" is the heartbeat of the Reformation. God's Word is sufficient, authoritative, and profoundly relevant for all of life and all of ministry.

Luther motivates me to crop the message of the life, death, resurrection, and final victory of Christ back into the picture of my counselees as saints, sons, and daughters who endure suffering and wrestle against sin in their sanctification journey.

How about you? After reading eleven chapters of *Counseling Under the Cross*, what difference is Luther's ministry making in your ministry?

Grace and Peace

Luther was imperfect. He would be the first to shout that news. That is why he clung tenaciously to Christ's grace and peace. Though imperfect, God used him . . . and continues to use him. I am thankful for Martin Luther and his continuing reforming impact on our lives and ministries.

With Martin Luther, I pray for you Christ's "grace and peace." Grace and peace—more than a salutation. "Grace" is our justification in Christ alone—the Father's words we all desperately need—"Forgiven!" "Peace" is our reconciliation in Christ alone—the Father's words we all urgently long for—"Welcome home!"

Grace and peace.

BIBLIOGRAPHY

Aden, LeRoy. "Comfort/Sustaining." Pages 193–95 in *Dictionary of Pastoral Care and Counseling*. Edited by R. J. Hunter. Nashville: Abingdon, 1990.

Alexander, Donald. *Christian Spirituality: Five Views of Sanctification*. Downers Grove, IL: InterVarsity, 1988.

Althaus, Paul. *The Theology of Martin Luther*. Philadelphia: Fortress, 1996.

Bainton, Roland. *Here I Stand: A Life of Martin Luther*. Nashville: Abingdon, 1978.

Bayer, O. "Luther's Ethics as Pastoral Care." *Lutheran Quarterly* 4 (1990): 125–42.

Becker, A. "Luther as Seelsorger: The Unexamined Role." Pages 136–50 in *Interpreting Luther's Legacy*. Edited by F. W. Meuser and S. D. Schneider. Minneapolis: Augsburg, 1969.

Begalke, M. "An Introduction to Luther's Theology of Pastoral Care." PhD Dissertation, University of Ottawa, 1980.

———. "Luther's *Anfechtungen*: An Important Clue to His Pastoral Theology." *Consensus* 8 (1982): 3–17.

Brecht, Martin. *Martin Luther: Shaping and Defining the Reformation: 1521–1532*. Minneapolis: Fortress, 1994.

Bucer, Martin. *Concerning the True Care of Soul*. Translated by Peter Beale. Edinburgh: Banner of Truth Trust, 1538/2009.

Bunyan, John. *Grace Abounding to the Chief of Sinners*. Philadelphia: Bradley and Garretson, 1666/1872.

Burck, J. "Reconciliation." Pages 1047–48 in *Dictionary of Pastoral Care and Counseling*. Edited by R. J. Hunter. Nashville: Abingdon, 1990.

Burck, J., and R. Hunter. "Pastoral Theology, Protestant." Pages 867–72 in *Dictionary of Pastoral Care and Counseling*. Edited by R. J. Hunter. Nashville: Abingdon, 1990.

Chesterton, G. K. *Orthodoxy*. Whitefish, MT: Kessinger, 2004.

Clebsch, William, and Charles Jaekle. *Pastoral Care in Historical Perspective*. New York: Harper and Row, 1964.

D'Aubigne, J. *The Life and Times of Martin Luther*. Translated by H. White. Chicago: Moody, 1950.

Delitzsch, Franz. *A System of Biblical Psychology*. Eugene, OR: Wipf & Stock, 1861.

Forde, G. "The Lutheran View." Pages 13–32 in *Christian Spirituality: Five Views of Sanctification*. Edited by D. L. Alexander. Downers Grove, IL: InterVarsity, 1988.

Gaston, N. "Martin Luther and Pastoral Ministry." *Journal of the Faculty of Religious Studies* 17 (1989): 5–12.

Graham, L. "Healing." Pages 497–501 in *Dictionary of Pastoral Care and Counseling*. Edited by R. Hunter. Nashville: Abingdon, 1990.

Grislis, E. "The Experience of *Anfechtungen* and Pure Doctrine in Martin Luther's Commentary on Genesis." *Consensus* 8 (1982): 19–31.

Hendrix, Scott. *Martin Luther: Visionary Reformer*. New Haven: Yale University Press, 2015.

———. *Recultivating the Vineyard: The Reformation Agenda of Christianization*. Louisville, KY: Westminster John Knox Press, 2004.

Hiltner, Seward. *Preface to Pastoral Theology*. New York: Abingdon, 1958.

Horton, Michael, *Covenant and Salvation: Union with Christ*. Louisville, KY: Westminster John Knox Press, 2007.

Ivarsson, H. "The Principles of Pastoral Care According to Martin Luther." *Pastoral Psychology* 13 (February, 1962): 19–25.

Jensen, G. "Some Help from Luther on Dealing with Suffering." *Touchstone* 9 (1991): 3–6.

Ji, W. "Significance of Tentatio in Luther's Spirituality." *Concordia Journal* 15 (April 1989): 181–88.

Kellemen, Robert. *Equipping Counselors for Your Church: The 4E Ministry Training Strategy*. Philipsburg, NJ: P&R Publishing, 2011.

———. *God's Healing for Life's Losses: How to Find Hope When You're Hurting*. Winona Lake, IN: BMH Books, 2010.

———. *Gospel-Centered Counseling: How Christ Changes Lives*. Grand Rapids: Zondervan, 2014.

———. *Gospel Conversations: How to Care Like Christ*. Grand Rapids: Zondervan, 2015.

———. "Spiritual Care in Historical Perspective: Martin Luther as a Case Study in Christian Sustaining, Healing, Reconciling, and Guiding." PhD Dissertation, Kent State University, 1997.

Kellemen, Robert, and Kevin Carson, editors. *Biblical Counseling and the Church: God's Care through God's People*. Grand Rapids: Zondervan, 2015.

Kellemen, Robert, and Karole Edwards. *Beyond the Suffering: Embracing the Legacy of African American Soul Care and Spiritual Direction*. Grand Rapids: Baker, 2007.

Kellemen, Robert, and Susan Ellis. *Sacred Friendships: Celebrating the Legacy of Women Heroes of the Faith*. Winona Lake, IN: BMH Books, 2009.

Kellemen, Robert, and Jeff Forrey, editors. *Scripture and Counseling: God's Word for Life in a Broken World*. Grand Rapids: Zondervan, 2014.

Kelly, R. "The Suffering Church: A Study of Luther's Theological Crucis." *Concordia Theological Quarterly* 50, no. 1 (1986): 3–17.

Kemp, C. *Physicians of the Soul: A History of Pastoral Counseling*. New York: Macmillan, 1947.

Kittleson, James. "Luther the Educational Reformer." Pages 95–114 in *Luther and Learning*. Edited by M. Harran. London: Associated University, 1983.

———. *Luther the Reformer: The Story of the Man and His Career.* Minneapolis: Fortress, 2003.

Kolb, R. "God Calling: 'Take Care of My People': Luther's Concept of Vocation in the Augsburg Confession and Its Apology." *Concordia Journal* 8 (1982): 4–11.

———. "Luther: The Master Pastor." *Concordia Journal* 9 (1983): 179–87.

———. "Luther as Seelsorger." *Concordia Journal* 2 (1985): 2–9.

———. *Luther and the Stories of God: Biblical Narratives as a Foundation for Christian Living.* Grand Rapids: Baker Academics, 2012.

Kraus, G. "Luther as Seelsorger." *Concordia Theological Quarterly* 98 (1984): 153–63.

Krey, Philip, and Peter Krey, editors and translators. *Luther's Spirituality.* New York: Paulist Press, 2007.

Lake, Frank. *Clinical Theology.* London: Darton, Longman, & Todd, 1966.

Lenker, John Nicholas, editor and translator. *Sermons of Martin Luther: The Church Postils,* Volumes 7–8. Grand Rapids: Baker Books, 1983.

Lewis, C. S. *The Problem of Pain.* Revised edition. New York: HarperOne, 2015.

Lischer, R. "Luther's Anthropology in Dialog." *Currents in Theology and Missions* 11 (1984): 279–84.

Lull, Timothy, and Derek Nelson. *Resilient Reformer: The Life and Thought of Martin Luther.* Minneapolis: Fortress, 2015.

Luther, Martin. *The Babylonian Captivity of the Church in Three Treatises.* Translated by P. Smith. Philadelphia: Muhlenberg, 1531/1947.

———. *The Bondage of the Will.* Translated by J. I. Packer and O. R. Johnston. Grand Rapids: Fleming H. Revell, 1525/1957.

———. "Career of the Reformer I." In *Luther's Works, Vol. 31.* Edited and Translated by Harold Grimm. Philadelphia: Fortress, 1957.

———. "Career of the Reformer II." In *Luther's Works, Vol. 32.* Edited and Translated by G. W. Forell. Philadelphia: Fortress, 1958.

———. "Career of the Reformer III." In *Luther's Works, Vol. 33*. Edited by P. S. Watson and H. T. Lehman. Translated by P. S. Watson. Philadelphia: Fortress, 1972.

———. "Career of the Reformer IV." In *Luther's Works, Vol. 34*. Edited by L. W. Spitz and H. T. Lehman. Translated by L. W. Spitz. Philadelphia: Fortress, 1960.

———. "The Catholic Epistles." In *Luther's Works, Vol. 30*. Edited by J. Pelikan and W. A. Hansen. Translated by M. H. Bertrom. Saint Louis: Concordia, 1967.

———. "The Christian and Society I." In *Luther's Works, Vol. 44*. Edited and Translated by J. Atkinson. Philadelphia: Fortress, 1966.

———. "Church and Ministry I." In *Luther's Works, Vol. 39*. Edited and Translated by E. W. Gritsch. Philadelphia: Fortress, 1970.

———. "Church and Ministry II." In *Luther's Works, Vol. 40*. Edited and Translated by C. Bergendoff. Philadelphia: Muhlenberg, 1958.

———. "Church and Ministry III." In *Luther's Works, Vol. 41*. Edited and Translated by E. W. Gritsch. Philadelphia: Fortress, 1969.

———. *Commentary on Galatians*. Translated by P. S. Watson. Grand Rapids: Fleming H. Revell, 1535/1988.

———. *Commentary on Romans*. Translated by J. T. Mueller. Grand Rapids: Kregel, 1516/1954.

———. "Devotional Writings I. In *Luther's Works, Vol. 42*. Edited and Translated by M. O. Deitrich. Philadelphia: Fortress, 1969.

———. "Devotional Writings II." In *Luther's Works, Vol. 43*. Edited and Translated by G. K. Wiencke. Philadelphia: Fortress, 1968.

———. "The Freedom of the Christian." Pages 69–90 in *Luther's Spirituality*. Edited and Translated by Philip Krey and Peter Krey. New York: Paulist, 2007.

———. "The Large Catechism." Pages 185–202 in *Luther's Spirituality*. Edited and Translated by Philip Krey and Peter Krey. New York: Paulist, 2007.

———. "Lectures on Genesis: Chapters 1–5." In *Luther's Works, Vol. 1.* Edited by J. Pelikan. Translated by G. V. Schick. Saint Louis: Concordia, 1958.

———. "Lectures on Genesis: Chapters 6–14." In *Luther's Works, Vol. 2.* Edited by J. Pelikan and D. F. Poellet. Translated by G. V. Schick. Saint Louis: Concordia, 1960.

———. "Lectures on Genesis: Chapters 21–25." In *Luther's Works, Vol. 4.* Edited by J. Pelikan and W. A. Hansen. Translated by G. V. Schick. Saint Louis: Concordia, 1964.

———. "Lectures on Genesis: Chapters 31–37." In *Luther's Works, Vol. 6.* Edited by J. Pelikan and H. C. Oswald. Translated by P. D. Paul. Saint Louis: Concordia, 1970.

———. "Lectures on Genesis: Chapters 45–50." In *Luther's Works, Vol. 8.* Edited by J. Pelikan. Translated by Paul Pahl. Saint Louis: Concordia, 1966.

———. "Lectures on Isaiah: Chapters 1–39." In *Luther's Works, Vol. 16.* Edited by J. Pelikan and H. C. Oswald. Translated by H. J. A. Bouman. Saint Louis: Concordia, 1969.

———. "Lectures on Isaiah: Chapters 40–66." In *Luther's Works, Vol. 17.* Edited by H. C. Oswald. Translated by H. J. A. Bouman. Saint Louis: Concordia, 1972.

———. "Lectures on the Minor Prophets II." In *Luther's Works, Vol. 19.* Edited by H. C. Oswald. Translated by C. D. Froehlich. Saint Louis: Concordia, 1974.

———. "Lectures on the Psalms." In *Luther's Works, Vol. 10.* Edited by H. C. Oswald. Translated by H. J. A. Bouman. Saint Louis: Concordia, 1974.

———. "Lectures on the Psalms II." In *Luther's Works, Vol. 11.* Edited by H. C. Oswald. Translated by H. J. A. Bouman. Saint Louis: Concordia, 1976.

———. "Letters I." In *Luther's Works, Vol. 48.* Edited and Translated by G. G. Krodel. Philadelphia: Fortress, 1963.

———. "Letters II." In *Luther's Works, Vol. 49*. Edited and Translated by G. G. Krodel. Philadelphia: Fortress, 1972.

———. "Letters III." In *Luther's Works, Vol. 50*. Edited and Translated by G. G. Krodel. Philadelphia: Fortress, 1975.

———. "Liturgy and Hymns." In *Luther's Works, Vol. 53*. Edited and Translated by U. S. Leupold. Philadelphia: Fortress, 1965.

———. "Selected Psalms I." In *Luther's Works, Vol. 12*. Edited by J. Pelikan. Translated by L. W. Spitz. Saint Louis: Concordia. 1955.

———. "Selected Psalms III." In *Luther's Works, Vol. 14*. Edited by J. Pelikan and D. E. Poelett. Translated by E. Sittler. Saint Louis: Concordia, 1958.

———. "Sermon on the Mount and the Magnificat." In *Luther's Works, Vol. 21*. Edited by J. Pelikan. Translated by A. T. Steinhaeuser. St. Louis: Concordia, 1955.

———. "Table Talk." In *Luther's Works, Vol. 54*. Edited and Translated by T. T. Tappert. Philadelphia: Fortress, 1967.

———. "Word and Sacrament II." In *Luther's Works. Vol. 36*. Edited by A. R. Wents and H. T. Lehman. Translated by A. T. W. Steinhauser. Philadelphia: Fortress, 1959.

McCue, J. "The Augsburg Confession." Pages 203–16 in *Luther's Ecumenical Significance: An Interconfessional Consultation*. Edited by P. Manns and H. Myers. Strausburg: International Consultation for Ecumenical Research, 1983.

MacDonald, James, Bob Kellemen, and Steve Viars, editors. *Christ-Centered Biblical Counseling: Changing Lives with God's Changeless Truth*. Eugene, OR: Harvest House, 2013.

McGrath, Alister. *Luther's Theology of the Cross: Martin Luther's Theological Breakthrough*. Hoboken, NJ: Wiley-Blackwell, 1991.

McNeil, John. *A History of the Cure of Souls*. New York: Harper and Row, 1951.

Manchester, William. *A World Lit Only by Fire: The Medieval Mind and the Renaissance: Portrait of an Age*. Boston: Back Bay, 1992.

Manns, P. "Catholic Luther Research." Pages 1–48 in *Luther's Ecumenical Significance: An Interconfessional Consultation*. Edited by P. Manns and H. Myers. Strausburg: International Consultation for Ecumenical Research, 1983.

Marty, Martin. "Luther's Living Legacy." *Christian History* 12 (1993): 51–53.

———. *Martin Luther*. New York: Viking, 2004.

———. *October 31, 1517: Martin Luther and the Day That Changed the World*. Brewster, MA: Paraclete Press, 2016.

Meuser, F. "The Changing Catholic View of Luther: Will Rome Take Him Back?" Pages 40–54 in *Interpreting Luther's Legacy*. Edited by F. W. Meuser and S. D. Schneider. Minneapolis: Augsburg, 1969.

Mildenberger, F. *Theology of the Lutheran Confession*. Translated by E. Lueker. Philadelphia: Fortress, 1986.

Miles, M. "The Rope Breaks When It Is the Tightest: Luther on the Body, Consciousness, and the Word." *Harvard Theological Review* 77, no 3–4 (1984): 239–58.

Nebe, August, editor. *Luther as Spiritual Adviser*. Translated by C. H. Hays. Philadelphia: Lutheran Publication Society, 1894.

Nichols, Stephen. *Martin Luther: A Guided Tour of His Life and Thought*. Philipsburg, NJ: P&R Publishing, 2002.

Oates, Wayne. *Protestant Pastoral Counseling*. Philadelphia: Westminster Press, 1962.

Oberman, Heiko. *Luther: Man between God and the Devil*. Translated by E. Walliser-Schwarzhart. London: Yale University Press, 1989.

———. *The Reformation: Roots and Ramifications*. Grand Rapids: Eerdmans, 1994.

Oden, Thomas. *Care of Souls in the Classic Tradition*. Philadelphia: Fortress, 1983.

———. *Pastoral Counsel*. Vol. 3 of Classical Pastoral Care. Grand Rapids: Baker, 1987.

———. "Whatever Happened to History?" *Good News* (January–February, 1993): 7.

Ozment, Steven. *The Age of Reform: 1250–1550*. London: Yale University Press, 1980.

———. "Reinventing Family Life." *Christian History* 12 (1993): 22–34.

Packer, J. I. *A Grief Sanctified: Passing Through Grief to Peace and Joy*. Ann Arbor, MI: Vine Books, 1997.

Rupp, Gordon. *The Righteousness of God: Luther Studies*. London: Hodder and Stoughton, 1953.

Scaer, D. "The Concept of *Anfechtungen* in Luther's Thought." *Concordia Theological Quarterly* 47 (1983): 15–30.

———. "Sanctification in Lutheran Theology." *Concordia Theological Quarterly* 4, no. 2–3 (1985): 181–97.

Schleiner, Winfried. "Renaissance Exampla of Schizophrenia: The Cure by Charity in Luther and Cervantes." *Renaissance and Reformation* 9, no. 3 (1985): 157–76.

Schwarz, Hans. *True Faith in the True God: An Introduction to Luther's Life and Thought*. Revised and Expanded Edition. Minneapolis, Fortress, 2015.

Smith, Preserved. *The Life and Letters of Martin Luther*. New York: Barnes and Noble, 1911.

Smith, Preserved, and C. M. Jacobs, editors. *Luther's Correspondence and Other Contemporary Letters* (Vol. 2). Philadelphia: Lutheran Publication Society, 1918.

Sproul, R. C., and Stephen Nicholas, editors. *The Legacy of Luther*. Orlando: Reformation Trust, 2016.

Steinmetz, D. *Luther in Context*. Grand Rapids: Baker, 1995.

Stott, John. *The Cross of Christ*. Downers Grove, IL: InterVarsity, 1986.

Strohl, J. "Luther's Fourteen Consolations." *Lutheran Quarterly* 3 (1989): 169–82.

Tappert, G. T., editor and translator. *Luther's Letters of Spiritual Counsel.* Vol. XVIII in The Library of Christian Classics. Edited by J. Baillie, J. T. McNeil, and H. P. Van Dusen). Philadelphia: Westminster Press, 1955.

Tinder, G. "Luther's Theology of Christian Suffering and Its Implications for Pastoral Care." *Dialog* (Minnesota) 25, no. 2 (1986): 108–13.

Tolkien, J. R. R. *The Hobbit.* Geneva, IL: Houghton Mifflin Harcourt, 2012

Vallée, G. "Luther and Monastic Theology: Notes on *Anfechtung* and *Conpunctio.*" *Archiv furReformations Queschichte* 75 (1984): 290–97.

Veith, Gene. "The Glory of God Alone: Luther on Vocation." Pages 178–90 in *The Legacy of Luther.* Edited by R. C. Sproul. Orlando: Reformation Trust, 2016.

Wende, Peter. *A History of Germany.* Hampshire: Palgrave, 2005.

Wengert, Timothy. *Martin Luther's 95 Theses: With Introduction, Commentary, and Study Guide.* Minneapolis, Fortress, 2015.

Won, Y. "Significance of Tentatio in Luther's Spirituality." *Concordia Journal* 15 (1989): 181–88.

Wood, A. "Spirit and Spirituality in Luther." *Evangelical Quarterly* 61 (1989): 311–33.

Wright, William. *Martin Luther's Understanding of God's Two Kingdoms: The Response to the Challenge of Skepticism.* Grand Rapids: Baker Academics, 2010.

Zersen, D. "Lutheran Roots for Small Group Ministry." *Currents in Theology and Mission* 8 (1981): 234–38.

ENDNOTES

Chapter 1

[1] Martin Luther, "Letters I" in *Luther's Works, Vol. 48.*, ed. and trans. by G. G. Krodel (Philadelphia: Fortress, 1963), 46.

[2] Ibid.

[3] John McNeil, *A History of the Cure of Souls* (New York: Harper and Row, 1951), 163.

[4] R. C. Sproul and Stephen Nicholas, eds., *The Legacy of Luther* (Orlando: Reformation Trust, 2016), 280.

[5] G. T. Tappert, ed. and trans., *Luther: Letters of Spiritual Counsel* (Philadelphia: Westminster Press, 1955), 13, emphasis added.

[6] Luther, "Career of the Reformer IV" in *Luther's Works, Vol. 34*, ed. by L. W. Spitz and H. T. Lehman, trans. by L. W. Spitz (Philadelphia: Fortress, 1960), 336.

[7] Heiko Oberman, *Luther: Man between God and the Devil*, trans. by E. Walliser-Schwarzhart (London: Yale University Press, 1989), 151.

[8] August Nebe, ed., *Luther as Spiritual Advisor*, trans. by C. H. Hays (Philadelphia: Lutheran Publication Society, 1894), iii.

[9] James Kittleson, *Luther the Reformer: The Story of the Man and His Career* (Minneapolis: Fortress, 2003), 88.

[10] Luther, *LW, Vol. 48*, 47.

[11] Ibid., 340–41.

[12] Kittleson, *Luther the Reformer*, 78–79.

[13] Martin Marty, *Martin Luther* (New York: Viking, 2004), 14, 9.

[14] Luther, *LW, Vol. 34*, 336–37.

[15] Martin Luther, "Table Talk" in *Luther's Works, Vol. 54*, ed. and trans. by G. T. Tappert (Philadelphia: Fortress, 1967), 188.

[16] Philip Krey and Peter Krey, ed. and trans., *Luther's Spirituality* (New York: Paulist Press, 2007), xxi.

[17] Kittleson, *Luther the Reformer*, 41.

[18] Luther, *LW, Vol. 54*, 19–20, emphasis added.

[19] Martin Luther, "Lectures on Genesis: Chapters 45–50" in *Luther's Works, Vol. 8*, ed. by J. Pelikan, trans. by Paul Pahl (Saint Louis: Concordia, 1966), 326.

[20] Luther, *LW, Vol. 54*, 15.

[21] Ibid., 193.

[22] Roland Bainton, *Here I Stand: A Life of Martin Luther* (Nashville: Abingdon, 1978), 31.

[23] Kittleson, *Luther the Reformer*, 56.

[24] Marty, *Martin Luther*, xii.

²⁵ Bainton, *Here I Stand*, 15.
²⁶ Marty, *Martin Luther*, 2.
²⁷ Luther, *LW, Vol. 48*, 332.
²⁸ Luther, *LW, Vol. 54*, 156–57.
²⁹ Bainton, *Here I Stand*, 30.
³⁰ Quoted in Scott Hendrix, *Martin Luther: Visionary Reformer* (New Haven: Yale University Press, 2015), 27, from WA 17:1, 309.
³¹ Bainton, *Here I Stand*, 34.
³² Ibid.
³³ Luther, *LW, Vol. 54*, 339–40.
³⁴ Ibid., 85.
³⁵ Ibid., 95.
³⁶ J. D'Aubigne, *The Life and Times of Martin Luther*, trans. by H. White (Chicago: Moody, 1950), 32.
³⁷ Luther, *LW, Vol. 54*, 340.
³⁸ Bainton, *Here I Stand*, 38.
³⁹ Luther, *LW, Vol. 54*, 237.
⁴⁰ D'Aubigne, *The Life and Times of Martin Luther*, 24.
⁴¹ Marty, *Martin Luther*, 14–15.
⁴² Luther, *LW, Vol. 54*, 94–95.
⁴³ Quoted in David C. Steinmetz, *Luther in Context* (Grand Rapids: Baker, 1995), 2, from WA 40. II.15, 15, trans. by Gordon Rupp, in *The Righteousness of God: Luther Studies* (London: Hodder and Stoughton, 1953), 104.
⁴⁴ D'Aubigne, *The Life and Times of Martin Luther*, 31.
⁴⁵ Martin Luther, *Commentary on Galatians*, trans. by P. S. Watson (Grand Rapids: Fleming H. Revell, 1535/1988), 125.

Chapter 2

¹ Luther, *LW, Vol. 48*, 12.
² Ibid.
³ Ibid.
⁴ Ibid., 13.
⁵ Ibid.
⁶ Ibid., 14.
⁷ Luther, *LW, Vol. 54*, 237.
⁸ Nebe, *Luther as Spiritual Advisor*, 9.
⁹ Luther, *LW, Vol. 54*, 50–51, brackets added.
¹⁰ G. Vallée, "Luther and Monastic Theology: Notes on *Anfechtung* and *Conpunctio*," *Archiv für Reformations Queschichte* 75 (1984): 294.
¹¹ Martin Luther, "Church and Ministry III" in *Luther's Works, Vol. 41*, ed. and trans. by E. W. Gritsch (Philadelphia: Fortress, 1969), xi.
¹² M. Begalke, "Luther's *Anfechtungen*: An Important Clue to His Pastoral Theology," *Consensus* 8 (1982): 16.

[13] Martin Luther, "Letters II" in *Luther's Works, Vol. 49*, ed. and trans. by G. G. Krodel (Philadelphia: Fortress, 1972), 48.

[14] D'Aubigne, *The Life and Times of Martin Luther*, 37.

[15] Luther, *LW, Vol. 48*, 64–70.

[16] Bainton, *Here I Stand*, 45.

[17] Nebe, *Luther as Spiritual Advisor*, 11–12.

[18] Ibid., 12.

[19] Luther, *LW, Vol. 48*, 65.

[20] Ibid.

[21] Ibid., 67.

[22] Ibid., 66.

[23] Ibid., 68.

[24] Nebe, *Luther as Spiritual Advisor*, 18, 19–20.

[25] Bainton, *Here I Stand*, 47–48.

[26] Ibid., 48–49.

[27] Martin Luther, *Commentary on Romans*, trans. by J. T. Mueller (Grand Rapids: Kregel, 1516/1954), xiii.

[28] Luther, *LW, Vol. 54*, 442–43.

[29] Luther, *Commentary on Romans*, xv.

[30] Ibid., xvi.

[31] Ibid., xvii.

[32] Luther, *Commentary on Galatians*, 182.

[33] Luther, *Commentary on Romans*, 89.

[34] Luther, *LW, Vol. 54*, 193–94.

[35] Ibid.,194.

[36] Ibid., 308–9.

[37] Bainton, *Here I Stand*, 49–50.

[38] P. Manns, "Catholic Luther Research" in *Luther's Ecumenical Significance: An Interconfessional Consultation*, ed. by P. Manns and H. Myers (Strausburg: International Consultation for Ecumenical Research, 1983), 1–48.

[39] Kittleson, *Luther the Reformer*, 146.

Chapter 3

[1] Martin Luther, "Letters III" in *Luther's Works, Vol. 50*, ed. and trans. by G. G. Krodel (Philadelphia: Fortress, 1975), 17–24, all quotes from the opening vignette in chapter 3 are taken from this letter.

[2] Luther, *Commentary on Galatians*, 21.

[3] Luther, *LW, Vol. 49*, 207.

[4] Luther, *LW, Vol. 48*, xv.

[5] Luther, *LW, Vol. 54*, ix–x.

[6] Ibid., 78.

[7] Tappert, *Luther: Letters of Spiritual Counsel*, 117.

[8] Luther, *LW, Vol. 50*, 77.

[9] Tappert, *Luther: Letters of Spiritual Counsel*, 118.

[10] Luther, *LW, Vol. 54*, 89.

[11] Luther, *Commentary on Galatians*, 249–50.

[12] Luther, "The Freedom of the Christian," in Krey, *Luther's Spirituality*, 72.

[13] Kittleson, *Luther the Reformer*, 168–69.

[14] Tappert, *Luther: Letters of Spiritual Counsel*, 14.

[15] Ibid., 15.

[16] Nebe, *Luther as Spiritual Advisor*, 18.

[17] Ibid.

[18] Luther, *LW, Vol. 54*, 165.

[19] Luther, *LW, Vol. 49*, 16.

[20] Luther, "The Large Catechism" in Krey, *Luther's Spirituality*, 187.

[21] Luther, *Commentary on Galatians*, 333, 126.

[22] Luther, *LW, Vol. 54*, 183.

[23] Ibid., 53–54.

[24] William Clebsch and Charles Jaekle, *Pastoral Care in Historical Perspective* (New York: Harper and Row, 1964), xii.

[25] McNeil, *A History of the Cure of Souls*, 85.

[26] Frank Lake, *Clinical Theology* (London: Darton, Longman, & Todd, 1966), 21.

[27] Clebsch and Jaekle, *Pastoral Care in Historical Perspective*, 4.

[28] Thomas Oden, *Care of Souls in the Classic Tradition* (Philadelphia: Fortress, 1983), 10.

[29] Martin Bucer, *Concerning the True Care of Souls*, trans. by Peter Beale (Edinburgh: Banner of Truth Trust, 1538/2009).

Chapter 4

[1] Martin Luther, "Devotional Writings I" in *Luther's Works, Vol. 42*, ed. and trans. by M. O. Deitrich (Philadelphia: Fortress, 1969), 98.

[2] Ibid., 119–66.

[3] Ibid., 128.

[4] Martin Luther, "Lectures on Isaiah: Chapters 1–39" in *LW, Vol. 16*, ed. by J. Pelikan and H. C. Oswald, trans. by H. J. A. Bouman (Saint Louis: Concordia, 1969), 214; *LW, Vol. 54*, 15; *LW, Vol. 48*, 12.

[5] Luther, *LW, Vol. 16*, 214. This version of the quote is from an older edition of notes from Luther's lecture on Isaiah from the hand of Antonius Lauterbach.

[6] Luther, *LW, Vol. 42*, 152–53.

[7] Martin Luther, *The Bondage of the Will*, trans. by J. I. Packer and O. R. Johnston (Grand Rapids: Fleming H. Revell, 1525/1957), 273–74. Luther, *Commentary on Romans*, 42–46, 51–64.

[8] Tappert, *Luther: Letters of Spiritual Counsel*, 27.

[9] Luther, *LW, Vol. 42*, 124.

[10] Ibid., 126, 131, 132, 147, 149, 135, 139, 143, 145.

[11] Ibid., 154.

[12] Ibid., 150.
[13] Ibid., 165.
[14] Ibid., 163.
[15] Ibid., 127.
[16] Ibid., 123, brackets added.
[17] Ibid., 124.
[18] Ibid.
[19] Tappert, *Luther: Letters of Spiritual Counsel*, 62.
[20] Ibid., 63, emphasis added.
[21] Martin Luther, "The Catholic Epistles" in *Luther's Works, Vol. 30*, ed. by J. Pelikan and W. A. Hansen trans. by M. H. Bertrom (Saint Louis: Concordia, 1967), 111.
[22] Luther, *LW, Vol. 42*, 141–42.
[23] Ibid., 162.
[24] Ibid., 163.
[25] Ibid., 163, 165.
[26] Ibid., 164.
[27] Ibid., 164, 165.

Chapter 5

[1] Tappert, *Luther: Letters of Spiritual Counsel*, 60.
[2] Luther, *LW, Vol. 54*, 18.
[3] Nebe, *Luther as Spiritual Advisor*, 41.
[4] Ibid.
[5] Luther, *LW, Vol. 54*, 275.
[6] Ibid., 276.
[7] Preserved Smith and Charles M. Jacobs, eds., *Luther's Correspondence and Other Contemporary Letters Vol. 2* (Philadelphia: Lutheran Publication Society, 1918), 213.
[8] Luther, *LW, Vol. 54*, 53.
[9] Ibid.
[10] Ibid., 53–54.
[11] Preserved Smith, *The Life and Letters of Martin Luther* (New York: Barnes and Noble, 1911), 402.
[12] Ibid.
[13] Luther, *LW, Vol. 54*, 132–33.
[14] Begalke, "Luther's *Anfechtungen*," 15.
[15] Luther, *LW, Vol. 54*, 430.
[16] Tappert, *Luther: Letters of Spiritual Counsel*, 30.
[17] Ibid., 48.
[18] Ibid., 41.
[19] Ibid., 31.

[20] Ibid., 27–28.

[21] Luther, *LW, Vol. 50*, 51.

[22] Tappert, *Luther: Letters of Spiritual Counsel*, 61.

[23] Ibid., 61–62.

[24] In the Bible of Luther's day, Luther noted this as Psalm 119. It is Psalm 120 in Bibles today.

[25] Tappert, *Luther: Letters of Spiritual Counsel*, 204.

[26] Luther, *LW, Vol. 54*, 30.

[27] Ibid., 30–31.

[28] R. Kolb, "Luther as Seelsorger," *Concordia Journal* 2 (1985): 3.

[29] Ibid.

[30] Luther, *LW, Vol. 54*, 105.

[31] Ibid., 17.

[32] Martin Luther, "Lectures on Genesis: Chapters 21–25" in *Luther's Works, Vol. 4*, ed. by J. Pelikan and W. A. Hansen, trans. by G. V. Schick (Saint Louis: Concordia, 1964), 149.

[33] Luther, *LW, Vol. 49*, 270.

[34] Ibid., 306.

[35] Tappert, *Luther: Letters of Spiritual Counsel*, 67.

[36] Ibid.

[37] Ibid.

[38] Ibid., 68–69.

[39] Luther, *LW, Vol. 54*, 45.

[40] Nebe, *Luther as Spiritual Advisor*, 157.

[41] Ibid., 158.

[42] Ibid., 138–39.

[43] Ibid., 148.

[44] Martin Luther, "The Christian and Society I" in *Luther's Works, Vol. 44*, ed. and trans. by J. Atkinson (Philadelphia: Fortress, 1966), 127.

[45] Martin Luther, "Word and Sacrament II" in *Luther's Works. Vol. 36*, ed. by A. R. Wents and H. T. Lehman, trans. by A. T. W. Steinhauser (Philadelphia: Fortress, 1959), 116.

[46] Nebe, *Luther as Spiritual Advisor*, 140.

[47] Luther, *LW, Vol. 54*, 268.

[48] Ibid., 140.

[49] Ibid., 275.

[50] Ibid., 276.

[51] Tappert, *Luther: Letters of Spiritual Counsel*, 91.

[52] Luther, *LW, Vol. 54*, 277.

[53] Tappert, *Luther: Letters of Spiritual Counsel*, 95.

[54] Smith, *Luther's Correspondence*, 216.

[55] Tappert, *Luther: Letters of Spiritual Counsel*, 95.

[56] Martin Luther, "Liturgy and Hymns" in *Luther's Works, Vol. 53*, ed. and trans. by U. S. Leupold (Philadelphia: Fortress, 1965), 13.

[57] D. Zersen, "Lutheran Roots for Small Group Ministry," *Currents in Theology and Mission* 8 (1981): 235.

[58] Ibid., 234–38.

[59] Luther, *LW, Vol. 53.*

Chapter 6

[1] Nebe, *Luther as Spiritual Advisor*, 154–56.

[2] Luther, *LW, Vol. 42*, 123.

[3] Tappert, *Luther: Letters of Spiritual Counsel*, 225.

[4] Nebe, *Luther as Spiritual Advisor*, 54.

[5] Ibid.

[6] Ibid., 54–55.

[7] Ibid., 55.

[8] Ibid., 141.

[9] Tappert, *Luther: Letters of Spiritual Counsel*, 218.

[10] Ibid., 219.

[11] Ibid., 37, emphasis added.

[12] Ibid.

[13] Luther, *LW, Vol. 42*, 125.

[14] Luther, *The Bondage of the Will*, 204, 242.

[15] Ibid., 273.

[16] Ibid., 158.

[17] Ibid., 275–76.

[18] Luther, *LW, Vol. 42*, 129–30.

[19] C. S. Lewis, *The Problem of Pain* Revised edition (New York: HarperOne, 2015), 23.

[20] Nebe, *Luther as Spiritual Advisor*, 171.

[21] Ibid., 172.

[22] Tappert, *Luther: Letters of Spiritual Counsel*, 41.

[23] Ibid.

[24] Clebsch and Jaekle, *Pastoral Care in Historical Perspective*, 210.

[25] Tappert, *Luther: Letters of Spiritual Counsel*, 56.

[26] J. Strohl, "Luther's Fourteen Consolations," *Lutheran Quarterly* 3 (1989): 171.

[27] Nebe, *Luther as Spiritual Advisor*, 188–89.

[28] Luther, *LW, Vol. 44*, 47.

[29] Luther, *LW, Vol. 54*, 75.

[30] Luther, *LW, Vol. 42*, 184.

[31] Nebe, *Luther as Spiritual Advisor*, 159.

[32] Ibid., 160–61.

[33] Alister McGrath, *Luther's Theology of the Cross: Martin Luther's Theological Breakthrough* (Hoboken, NJ: Wiley-Blackwell, 1991), 171.

34 F. Mildenberger, *Theology of the Lutheran Confession*, trans. by E. Lueker (Philadelphia: Fortress, 1986), 41.

35 Vallée, "Luther and Monastic Theology," 292.

36 McGrath, *Luther's Theology of the Cross*, 170.

37 Tappert, *Luther: Letters of Spiritual Counsel*, 165.

38 Lake, *Clinical Theology*, 97.

Chapter 7

1 Tappert, *Luther: Letters of Spiritual Counsel*, 198.

2 Ibid., 198.

3 Ibid.

4 Ibid.

5 Ibid., 199.

6 Nebe, *Luther as Spiritual Advisor*, 175.

7 Ibid., 177.

8 Ibid., 179.

9 Ibid., 189–90.

10 Ibid., 180–81.

11 Ibid., 184–85.

12 Ibid., 192.

13 Ibid., 193.

14 Ibid.

15 Ibid., 213–15.

16 Ibid., 215.

17 Tappert, *Luther: Letters of Spiritual Counsel*, 92.

18 Luther, *LW, Vol. 16*, 214.

19 Nebe, *Luther as Spiritual Advisor*, 183.

20 Ibid.

21 Tappert, *Luther: Letters of Spiritual Counsel*, 67.

22 Ibid., 68.

23 Ibid., 69.

24 Ibid., emphasis added.

25 Ibid., 101, emphasis added.

26 Winfried Schleiner, "Renaissance Exempla of Schizophrenia: The Cure by Charity in Luther and Cervantes," *Renaissance and Reformation* 9, no. 3 (1985): 157–76.

27 Ibid., 159.

28 Ibid., 158.

29 Ibid., 163.

30 Ibid., 163, 165.

31 Ibid., 163.

32 Ibid.

[33] Ibid., 173.

[34] Ibid., 166.

[35] Ibid., 172.

[36] Nebe, *Luther as Spiritual Advisor*, 13.

[37] Schleiner, "Renaissance Exempla of Schizophrenia," 164.

[38] Ibid.

[39] McGrath, *Luther's Theology of the Cross*, 168–69.

[40] Grislis, "The Experience of *Anfechtungen* and Pure Doctrine in Martin Luther's Commentary on Genesis," *Consensus* 8 (1982): 19–31.

[41] Ibid.

[42] Ibid., 24.

[43] Ibid.

[44] Nebe, *Luther as Spiritual Advisor*, 175–76.

[45] Ibid., 176.

[46] Ibid.

[47] Ibid., 178.

[48] Ibid., 179.

[49] Ibid., 180.

[50] Ibid.

[51] Tappert, *Luther: Letters of Spiritual Counsel*, 31.

[52] Ibid., 31–32.

[53] G. Jensen, "Some Help from Luther on Dealing with Suffering," *Touchstone* 9 (1991): 4.

[54] Nebe, *Luther as Spiritual Advisor*, 158.

[55] Ibid.

[56] Ibid., 160

[57] Ibid.

[58] Tappert, *Luther: Letters of Spiritual Counsel*, 82.

[59] Ibid.

[60] Nebe, *Luther as Spiritual Advisor*, 52.

[61] Ibid.

[62] Ibid.

[63] Tappert, *Luther: Letters of Spiritual Counsel*, 142.

[64] Ibid., 147.

[65] Ibid.

[66] Ibid., 154.

[67] Ibid., 155.

[68] Ibid., 156–57.

[69] Ibid., 157.

[70] Ibid., 147.

[71] Ibid., 160.

[72] Martin Luther, "Devotional Writings II" in *Luther's Works, Vol. 42*, ed. and trans. By G. K. Wiencke (Philadelphia: Fortress, 1968), 146.

[73] Nebe, *Luther as Spiritual Advisor*, 201–2.

74 Tappert, *Luther: Letters of Spiritual Counsel*, 72–73.

Chapter 8

1 Quotations taken from the combined sources of, Nebe, *Luther as Spiritual Advisor*, 204–5: and Tappert, *Luther: Letters of Spiritual Counsel*, 115.

2 Nebe, *Luther as Spiritual Advisor*, 207, and Tappert, Luther: Letters of Spiritual Counsel, 116.

3 Tappert, *Luther: Letters of Spiritual Counsel*, 116.

4 Ibid., 115.

5 Ibid., 116.

6 Ibid., 117.

7 Clebsch & Jaekle, *Pastoral Care in Historical Perspective*, 9.

8 Franz Delitzsch, *A System of Biblical Psychology* (Eugene, OR: Wipf & Stock, 1861), xiii.

9 Luther, *LW, Vol. 54*, 69–70.

10 Robert Kellemen, *Gospel Conversations: How to Care Like Christ* (Grand Rapids: Zondervan, 2015), 114.

11 Luther, *LW, Vol. 54*, 70.

12 Ibid.

13 Ibid.

14 Luther, *Commentary on Galatians*, 369.

15 Ibid., 367.

16 Ibid., 363–64.

17 Ibid., 366.

18 Ibid.

19 Ibid., 368.

20 Ibid., 369.

21 Ibid.

22 Delitzsch, *A System of Biblical Psychology*, 3.

23 Luther, *Commentary on Romans*, 43.

24 Ibid., 44–45.

25 Kolb, "Luther as Seelsorger," 4.

26 Ibid.

27 Luther, *LW, Vol. 54*, 17.

28 Ibid.

29 Ibid.

30 Ibid.

31 Kolb, "Luther as Seelsorger," 3.

32 Luther, *Commentary on Romans*, 45.

33 Kolb, "Luther as Seelsorger," 3.

[34] Martin Luther, "Lectures on Genesis: Chapters 6–14" in *Luther's Works, Vol. 2*, ed. by J. Pelikan and D. F. Poellet, trans. by G. V. Schick (Saint Louis: Concordia, 1960), 22.

[35] Luther, *Commentary on Romans*, 45.

[36] Kolb, "Luther as Seelsorger," 5.

[37] Martin Luther, "Lectures on Isaiah: Chapters 40–66" in *Luther's Works, Vol. 17*, ed. by H. C. Oswald, trans. by H. J. A. Bouman (Saint Louis: Concordia, 1972), 89.

[38] Tappert, *Luther: Letters of Spiritual Counsel*, 102–3.

[39] Nebe, *Luther as Spiritual Advisor*, 207, and Tappert, *Luther: Letters of Spiritual Counsel*, 116.

[40] Luther, *LW, Vol. 54*, 70.

[41] Luther, *LW, Vol. 54*, 17.

[42] Luther, *Commentary on Galatians*, 372.

[43] Ibid.

[44] Luther, *LW, Vol. 50*, 21.

Chapter 9

[1] Tappert, *Luther: Letters of Spiritual Counsel*, 338.

[2] Ibid.

[3] Ibid.

[4] Ibid.

[5] Ibid.

[6] Ibid.

[7] Ibid., 338–39, brackets added.

[8] Ibid., 339.

[9] Ibid.

[10] Kolb, "Luther as Seelsorger," 2.

[11] Ibid., 4.

[12] Luther, *LW, Vol. 54*, 321.

[13] Luther, *Commentary on Galatians*, 390.

[14] Ibid.

[15] Ibid., 391.

[16] Nebe, *Luther as Spiritual Advisor*, 189.

[17] Luther, *LW, Vol. 54*, 37.

[18] Nebe, *Luther as Spiritual Advisor*, 187.

[19] Ibid., 186.

[20] Ibid., 217–18.

[21] Luther, *LW, Vol. 54*, 106.

[22] Ibid.

[23] Luther, *Commentary on Galatians*, 391.

[24] Luther, *LW, Vol. 42*, 442.

[25] Ibid., 443.
[26] Ibid., 15.
[27] Ibid., 70.
[28] Ibid., 127.
[29] Luther, *Commentary on Romans*, 122.
[30] Luther, *LW, Vol. 54*, 86.
[31] Ibid.
[32] Ibid., 87.
[33] Ibid., 143.
[34] Ibid.
[35] Luther, *Commentary on Galatians*, 314.
[36] Ibid., 315.
[37] Ibid., 314.
[38] Luther, *Commentary on Romans*, 168.
[39] Ibid.
[40] Ibid., 168–69.
[41] Nebe, *Luther as Spiritual Advisor*, 181.
[42] Ibid., 179.
[43] Ibid., 181–82.
[44] Ibid., 217.
[45] Ibid., 179–80.
[46] Ibid., 193.
[47] Tappert, *Luther: Letters of Spiritual Counsel*, 121.
[48] Martin Luther, "Church and Ministry II" in *Luther's Works, Vol. 40*, ed. and trans. by C. Bergendoff (Philadelphia: Muhlenberg, 1958), 296.
[49] Luther, *LW, Vol. 54*, 334.
[50] Martin Luther, *The Babylonian Captivity of the Church in Three Treatises*, trans by P. Smith (Philadelphia: Muhlenberg, 1531/1947), 201.
[51] H. Ivarsson, "The Principles of Pastoral Care According to Martin Luther," *Pastoral Psychology* 13 (February, 1962): 21.
[52] Luther, *LW, Vol. 40*, 21.
[53] Nebe, *Luther as Spiritual Advisor*, 215.
[54] Ibid., 216.
[55] Ibid., 103.
[56] Ibid., 115, 116, 117.
[57] Ibid., 117.
[58] Ibid., 185.
[59] Ibid., 187.
[60] Ibid., 186.
[61] Ibid., 183.
[62] G. Forde, "The Lutheran View," in Donald Alexander, *Christian Spirituality: Five Views of Sanctification* (Downers Grove, IL: InterVarsity, 1988), 13.

Chapter 10

[1] Luther, *Commentary on Galatians*, 125.

[2] Ibid., 126.

[3] Ibid., 36.

[4] Ibid., 38.

[5] Ibid., 38–39.

[6] Ibid., 21, emphasis added.

[7] Luther, *Commentary on Galatians*, 39–40.

[8] Ibid., 283–84.

[9] Luther, *LW, Vol. 54*, 143.

[10] Luther, *Commentary on Galatians*, 39.

[11] Ibid.

[12] Ibid., 18.

[13] Ibid., 30–31.

[14] Ibid., 251.

[15] Ibid., 253.

[16] Luther, *LW, Vol. 54*, 34.

[17] Luther, *Commentary on Galatians*, 333.

[18] Martin Luther, "Sermons on Epistle Texts for Trinity Sunday to Advent" in *Sermons of Martin Luther: The Church Postils, Vol. 8*, ed. By John Nicholas Lenker, trans. By John Nicolas Lenker (Grand Rapids, Baker Books, 1983), 304.

[19] Ibid., 305, emphasis added.

[20] Ibid.

[21] Ibid., 306.

[22] Ibid., 308.

[23] Ibid., 306.

[24] Ibid., 308, emphasis added.

[25] Ibid., 308–9.

[26] Luther, *Commentary on Galatians*, 230.

[27] R. Kolb, *Luther and the Stories of God: Biblical Narratives as a Foundation for Christian Living* (Grand Rapids: Baker Academics, 2012), 23, brackets added.

[28] Luther, *Sermons of Martin Luther, Vol. 8*, 310.

[29] Luther, *LW, Vol. 49*, 212–13.

[30] Luther, *Commentary on Galatians*, 25–26.

[31] Scripture translations from Galatians in this section are Luther's translations from his *Commentary on Galatians*.

[32] Ibid., 347.

[33] Ibid.

[34] Ibid., 347–48.

[35] Ibid., 348.

[36] Ibid., 163.

[37] Ibid., 162–63.

[38] Ibid., 176.

[39] Ibid., 335.

[40] Martin Luther, "Lectures on Genesis: Chapters 31–37" in *Luther's Works, Vol. 6*, ed. by J. Pelikan and H. C. Oswald, trans. by P. D. Paul (Saint Louis: Concordia, 1970), 348.

[41] Luther, *Commentary on Galatians*, 351.

[42] Tappert, *Luther: Letters of Spiritual Counsel*, 15.

[43] Luther, *Commentary on Galatians*, 335.

[44] Ibid.

[45] Ibid., 344–45.

[46] Luther, "The Freedom of the Christian," in Krey, *Luther's Spirituality*, 82.

[47] Luther, *Commentary on Romans*, xxiv.

Chapter 11

[1] Nebe, *Luther as Spiritual Advisor*, 210.

[2] Ibid.

[3] Ibid.

[4] Ibid.

[5] Ibid., 212.

[6] Ibid.

[7] Ibid.

[8] Ibid., 213.

[9] Bucer, *Concerning the True Care of Souls*.

[10] Luther, *LW, Vol. 50*, 19.

[11] Ibid.

[12] Ibid., 21.

[13] Luther, *Commentary on Romans*, xvii.

[14] Ibid.

[15] Ibid.

[16] Luther, "The Freedom of a Christian," in Krey, *Luther's Spirituality*, 71–72.

[17] Ibid., 77–78.

[18] Ibid., 80.

[19] Luther, *LW, Vol. 49*, 306.

[20] Ibid., 307.

[21] Ibid.

[22] Ibid., 309.

[23] Ibid., 309–10, brackets added.

[24] Luther, *LW, Vol. 48*, 216.

[25] Ibid., 232.

[26] Luther, *LW, Vol. 50*, 306.

[27] John Bunyan, *Grace Abounding to the Chief of Sinners* (Philadelphia: Bradley and Garretson, 1666/1872), 51.

[28] Martin Luther, "Lectures on Genesis: Chapters 1–5" in *Luther's Works, Vol. 1*, ed. by J. Pelikan, trans. by G. V. Schick (Saint Louis: Concordia, 1958), 148.

[29] Tappert, *Luther: Letters of Spiritual Counsel*, 100.

[30] Nebe, *Luther as Spiritual Advisor*, 200.

[31] Ibid., 199.

[32] Ibid., 200.

[33] Ibid., 199.

[34] Ibid., 203.

[35] Ibid., 202.

[36] Sinclair B. Ferguson, "Grace Alone: Luther and the Christian Life" in Sproul, *The Legacy of Luther*, 154.

[37] Ibid.

[38] Luther, *LW, Vol. 50*, 182.

[39] Luther, *LW, Vol. 49*, 97–99.

[40] Luther, *LW, Vol. 48*, 258.

[41] Ibid., 256–63.

[42] Luther, *LW, Vol. 54*, 74.

[43] Luther, *Commentary on Galatians*, 352.

[44] Luther, "The Freedom of a Christian," in Krey, *Luther's Spirituality*, 87.

[45] Ibid.

[46] Kolb, *Luther and the Stories of God*, 10.

[47] Scott Hendrix, *Recultivating the Vineyard: The Reformation Agenda of Christianization* (Louisville, KY: Westminster John Knox Press, 2004), 59–60.

[48] Robert Kellemen, "Spiritual Care in Historical Perspective: Martin Luther as a Case Study in Christian Sustaining, Healing, Reconciling, and Guiding," PhD Dissertation, Kent State University, 1997, 197–206.

[49] Luther, *LW, Vol. 41*, 114.

[50] Luther, *Commentary on Romans*, 206.

[51] Nebe, *Luther as Spiritual Advisor*, 135.

[52] Luther, "The Freedom of a Christian," in Krey, *Luther's Spirituality*, 90.

[53] Tappert, *Luther: Letters of Spiritual Counsel*, 137.

[54] Gene Edward Veith, "The Glory of God Alone: Luther on Vocation" in Sproul, *The Legacy of Luther*, 178–90.

[55] Ibid., 179.

[56] Quoted in Veith, "The Glory of God Alone," 184–85.

[57] Martin Luther, "Selected Psalms III" in *Luther's Works, Vol. 14*, ed. by J. Pelikan and D. E. Poelett, trans. by E. Sittler (Saint Louis: Concordia, 1958), 115.

[58] Martin Luther, "Sermon on the Mount and the Magnificat" in *Luther's Works, Vol. 21*, ed. by J. Pelikan, trans. by A. T. Steinhaeuser (St. Louis: Concordia, 1955), 237.

[59] J. R. R. Tolkien, *The Hobbit* (Geneva, IL: Houghton Mifflin Harcourt, 2012), 51–52.